GREAT LINERS AT WAR

Stephen Harding

Motorbooks International
Publishers & Wholesalers ®

First published in 1997 by Motorbooks International Publishers & Wholesalers, PO Box 1, 729 Prospect Avenue, PO Box 1, Osceola, WI 54020-0001 USA

Motorbooks International books are also available at discounts in bulk quantity for industrial or sales-promotional use. For details write to Special Sales Manager at the Publisher's address

Library of Congress Cataloging-in-Publication Data Available

ISBN 0-7603-0346-0

On the front cover: This artist's impression gives a good idea of what the attack on *Lusitania* must have looked like, despite the fact that the artist has the ship being hit by two torpedoes (note the hole just below the starboard bridge wing). In reality, *U-20*'s single G-type torpedo was enough to doom the liner. *Library of Congress*

On the back cover, top: Shifted to repatriation duty following the Armistice, *Leviathan* routinely carried between 8,000 and 12,000 troops on each westbound crossing. Here she moves toward her New York pier on 16 December 1918, loaded with 9,000 returning servicemen. Note that the dazzle camouflage scheme has been removed from her hull but she still carries her full complement of 6-inch guns. *USNHC*

On the back cover, bottom: Clad in dress whites, *Imperator*'s crew mans her railings on the day of her decommissioning. Sister ships and fellow wartime members of the Cruiser and Transport Force, *Leviathan* and *Imperator* became commercial rivals after leaving military service. *Imperator* became the Cunard Line's *Berengaria*, while *Leviathan* joined the United States Line. *National Archives*

Printed in the United States of America

CONTENTS

FOREWORD

Few topics in maritime history are as interesting, or as often overlooked, as the military exploits of the world's great passenger steamships. This is odd, in that these seagoing grand hotels proved immensely valuable as wartime naval auxiliaries almost from the time of their origin as a distinct vessel type. Most of the ships we now acknowledge as Great Liners—passenger vessels whose size, performance, beauty, and style set them above lesser craft—have served as troop transports, hospital ships, and armed merchant cruisers. The Great Liners have seen duty in conflicts from the Crimean War of 1854 to the 1982 battle for the Falkland Islands, and in almost every case have shown themselves to be important—though sometimes tragically vulnerable—additions to the existing fleets. Indeed, in some cases the liners proved to be of greater value as naval vessels than they had ever been in commercial service.

This volume is an introduction to the military exploits of some of the world's greatest ocean liners. The ships I have included span 70 years of maritime history, and thus represent a wide range of designs and abilities. Yet each vessel has much in common with the others. All were originally intended to be the ultimate passenger liner and rule the seas in style, splendor, and speed. Yet each was also eventually called away from commercial service to take part in a rivalry potentially far more lethal than any envisioned by her builders. Stripped of the trappings of luxury, these queens of the seas circled the globe on errands both merciful and militaristic, their speed, endurance, and capacity dedicated to the service of causes both noble and contemptible. For some of the ships, it was a trial by fire they would not survive.

Stephen Harding
October 1996

INTRODUCTION

The use of merchant ships as wartime naval auxiliaries is a practice as old as seafaring itself, and the world's maritime nations have long regarded their respective commercial fleets as vital adjuncts to their existing naval forces. Passenger ships have always been of particular interest to military planners because the ability to rapidly transport significant numbers of troops across vast distances has always been the foundation upon which great empires have been built. The development of the passenger steamship as an economically feasible and mechanically reliable mode of transportation thus had, from the beginning, important military ramifications.

True, the early steamers were slow, fragile vessels that could not seriously compete—commercially or militarily—with contemporary sailing ships. But advances in naval architecture and steam-driven propulsion systems soon led to the construction of progressively larger and more capable steamships that, unlike sailing vessels, were not subject to unfavorable winds and contrary currents. This advantage allowed steam-powered ships to maintain regular schedules, something wind-driven vessels had never been able to do, and it was a development that revolutionized military sea transport as much as it did commercial shipping.

As with many later ships, wartime requisitioning saved the P&O Line's 3,438-ton *Himalaya* from the embarrassment of financial ruin. The huge vessel was deeply in the red when called up for service as a British troopship in the Crimean War, a role in which she excelled. Purchased by the British government, the ship served long and well, finally succumbing to German bombs while serving as a World War II storage hulk in Britain's Portland Harbor. *U.S. Naval Historical Center*

The first recorded military use of a passenger steamship occurred in 1826, when the British liner *Enterprize* transported Indian Army troops from Calcutta to Rangoon during the First Burmese War. But this was more an expedient answer to a specific need than a true innovation, and it was not until 1833 that the first large-scale trooping effort was organized around steam-powered passenger ships. In that instance Britain's Peninsular and Oriental Steam Navigation Company chartered several steamers to the Queen of Portugal for the transport of Royalist troops during the Portuguese civil war. Two years later P&O ships carried both Spanish and British troops into action in the first Spanish civil war.

But in each of these early cases, liners were used in a piecemeal and uncoordinated way, and the military value of passenger steamships thus remained essentially theoretical until the 1851 outbreak of the "Kaffir War" in South Africa. The start of hostilities took the British government by surprise, and the Admiralty was unprepared to transport a significant relief force to the Cape. The directors of the P&O Line quickly volunteered several of the firm's larger vessels, including the new liner *Singapore*, for trooping duty. Her Majesty's Government accepted the offer, and the first 500 British troops disembarked at Cape Town within a month. The Admiralty was impressed with P&O's organizational abilities, as well as with the excellent performance of the firm's liners in the heavy seas around the Cape of Good Hope, and shortly after the conclusion of hostilities the British government announced that all subsequent trooping duties would be performed exclusively by steam-powered ships.

Britain's decision to switch to steam-powered troopships was vindicated during the Crimean War. The Admiralty began calling up passenger steamships for military duty soon after Britain entered the conflict in 1854, and most of the nation's shipping lines eventually contributed vessels to the war effort. Several well-known liners served in the British transport fleet, including the former P&O liner *Himalaya*, the largest ship afloat when launched in 1852, and *Germania*, which as the Cunard Line's *Acadia* had been one of Britain's first four Royal Mail steamers. Passenger liners carried men and horses to both the Baltic and Black Sea theaters, and without their efforts the landings at Varna and the siege of Sevastopol would have been impossible. The ships undertook other duties as well, including the evacuation of casualties to rear-area hospitals. This marked the first use of passenger steamships in the medical-evacuation role, a duty that many famous liners would perform in future conflicts.

The latter half of the nineteenth century was characterized by armed struggle in many parts of

The Cunard Line's first iron-hulled transatlantic passenger steamship, the 3,300-ton *Persia*, made her trooping debut in the autumn of 1861. Working in concert with the huge *Great Eastern* and Cunard's 2,750-ton *Australasian*, *Persia* rushed British troops to Halifax to bolster Canada's neutrality during the American Civil War. *Cunard Line*

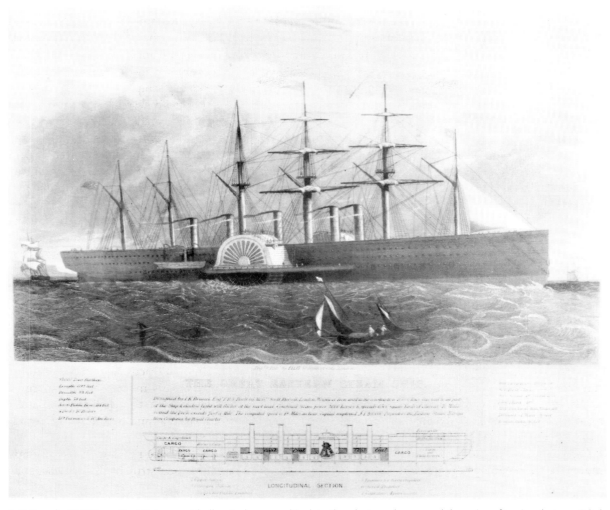

I. K. Brunel's 22,500-ton *Great Eastern* was ideally suited to troopship duty, though storm damage and the easing of tensions between Britain and the United States kept her from undertaking further trooping voyages. The huge ship never attained the level of success envisioned for her and, despite her important role in the laying of the first transatlantic telegraph cable, she fell into decline and ended her days as a beached tourist attraction. *USNHC*

the world, and passenger steamers were called up for military service with increasing frequency. The British government requisitioned or chartered more than 60 liners during the 1857 Sepoy Mutiny, including I. K. Brunel's *Great Britain*, the first iron-hulled passenger steamship and, at the time of its requisitioning, the largest vessel afloat.

The United States, for its part, first used liners as naval auxiliaries during the American Civil War. Several well-known passenger steamers saw service on the Union side during that conflict, including *Atlantic* and *Baltic* of the prewar Collins Line. These were the largest ships operated by the United States during the war, and both saw extensive trooping service along the United States' eastern seaboard.

The famous British liner *Great Eastern*, Brunel's immense successor to his earlier *Great Britain*, also saw trooping service during the course of the American Civil War. The huge ship joined the Cunard liners *Australasia* and *Persia* in carrying British soldiers to Canada to reinforce Britain's neutrality. On a single voyage to Quebec, *Great Eastern* transported more than 2,100 troops, 473 accompanying wives and children, and 122 horses. It was an immensely effective demonstration of both the military value and commercial potential of passenger steamships.

Trooping remained the passenger steamer's primary military task until the 1880s, when several nations began experimentally converting liners into armed merchant cruisers (AMCs). It was hoped that armed and armored liners would be able to undertake the escort and reconnaissance duties normally assigned to a navy's smaller ships of the line, thereby freeing the warships for more aggressive tasks elsewhere. Britain was a leader in the development of AMCs, and much of what ultimately became standard procedure for the employment of such vessels resulted from tests the Royal Navy conducted aboard the converted Cunarder *Oregon* in 1885.

The United States was equally interested in the potential of AMCs, and the American Line's *St. Louis* and *St. Paul* of 1894 and 1895, respectively, were the first passenger steamers specifically designed for wartime use as auxiliary cruisers. Each vessel incorporated strategically placed armor plate and other features not normally found on merchant ships, and it was claimed the liners could be completely converted from civilian to military status in just five days. This was, as it turned out, fairly accurate, because when *St. Louis* and *St. Paul* were called up for service in the Spanish-American War of 1898 they required less than a week for conversion.

America's war with Spain marked the AMC's combat debut, and the successes enjoyed by *St. Louis* and *St. Paul* seemed to vindicate the armed-liner concept. The first British vessels purposely designed for wartime AMC duty, the White Star

Like their American Line running mates *St. Louis* and *St. Paul*, the elegant sisters *Paris* and *New York* helped pioneer the military use of passenger steamships during the Spanish-American War. Following brief duty as the auxiliary cruisers USS *Yale* and USS *Harvard*, respectively, the vessels were transferred to the much more suitable task of troop transportation. Both *Yale* (seen here after off-loading troops at Santiago de Cuba) and *Harvard* also saw trooping service in World War I. *USNHC*

Line's *Teutonic* and *Majestic*, were commissioned in 1899, and Germany, Russia, and Japan launched similarly designed ships soon thereafter. Armed liners saw service in the Boer and Russo-Japanese wars, but it was not until World War I that such vessels were used to any appreciable degree.

The military value of the passenger steamship remained a moot point between 1905 and 1914 because the major powers were at peace and the only battles in which most liners engaged were commercial. Yet this economic conflict had important military consequences; the increasingly fierce competition among the world's leading steamship companies helped stimulate the construction of progressively larger, faster, and more technically advanced passenger ships. The express steamers launched during this period incorporated a range of innovations, and the characteristics that were to make them so commercially successful—rugged construction, high speed, long range, and large passenger capacity—also promised to make them outstanding naval auxiliaries.

The military potential of this new generation of passenger steamships was not lost on the world's admiralties, and it quickly became common for governments to subsidize the construction and operation of the larger liners. Such subsidies were not new; various nations had long supported their shipping firms in return for a share of the commercial profits. But, though profits continued to be an important consideration, it became increasingly customary for governments to subsidize steamship lines primarily to ensure the wartime availability of naval auxiliaries. This sort of arrangement was eminently acceptable to both parties because it satisfied the needs of both the government and the shipping firm. In exchange for its financial aid the former was guaranteed the wartime use of ships that were often superior to existing naval vessels, while the latter, in return for adapting the vessels' design to increase military potential, received a steady injection of capital that was not subject to the vagaries of commerce.

By 1910 most of the world's more advanced navies had come to consider passenger steamers a vital part of the fleet. During the years just before the outbreak of World War I, each of the major powers developed contingency plans for the military employment of chartered and requisitioned liners. The June 1914 assassination of Austrian Archduke Franz Ferdinand set those and other,

Norddeutscher Lloyd's 14,300-ton *Kaiser Wilhelm der Grosse* was the first of five large, fast German passenger ships specifically designed for wartime use as naval auxiliaries. The ship, seen here in Bremen just before her August 1914 requisitioning, was converted, armed, and provisioned for sea in only two days. *The Mariner's Museum*

more drastic plans inexorably in motion. The outbreak of a general European war the following August led to the cancellation of most liner sailings as the belligerents began calling up their passenger fleets. Those vessels in home waters were quickly stripped of their luxury fittings and militarized, while liners still at sea were ordered to make for the nearest friendly or neutral port.

Most French and British liners did not sit idle in foreign harbors for long; the Allies ruled the seas and warships quickly appeared to shepherd the liners home. German passenger steamers caught in neutral ports did not fare as well, however, because the German Navy was effectively blockaded in the Baltic and North seas and could offer no assistance. Many of Germany's finest liners were therefore trapped abroad, the ships unable or their masters unwilling to run the gauntlet of Allied warships that lay in wait just outside the neutral nation's territorial waters.

Such was the case for twenty steamers of Germany's Hamburg-Amerika (HAPAG)[1] and Norddeutscher Lloyd (NDL) lines trapped in the United States at the outbreak of war. These ships, which included HAPAG's 54,000 ton *Vaterland*, the largest vessel afloat at that time, were forced to remain at their piers until interned by the U.S. government in 1917. This was to prove a severe blow to the German war effort because the interned vessels totaled over 500,000 gross tons and represented a significant portion of the German Navy's potential troop transport and AMC tonnage.

Chartered and requisitioned passenger steamers undertook a range of military duties in World War I. During the first months of the conflict, commerce-raiding and AMC duty predominated, and several liners on both sides made names for themselves as men o' war. Among the more successful were the German steamers

Among the many German passenger steamers caught in U.S. ports by the outbreak of World War I was NDL's 19,300-ton *Kronprinzessin Cecilie*. The liner sought shelter in Bar Harbor, Maine (and is seen here entering that port wearing the funnel colors of Britain's White Star Line as deceptive camouflage) and was interned. Pressed into U.S. service in 1917, she saw extensive trooping duty as USS *Mount Vernon*. *USNHC*

Trapped in Boston, the Hamburg-Amerika Line's *Amerika* was interned until seized by federal agents in April 1917. Seen here at Boston Navy Yard eight days after her 6 August commissioning as USS *America*, the 22,220-ton vessel went on to serve as a U.S. troopship in both world wars. *National Archives*

Kronprinz Wilhelm and *Prinz Eitel Friedrich*, and Britain's *Carmania*.

But by mid-1915 it had become obvious that merchant vessels—no matter how well armored—were too vulnerable to be of much use in offensive roles. The belligerents consequently began shifting liners to such other, more appropriate tasks as troop transportation and medical evacuation, and most of the better known French and British liners eventually served in these capacities. Germany, for her part, was unable to make widespread use of passenger ships, primarily because of the internment of her more capable liners and Allied control of the seas.

Though a few vessels did participate in the Kaiser's war effort, Germany's greatest (albeit unwilling) contribution was to the United States' troop-transport effort. More than 100 German merchant vessels were seized for U.S. military use following the United States' entry into the war. These vessels, overhauled and commissioned into the U.S. Navy, formed the backbone of the United States' immense trooping program. And once the war ended, captured German liners helped speed the repatriation of the American Expeditionary Force.

Norddeutscher Lloyd's aptly named *George Washington* also saw U.S. trooping duty in World War I. Caught in New York by the outbreak of war, she is seen here just after her 1917 seizure. The ship's wartime service included carrying President Woodrow Wilson and other dignitaries to France for the Paris Peace Conference. *USNHC*

USS *Agamemnon* arrives in Boston in 1918 with U.S. troops returning from Europe. Formerly Norddeutscher Lloyd's *Kaiser Wilhelm II*, the liner was another of the major German steamships trapped in U.S. ports by the 1914 outbreak of World War I. The loss of these vessels was a severe blow to Germany's war effort, and their ultimate service in the U.S. Navy was a key reason for the success of the United States' trooping effort. *USNHC*

Sister ship to the ill-fated *Lusitania*, Cunard's 31,938-ton *Mauretania* made six voyages to the Dardanelles early in World War I. After a two-year layup she was shifted to the North Atlantic trooping service, carrying U.S. troops to France. This 1924 painting by Burnell Poole depicts her in the "dazzle" paint scheme widely applied to Allied ships. *USNHC*

Called up for military service in September 1915, the White Star Line's 45,300-ton *Olympic* ultimately carried British, Canadian, and U.S. troops during the course of her World War I career. Seen here in Halifax during an early crossing in 1916 the liner, sister ship to the ill-fated *Titanic*, still wears a modified form of her commercial color scheme. *John H. Shaum Collection*

The end of World War I allowed the great passenger liners to return to the peacetime tasks for which they'd been designed. For surviving German steamers this entailed a change of ensign as well as a change of name because the victorious Allies divided the vessels among themselves. The French, British, and U.S. steamship lines, rejuvenated by their absorption of the German vessels, returned to business as usual on the lucrative transatlantic passenger routes.

Business did not remain usual for long, however, because in 1921 the United States imposed strict immigrant-entry quotas. The carriage of immigrants was the foundation of the transatlantic passenger industry, and the restriction of immigration was a serious economic blow. Fortunately, the postwar economic boom had created a new type of international traveler, the affluent tourist who wished to see Europe and the Americas firsthand, and after a few difficult years the major steamship lines adapted themselves to the new economic order.

Indeed, by the mid-1920s the tourist trade had become so profitable, and the increasingly worldly

World War I forced the return to U.S. military service of several older passenger liners that had seen duty in the Spanish-American War. Among them was the former *New York* (ex-*City of New York* and USS *Harvard*), which as USS *Plattsburg* carried troops both to and from France. She is seen here in Brest, just after unloading troops in September 1918. *USNHC*

tourists so fond of luxury afloat, that the major shipping firms began replacing their aging vessels with newer and considerably larger liners. The newly reborn German steamship industry soon became a leader in the construction of fast, technically advanced ships, and thereby sparked the sort of international building frenzy that had characterized the decade prior to World War I. France, Britain, and the United States all laid down new liners during this period, despite increasingly frequent indications of an impending worldwide economic crisis.

The advent of that crisis in 1928 and 1929 struck the steamship industry hard, and many of the smaller firms failed. The larger companies weathered the storm only by curtailing services, suspending new construction, and seeking enormous amounts of financial aid from their respec-

tive governments. In many cases such aid was given only after two or more firms had agreed to merge to form a single "national line"; such was the case with the 1934 merger of Britain's Cunard and White Star lines. In any case, the steamship industry was just beginning to recover from the Great Depression when war once engulfed Europe.

The September 1939 outbreak of World War II sparked the same type of industrial mobilization that had characterized World War I. And, as in that earlier conflict, the passenger liners of the world's great steamship companies were destined to play a vital role. During the first months of the war, most of the liners lay safely in neutral ports. Indeed, the outbreak of hostilities trapped the two largest passenger steamships then in service, Cunard-White Star's 81,000-ton *Queen Mary* and the 83,423-ton

The end of World War I did not halt Allied requisitioning of German passenger liners because the Armistice agreement stipulated that Germany was to give up certain ships as war reparations. Among those vessels was Hamburg-Amerika's 51,950-ton *Imperator*, seen here on her 1913 maiden arrival in New York. Sister ship to *Vaterland/USS Leviathan, Imperator* served as a U.S. troopship in 1919 and 1920 before joining Britain's Cunard Line as *Berengaria*. *USNHC*

Normandie of France's Compagnie Général Transatlantique, in New York. In March 1940 the two ships were joined by Cunard-White Star's 83,600-ton *Queen Elizabeth* which, though launched 18 months earlier, had not entered commercial service. The British government had ordered the vessel to New York to protect her from German attack, and all three liners were to spend three weeks laying side by side at their Hudson River piers.

The 1942 sinking in New York of the French Line's 83,423-ton *Normandie* was a dramatic reminder of the tremendous vulnerability of ships designed for commerce rather than war. Seized by the United States and destined for trooping service, the once-proud liner burned at her pier during her trooping conversion and was ultimately scrapped. *USNHC*

On 21 March *Queen Mary* left New York bound for Australia and war service, and in mid-September *Queen Elizabeth* set sail for Singapore and her own conversion into a naval auxiliary. *Normandie*, flagship of the French Line, remained in New York and was eventually interned. The ship was requisitioned for U.S. service soon after the December 1941 Japanese attack on Pearl Harbor,

but caught fire and sank at her pier while being converted into a troopship. She was thus the first, but certainly not the last, of the great liners to be lost in World War II.

The tasks undertaken by passenger steamships in World War II were much the same as those performed by express liners during World War I. In the first months of World War II some smaller steam-

Overshadowed by *Normandie* in commercial service, the French Line's 44,356-ton *Ile de France* excelled as a World War II troopship. Operated by British and, later, Free French crews, the liner hauled Allied troops in both the Mediterranean and Atlantic theaters. *USNHC*

Launched in 1939, the second Cunard liner to bear the proud name *Mauretania* saw extensive World War II trooping service. Though not as large as some of the other converted liners with which she operated, the 35,738-ton *Mauretania* did yeoman service hauling troops, wounded, and Axis prisoners throughout the war. *USNHC*

ers were fitted out as AMCs, though both the Allied and Axis powers remembered the lessons of World War I and did not use their larger liners for offensive tasks. Almost from the beginning the Allies dedicated their larger ships to troop transportation and medical evacuation, duties for which the vessels were supremely well-equipped. Both *Queen Mary* and *Queen Elizabeth* spent the war crisscrossing the globe loaded with troops, as did *Aquitania*, *Mauretania*, Holland's *Nieuw Amsterdam*, France's *Ile de France,* and the United States' *America*. These vessels, and dozens of smaller passengers liners as well, played a vital role in the Allied war effort. Indeed, without the trooping capacity provided by these passenger steamships the Allies would have been hard-pressed to sustain their offensives against the Axis powers in the Pacific and Atlantic theaters of war.

The Axis powers, for their part, did not make extensive use of requisitioned passenger steamships. Germany's two finest liners, *Bremen* and *Europa*, were partially converted to troopship status in preparation

The Netherlands' contribution to the World War II Allied trooping effort, Holland-America Line's 36,982-ton *Nieuw Amsterdam*, is seen here entering San Francisco Bay in 1943. The liner spent the war years roaming the Atlantic, Pacific, and Indian oceans, carrying her vital human cargoes wherever they were needed. *USNHC*

for the planned invasion of Britain. But the Luftwaffe's inability to destroy the Royal Air Force made any such invasion suicidal, and *Bremen* and *Europa* were shifted to Bremerhaven for use as accommodation vessels once preparations for the cross-Channel attack were canceled. *Bremen* caught fire and sank at her pier in March 1941, and her running mate was captured intact by Allied troops in May 1945.

Italy's greatest prewar liners, the 51,000-ton *Rex* and 48,500-ton *Conte de Savoia*, fared no better than their German counterparts. Both vessels were withdrawn from commercial service in early 1940 and laid up. Plans to convert the liners into aircraft carriers never came to fruition and, but for a single short trooping voyage by *Conte de Savoia* in 1943, neither liner played any appreciable role in the Italian war effort. Both ships were eventually sunk by Allied aircraft when it became apparent that retreating German forces intended to use them to block the entrances to important Adriatic ports.

Cunard's famed 81,237-ton *Queen Mary* races across the North Atlantic in this 1943 photograph. Able to transport up to 16,000 human beings at a time, the liner was arguably the most capable troopship the world has ever seen. She and her sister *Queen Elizabeth* formed the backbone of the Allies' World War II trooping effort, in the process proving the immense strategic value of properly employed passenger steamships. *National Archives of Canada*

Younger, larger, and decidedly more stylish than *Queen Mary*, Cunard's 83,673-ton *Queen Elizabeth* was equally successful in wartime service. Drafted for trooping duty even before her commercial debut, the liner crisscrossed the globe throughout the war years, ferrying troops, wounded, prisoners, and returning servicemen. *The Cunard Line*

The Axis powers made wider use of small coastal passenger steamers, using them to transport men and supplies in the Baltic, Adriatic, and Aegean seas. However, increasing Allied air and naval superiority eventually made even this limited use unacceptably dangerous, and the Axis' continued reliance on these almost defenseless ships ultimately led to such tragedies as the sinking of the *Wilhelm Gustloff*.

On January 30, 1945, the 25,400-ton ship, originally built as a coastal cruise liner intended for use by Nazi Party members, left East Prussia loaded with 8,000 troops and refugees attempting to escape the advancing Soviet Army. The small convoy in which she was traveling was attacked by Russian submarines in the Baltic, and *Wilhelm Gustloff* was torpedoed and sunk with the loss of

almost all aboard. This remains the greatest maritime disaster in history, and is a vivid demonstration of the perils involved in the military use of commercial ships.

The end of World War II sparked a boom in the passenger steamship industry and those great liners that had survived the war were soon shuttling paying passengers across the Atlantic. Business was so good in the 10 years following the end of the war that the period is often referred to as the "Golden Age" of the great transatlantic steamships.

But technological progress, like time, marches onward, and by the mid-1960s the popularity of air travel had brought the "Golden Age" to an end. Passengers were no longer willing to spend four to six days crossing the ocean by ship when the same journey could be made by airliner in six hours. The

Italy's premier prewar passenger liner, the 51,062-ton *Rex*, begins to burn after repeated rocket hits inflicted by RAF fighter-bombers on September 8, 1944. Though other major passenger steamers have been attacked from the air, *Rex* holds the dubious distinction of being the only one not to survive the experience. *USNHC*

great steamship lines struggled to remain competitive but, faced by skyrocketing costs and plummeting revenues, one after another retired their liners in favor of all-cargo ships and smaller, more profitable cruise liners. By 1967 Britain's Cunard Line was the only firm offering regular transatlantic service of the traditional sort, but this was only possible because the 67,000-ton *Queen Elizabeth 2* spent most of the year cruising.

The development of international air travel brought about equally fundamental changes in military transportation. Though France used *Ile de France* for trooping in the early stages of the war in Indochina, and though Britain continued to use medium-sized liners to shuttle troops around the remaining outposts of empire until 1962, jet aircraft inexorably took over those transport tasks pre-viously performed by impressed passenger ships. This seemed, at first glance, to be a logical and desirable development because common sense indicated that aircraft could transport troops or evacuate casualties far faster than ships could. And most of the world's navies had commissioned specialized assault transport ships for use in those rare cases when aircraft could not fill a specific tactical need.

But a few governments, most notably that of Great Britain, maintained the organizations and plans necessary to impress larger, faster, and more capable commercial vessels in wartime. These governments realized that aircraft had limitations as well and knew that, under certain circumstances, large, fast, passenger-carrying ships would be the only way to transport a significant number of troops to a specific hot spot.

Germany's premier passenger liners, Norddeutscher Lloyd's *Bremen* and *Europa*, spent virtually all of World War II trapped in German ports. *Bremen* was ultimately destroyed by fire, while *Europa,* seen here in New York in early 1946, saw limited service as a U.S.-operated trooper following her capture by advancing Allied forces. *USNHC*

This belief was vindicated, of course, during the 1982 Anglo-Argentine War for the Falkland Islands. The geographic remoteness of the battle zone, the sheer mass of troops and equipment required, and the prevailing tactical situation jointly decreed that all British land forces used to recapture the islands had to be brought in by ship. Indeed, the number of transport aircraft required to move the necessary troops and their equipment would have been prohibitive, and the threat posed to any British "air bridge" by Argentine aircraft and anti-aircraft defenses made movement by sea the only viable alternative. Without the trooping capacity provided by the impressed liners *Canberra* and *Queen Elizabeth 2*, supported by dozens of smaller commer-

cial vessels, the British government's vow to reclaim the islands by force would have been an empty threat.

Britain's ability to quickly requisition suitable merchant ships for military use during the Falklands War was a major factor in the British victory because without the lift capacity provided by the dozens of impressed vessels the men and materiel necessary to conduct a successful campaign could never have been transported to the war zone. This fact was not lost on the world's naval planners, and in the years since the end of the Falklands conflict several nations have initiated feasibility studies concerning the increased use of requisitioned merchant ships for military use in wartime.

That the military establishments of some of

Unable to build their troop-transport efforts around larger liners, the Germans turned to smaller passenger vessels such as the 25,400-ton coastal steamer *Wilhelm Gustloff*. Torpedoed by a Russian submarine while evacuating troops and refugees from East Prussia, the liner sank with the loss of 8,000 lives. *Library of Congress*

the world's greatest powers should be actively planning for the military use of car ferries, roll-on/roll-off cargo vessels, and cruise ships is not surprising. For even in this age of long-range jet aircraft the fact remains that, in many cases, the only way to move large numbers of troops and their equipment to a hot spot halfway around the globe is by ship. And, in an age when even the wealthiest nations cannot afford to build and maintain large fleets of cargo and troop transports, and cannot hope to effectively perform the many and varied tasks assigned to those vessels they do have, the wartime requisitioning of existing commercial ships is an increasingly more sensible economic and military option.

CHAPTER ONE

GREAT EASTERN

Builder: J. Russell Scott, London

Launched: 1859

Length overall: 689 feet

Width: 82 feet

Gross tonnage:

    Commercial: 18,915 tons

    Military: 22,500 tons

Propulsion: Two steam engines: one of 1,000 hp driving the side-mounted paddle wheels, and one of 1,600 hp driving the single screw. Also carried 6,500 square feet of sail on six masts.

Top speed: 13.5 knots

Capacity:

    Crew: 400

    Passengers: 596 Cabin, 2,400 Steerage (as designed, though the ship never actually embarked this many commercial passengers).

    Troops: 2,617 troops and dependents

Disposition: Scrapped in England, 1889–1891.

Isambard Kingdom Brunel was undoubtedly one of the greatest of the pioneering nineteenth-century engineers; his most impressive creation, the steamship *Great Eastern*, remains one of the best known of the early passenger liners. The vessel's renown is not a product of her commercial activities, however, because despite her unprecedented size and numerous technological innovations, *Great Eastern*'s career on the North Atlantic was one of the least successful on record. Her fame is the result of accomplishments in other, less glamorous roles, the most often cited of which is her laying of the first transatlantic telegraph cable in 1865–1866. But it was during the course of an earlier trooping voyage that *Great Eastern* first demonstrated her remarkable versatility and, at the same time, underscored the enormous military value of large, fast passenger steamships.

It was almost inevitable that *Great Eastern* would eventually serve as a troopship because Brunel had unknowingly incorporated in her design several features that unique-

Though fitted with six masts capable of flying 6,500 square feet of sail, *Great Eastern* normally relied on her twin paddle wheels for propulsion. This T. G. Dutton painting depicts the liner setting out on yet another journey, though in reality such departures were rare: *Great Eastern* made only two commercial passages before her requisitioning for trooping duty. *USNHC*

Her massive bulk dwarfing the shipyard workers plating her immensely strong, cellular double hull, *Great Eastern* takes shape at Millwall, London, in July 1855. The ship's size was intended to give her both stability and load-carrying capacity on the Australasian and Far East routes, but also made her an extremely capable transatlantic troopship. *USNHC*

ly equipped her for such duty. The liner had been intended for service on the grueling Australia and Far East routes, and Brunel had based his design on an immensely strong cellular double hull that ensured excellent watertight integrity. This was, of course, an important consideration for both a merchant vessel facing the perils of the southern seas and a troopship subject to hostile fire.

Great Eastern's size was another important factor; at 689 feet and 22,500 tons she was nearly five times larger than her nearest competitor and could carry 10,000 tons of coal, 6,000 tons of cargo, and nearly 2,300 passengers and crew. The liner's wide and relatively uncluttered upper deck offered space for quartering and drilling troops and horses, and her decent sea-keeping abilities increased the chances that her troops would arrive at their ultimate destination in fighting trim. Moreover, *Great Eastern*'s twin paddle wheels and single screw

pushed her along at a steady six knots and could, if necessary, be augmented by 6,500 square feet of sail on six masts. Finally, and most important to a nation that still ruled a worldwide empire, *Great Eastern*'s fully laden nonstop range of 22,000 miles was far beyond the capabilities of any other contemporary steamship.

All of these attributes served to make *Great Eastern* an attractive candidate for military service, and the British Admiralty kept a close eye on the liner from the time of her launching in January 1858. But, despite her obvious suitability for trooping, the liner probably would never have been called up for such service had she fulfilled her designer's commercial expectations. A ship of her size gainfully employed in carrying people and goods to and from Australasia would have been tremendously important to the economic and political life of the Empire, and her arbitrary trans-

Builder of bridges and railways as well as ships, Isambard Kingdom Brunel supervised every aspect of *Great Eastern*'s construction. Seen here posed before the huge ship's launching chains, Brunel envisioned her as the ultimate ocean liner. He did not live to see his creation take to the seas, however; he died before her maiden voyage. *Smithsonian Institution*

fer to trooping service would have been both short-sighted and an economic blunder of the first order.

But *Great Eastern* never traveled the route for which she had been designed and her commercial career was, at best, undistinguished. The enormous

cost of building the ship drove her original owners to ruin, and the money spent repairing damage caused by an explosion during her sea trials forced a second consortium out of business as well. The liner was eventually purchased by yet another group of investors, who put her into North Atlantic service despite Brunel's warnings that such a limited domain could not provide sufficient employment for his huge ship. Brunel died before *Great Eastern*'s June 1859 maiden voyage to the United States, but his prophecy proved accurate. Though the liner attracted much favorable attention from the press and public in both Great Britain and the United States, she was unable to entice aboard enough paying customers to defray her enormous operating costs. To conserve their remaining capital, the ship's owners withdrew her from service upon her return to Britain and laid her up for the winter. A second crossing to New York in May 1861 was no more successful, and upon her return *Great Eastern* was again laid up while her owners pondered her ultimate fate.

The "Great Iron Ship" might well have ended her short and unhappy career at that point had it not been for the Confederate bombardment of a Union fortress in the harbor at Charleston, South Carolina, six weeks earlier. The April attack on Fort Sumter had fanned the long-smoldering differences between the United States' northern and southern states into civil war and, at the same time, had kindled British fears that Fenian groups in the United States might attempt military action against British Canada while the attention of the U.S. government was focused elsewhere. Canada was ill-equipped to resist assault because there were only 4,300 British regulars and 10,000 volunteer militiamen in the entire country. The British government therefore ordered Canada's immediate reinforcement, and the Admiralty chose the economically becalmed *Great Eastern* as the vessel best suited to the task.

The ship's owners were overjoyed by the prospect of a one-time trooping charter because the fee the British government offered would provide a desperately needed injection of capital. There was also the possibility that the voyage to Canada might lead to a full-time trooping career for the financially troubled liner. Britain still maintained garrisons in several far-flung outposts of empire, and Brunel's ship was ideally qualified to replace the smaller and less capable vessels then

Men of the 30th Regiment of Foot board *Great Eastern* on 24 June 1861. On her voyage to Canada the liner carried 2,144 soldiers, 473 women and children, and 400 crew members. This was by far the greatest number of human beings that had yet voyaged in a single vessel, and foreshadowed the huge numbers of men that would routinely be packed aboard later troopers. *National Archives of Canada*

the holds for human habitation by attaching hammock supports and a few folding-frame beds to the bulkheads and installed large wooden staircases that provided access to the main deck. Meals for the enlisted men would be prepared in covered areas on the aft end of the promenade deck, where brick ovens and grills were erected for that purpose.

Carpenters installed rifle and equipment racks in each of *Great Eastern*'s troop berthing areas and built stall-like enclosures on the promenade deck for the storage of wheeled light-artillery pieces. Other equipment was to be stowed wherever possible, and 120 horses were to be stabled with other livestock on the main deck. Officers and the women and children accompanying the force were to be housed in the ship's existing staterooms, most of which retained their furnishings and fittings. The first class dining room was set aside as the officer's mess, and the removal of a single interior wall allowed the vessel's small infirmary to be doubled in size. *Great Eastern* was to retain her original paint scheme, though her silhouette was altered by the addition of eight extra lifeboats suspended from specially built davits fixed along both sides of the promenade deck. Finally, as a further concession to safety, over a thousand life rings were stowed around the ship.

Great Eastern's metamorphosis was completed by the third week of June 1861, and embarkation of troops began on the morning of the 24th. In all, 2,144 officers and men boarded the vessel during the next 24 hours, as did 473 women and children and 122 horses. The troops, which had been drawn from the Royal Artillery and five rifle regiments, settled in and then assisted in the loading of provisions. Nearly 200 tons of fresh and preserved food were brought aboard, as were several dozen chickens; 10 pigs; kegs of ale, rum, and brandy; and almost a ton of animal fodder. An additional 300 tons of miscellaneous equipment was lashed to the decks and 6,500 tons of coal disappeared into *Great Eastern*'s bunkers.

Loading of the huge liner for her inaugural trooping voyage was accomplished in just two days and on the evening of 26 June the ship's Master, Captain James Kennedy, ordered her boilers fired in preparation for departure the following morning. At this point, however, a problem developed that threatened to disrupt the Captain's schedule. About 100 of *Great Eastern*'s 400-man crew collec-

being used to shift British forces from one area to another. Such a development would have pleased *Great Eastern*'s owners because it would guarantee steady employment for the ship and a regular dividend for the stockholders. The desire to impress the Admiralty, and thereby increase the Great Ship Company's chances for survival, ensured the firm's total cooperation in hastening the liner's availability for her new task.

Conversion of *Great Eastern* from liner into troop transport began at the Birkenhead Iron Works in Milford Haven, Wales, during the first week of June 1861. The Admiralty anticipated that the liner would embark 2,000 troops, most of whom could be accommodated in the ship's cavernous holds. The Birkenhead workers prepared

tively decided that the voyage to Canada was one in which they did not care to participate, and all 100 consequently went looking for better jobs elsewhere. As this left the vessel short of stokers and deckhands, Kennedy resorted to the time-honored tradition of sending press gangs out to shanghai suitably brawny individuals. Within hours *Great Eastern*'s complement was up to strength, though many of the 100 new crew members were distinctly unhappy with the way in which they'd been enlisted.

The anger of the shanghaied men increased dramatically once *Great Eastern* sailed on the morning of 27 June. Kennedy's Admiralty orders directed him to make for Quebec with all haste, and the 30-year-old Master was determined to do just that. Within minutes of clearing port the liner was building up speed for the dash across the Atlantic, and the sailors in the stoke holds were soon working like men possessed to keep the ship's 10 boilers at peak temperature. By mid-morning several voices were loudly questioning the need for such speed, and just before noon a handful of the impressed seamen announced that they would do no more stoking and demanded to be put ashore immediately.

Kennedy's reaction to this mutinous outburst was both rapid and direct: a 20-man detachment of armed troops was sent into the

Watched by sailors and a group of female passengers, troops muster on *Great Eastern*'s vast main deck during the breakneck passage to Quebec. Enlisted soldiers were housed in the ship's holds, officers and the women and children used the liner's existing staterooms, and the 122 embarked horses were stabled with other livestock on deck. *Illustrated London News*

stoke holds and the mutineers were forced topside at bayonet point. Ordered up the masts and out onto the yards, the reluctant stokers remained exposed to the elements and the smoke from the ship's five funnels for the rest of the day. By nightfall the mutineers were ready to admit the error of their ways and, after doing so, were allowed down. Kennedy gave a brief speech in which he pointedly reminded the men that the liner was on a military mission and her crew was therefore subject to military discipline, and ended by pointing out that under such discipline mutineers could be executed. There were no further breaches of discipline.

Great Eastern kept up her breakneck pace day and night for the next week, and by 2 July was within 800 miles of the St. Lawrence. At that point, however, the liner encountered a thick fog bank, and it appeared that her speed would have to be drastically reduced if she were to avoid a mid-ocean collision with an iceberg or another vessel. Kennedy discussed the situation with his senior officers and the commander of the embarked troops, and all agreed that the need to reach Quebec with the utmost dispatch outweighed the need for caution. The Master therefore ordered additional lookouts into the yards and onto the bowsprit, and *Great Eastern* raced on. The ship easily avoided the several small icebergs she encountered during the next 24 hours, and managed to cover nearly 320 miles.

By the afternoon of 4 July the liner was nearing Cape Race and the fog had grown thicker. Just after three o'clock the bow lookout sighted the figurehead of another liner, the 2,400-ton Cunarder *Arabia*, looming out of the fog and screamed out a warning. Men stationed along *Great Eastern*'s promenade deck relayed the news to the crewmen manning the ship's giant tiller, and the liner's immense bow slowly came about. For a moment it looked like disaster could not be avoided; it seemed the two ships were being drawn inexorably together. Then, at the last possible moment, each ship veered away from the other and continued, undamaged, into the fog.

Captain Kennedy's insistence on the fastest possible passage might have seemed foolhardy to some of his passengers, but it made him a hero in Canada. *Great Eastern* dropped anchor at Quebec exactly eight days and six hours after leaving England, thereby establishing a new record for the

Pictured here during calmer times, Cunard's 2,400-ton *Arabia* very nearly became the victim of Captain Kennedy's headlong rush toward Canada. Herself a veteran of trooping service during the Crimean War, *Arabia* was almost rammed by *Great Eastern* while both were plowing through a fog bank off Cape Race. The liners passed within yards of each other, narrowly averting what undoubtedly would have been the greatest maritime disaster the world had yet seen. *National Archives of Canada*

fastest Atlantic crossing. Crowds of jubilant Canadians lined the Quebec piers for a look at the ship, and her Captain and senior officers were feted at a round of parties and receptions. The troops were off-loaded by lighters over the next two days, and they too were cheered as they set off for camps outside the city.

Great Eastern was lionized in the local press, and "knowledgeable individuals" wrote editorials predicting that the liner would be shifted to full-time trooping upon her return to Britain. This belief, which seemed fully justified by *Great Eastern*'s excellent performance on her first military voyage, was shared by the board of directors of the Great Ship Company. The firm's Canadian representative was instructed to inform Kennedy that he and his crew could enjoy a well-earned three-week rest in Quebec, after which *Great Eastern* should make for Liverpool to take up a probable full-time troop-

ing career. Kennedy used the brief sojourn in Canada to make minor repairs to his ship, and the liner was ready to depart by the first week in August. After embarking 350 paying passengers, Kennedy set a course for England and what promised to be a long and lucrative period of military service for *Great Eastern*.

But like so many other aspects of the huge liner's troubled life, her anticipated trooping career did not work out as expected. By the time *Great Eastern* returned to England, the threat of a Fenian incursion into Canada had evaporated. The Admiralty therefore informed the Great Ship Company that the one-time charter agreement would not be renewed because Her Majesty's government had no immediate need for the vessel and did not wish to needlessly hamper her commercial operations.

The possibility of further military service was not ruled out, but *Great Eastern*'s owners could not

USS *San Jacinto* (at right) lies near the British mail steamer *Trent* as a U.S. boarding party removes the Confederate commissioners Mason and Slidell on 8 November 1861. Britain's desire to further increase the number of troops in Canada in response to this incident nearly led to *Great Eastern*'s second requisitioning. She was still under repair, however, and was passed over in favor of the Cunarders *Australasia* and *Persia*. USNHC

afford to wait for a military charter that might never materialize. The liner therefore returned to civilian service and left for New York in September 1861 with a respectable number of passengers and a fair amount of cargo. Unfortunately, three days out of Liverpool *Great Eastern* ran into heavy weather and was damaged by high seas. The ship was taken back into Queenstown, Ireland, under screw power because both paddle wheels had been disabled. Repairs were begun immediately, but were not completed in time for *Great Eastern* to make what might have been one of the most important voyages of her career.

On 8 November 1861 the U.S. steam frigate USS *San Jacinto*, commanded by Captain Charles Wilkes, stopped the British mail steamer *Trent* 230 miles east of Havana, Cuba. Wilkes led an armed boarding party onto the English vessel and forcibly removed two Confederate diplomats who had been bound for Europe to drum up support for the Southern cause. *Trent* was allowed to resume her journey once the prisoners had been transferred to

San Jacinto, and the U.S. vessel subsequently set a course for the United States.

Wilkes was greeted as a hero upon the frigate's arrival at Norfolk, Virginia, despite the fact that he had acted without the sanction of the U.S. government. News of the incident reached England on 27 November, and the Foreign Office quickly expressed its outrage at such a blatant violation of Britain's neutrality. A strong protest was lodged with the U.S. ambassador in London, as was a demand for a formal apology and the release of the imprisoned Southern diplomats. To underscore the seriousness of the matter, Her Majesty's government decided to increase the number of British troops in Canada, and the Admiralty again approached the Great Ship Company with the offer of a one-time trooping charter for *Great Eastern*. It soon became apparent, however, that repairs to the liner would not be completed in time for the ship to meet the Admiralty deadline, and the charter was there-

Attended by smaller vessels, *Great Eastern* is seen here at Trinity South, Newfoundland, in 1866. The liner had just finished laying the first transatlantic telegraph cable, a feat that was the highlight of her post-trooping years. Brunel's Great Iron Ship never achieved the commercial glory he intended for her, and was ignominiously scrapped in 1888. *National Archives of Canada*

fore awarded to Cunard for the use of its liners *Australasian* and *Persia*.

These two vessels together transported 1,525 troops to Canada in December 1861, though America's decision to release the Confederate envoys and formally apologize to Britain for Wilkes' rash act prevented an outbreak of hostilities and eliminated the need for further transatlantic troop lifts. *Great Eastern*'s mid-ocean breakdown, and her resultant layup for repairs, thus probably changed the course of her subsequent career. Had the liner been available for the second trooping voyage to Canada, and had she performed as well as she had on her first journey, it is likely the Admiralty would have taken her into full-time military service. This was not to be, however, and *Great Eastern* returned to the North Atlantic passenger trade following the January 1862 completion of her repairs.

The story of *Great Eastern*'s ensuing commercial career has been well told elsewhere and will not be repeated here. Suffice it to say that she never attained the level of success Brunel had envisioned for her and, despite her important role in laying the first transatlantic telegraph cable, she ultimately fell into decline and spent the two years prior to her 1889 scrapping as a beached tourist attraction in England.

Yet, despite the way she ended her days, *Great Eastern* remains one of the most important vessels in the history of military sea transportation. In the course of her single trooping voyage, she carried a greater number of human beings than had ever before embarked in a single ship. The number of soldiers she carried on that crossing remained a troopship record for 50 years. But, more importantly, *Great Eastern*'s capacity, coupled with the speed of her crossing and the ease with which she overcame obstacles that would have thwarted lesser vessels, proved the enormous value of the large passenger steamship in both peace and war. Her pioneering efforts paved the way, both militarily and commercially, for those superliners that followed.

Builder: Vulkan Yards, Stettin
Launched: 1901
Length overall: 663 feet
Width: 66 feet
Gross tonnage:
Commercial (as built): 14,908 tons
Military: 23,500 tons (in U.S. service)
Propulsion: Two six-cylinder, quadruple-expansion steam engines with total output of 36,000 hp driving twin screws.
Top speed: 23 knots
Capacity:
Commercial crew: 431
Military crew: 309 (German); 540 (U.S.)
Passengers: 367 First Class, 340 Second Class, 1,054 Steerage Class
Troops: 1,200 (1917); 3,000 (1918); 3,100 (1919)
Armament:
German service: Two 8.8 cm guns, one 7.62 mm machine gun, two 12 cm guns capable of firing only blanks
U.S. service: Eight 5-inch guns, four 3-inch guns, two 3-inch anti-aircraft guns, four 1-pounder cannon, eight .30-caliber machine guns, and two 10-round depth charge rails.
Disposition: Scrapped by Boston Metal Co., Baltimore, Maryland, 1923–1924.

CHAPTER TWO

KRONPRINZ WILHELM

Norddeutscher Lloyd's 14,908-ton *Kronprinz Wilhelm* was launched in 1901 as the second member of the four-ship "Royal Family" of advanced transatlantic express steamers that began with *Kaiser Wilhelm der Grosse.* An elegant and capable ship, *Kronprinz Wilhelm* became a favorite of the traveling public and one of the better-known liners of the early twentieth century. But it was not solely her commercial achievements that made her famous: during World War I she achieved equal renown for her exploits as a warship. During the course of a single eight-month cruise as a German Navy commerce raider, *Kronprinz Wilhelm* proved to be a deadly efficient hunter and firmly established herself as history's most successful passenger liner-turned-auxiliary cruiser. And though her designers could scarcely have imagined it the liner, so quintessentially German in style and ambiance, went on to provide equally sterling service to the U.S. Navy.

Military glory was the farthest thing from the minds of NDL's directors when they commissioned the Vulkan Yards of Stettin to build *Kronprinz Wilhelm.* It was, instead, good business sense that provided the impetus for the vessel's construction because the new liner was

The paint worn from her bow plates by the speed of her passage, *Kronprinz Wilhelm* rests at a New York pier after a 1902 crossing. In September of that year the liner, built as part of NDL's planned four-ship "Royal Family" of express liners, broke the westbound Atlantic crossing record set in 1901 by HAPAG's *Deutschland. Shaum Collection*

As the first ship of NDL's "Royal Family" *Kaiser Wilhelm der Grosse* (seen here entering New York at the end of her 1897 maiden voyage) was the pattern for *Kronprinz Wilhelm*. However, the younger vessel differed in significant respects, and was both faster and moderately more popular than her older sister. *Library of Congress*

intended to capitalize on the commercial success enjoyed by *Kaiser Wilhelm der Grosse* and at the same time compete directly with the Hamburg-Amerika Line's premier transatlantic passenger steamer, *Deutschland*.

Kronprinz Wilhelm was designed to be a somewhat larger and rather more capable version of *Kaiser Wilhelm der Grosse*, and therefore shared the earlier vessel's general layout and silhouette. Like her predecessor, *Kronprinz Wilhelm* had four slightly raked, paired funnels, a knife-like bow, and a counter stern. She was, however, 10 feet longer and 600 tons heavier than her older running mate, and was powered by two sets of quadruple expansion engines instead of the triple expansion powerplants aboard *Kaiser Wilhelm der Grosse*.

Kronprinz Wilhelm's twelve single-ended and four double-ended boilers were divided among four boiler rooms, each of which fed into a separate funnel, and provided the ship's twin screws

with nearly 36,000 horsepower at maximum output. This impressive performance was not without its price, however, because in order to maintain the liner's top speed of 23 knots her furnaces required more than 500 tons of high-grade coal every 24 hours.

Though furnished in the same sort of sumptuous "early German" style as *Kaiser Wilhelm der Grosse*, *Kronprinz Wilhelm* carried her 367 First Class, 340 Second Class, and 1,054 Steerage Class passengers in quarters made much lighter and less oppressively Teutonic through greater use of light-colored woods and larger open spaces. She was, by all accounts, an attractive and capable vessel that struck a fair balance between comfort and speed.

Like *Kaiser Wilhelm der Grosse*, *Kronprinz Wilhelm* was intended from the start for wartime service as a First Line naval auxiliary. She thus had deck plates strengthened to support gun mounts, extra plating over her more sensitive areas, and several specially constructed storage rooms meant to serve as arms rooms and magazines. In addition, the liner's innovative design included features that, though not specifically military, were also important to a potential warship. Among these were an extensive telephone system that permitted instantaneous communication between the bridge and most other parts of the ship, a radio room packed with state-of-the-art equipment, and refrigerated food lockers that allowed the vessel to carry far more provisions than most other contemporary commercial or naval vessels. Taken together these various innovative structural and equipment features made *Kronprinz Wilhelm* potentially the most capable auxiliary cruiser to enter commercial service during the first decade of the twentieth century.

Though prepared for war, *Kronprinz Wilhelm* had been built to fight the vastly more profitable commercial battle of the North Atlantic, and it was a contest in which she excelled. The liner made her maiden voyage in September 1901, and 12 months later broke the record for the fastest westbound Atlantic crossing set the previous year by HAPAG's *Deutschland*. *Kronprinz Wilhelm* quickly became a favorite of the rich and famous of two continents and developed a reputation for comfort, dependability, and respectable speed.

NDL's commissioning of *Kaiser Wilhelm II* in 1903 and *Kronprinzessin Cecilie* four years later completed the four-ship "Royal Family" of express liners. *Kronprinz Wilhelm* continued to play an important role in that partnership well into her middle age. Indeed, by the spring of 1914 the ship was firmly established as a vigorous and profitable member of the quadrumvirate, and a long and prosperous career seemed assured.

The rosy future envisioned for *Kronprinz Wilhelm* by her owners was destined not to be, however; the June 1914 assassination of Austrian Archduke Franz Ferdinand set in motion a chain of events that irrevocably altered the course of the liner's destiny. The murder triggered a seemingly unstoppable drift toward war that saw massive and widespread military mobilization throughout Europe.

For its part the German government, determined not to be caught napping should hostilities break out, began implementing its detailed war plans within days of the archduke's assassination. The men and ships of the Kaiser's naval and merchant fleets figured prominently in those plans,

and the German Admiralty was consequently directed to begin the well-rehearsed shift to a war footing with all speed. Throughout the first weeks of July 1914 dozens of German warships laying in home waters began taking on additional crew members, provisions, ammunition, and coal in preparation for anticipated sorties against the Royal Navy.

Scores of smaller naval and merchant vessels equipped as sea-going supply ships set out for previously established rendezvous points in the Atlantic, Pacific, and Indian oceans, while some of the larger merchant ships previously earmarked for wartime use were brought into shipyards along Germany's Baltic and North Sea coasts for needed reconditioning or conversion work. Most of the larger German passenger steamers were not immediately called up, however. The major steamship companies—loathe to disrupt their sailing schedules in the middle of the summer travel season—convinced the Kaiser's government that the too-hasty withdrawal from service of the nation's preeminent steamers would be a huge public relations gaffe, as well as prematurely eliminating an important source of national revenue.

So it was that the last week of July found *Kronprinz Wilhelm* in New York. Her arrival on the 29th was attended by crowds of well-wishers, though the welcome accorded the German liner was uncharacteristically restrained. Despite the specter of world war looming on the horizon, NDL's New York office seemed determined to conduct business as usual and ordered the liner's master, Captain Karl Grahn, to coal and provision his ship in the usual manner. However, on 31 July the Line's home office directed Grahn to take aboard an additional 2,000 tons of coal and several extra tons of fresh water. The next day NDL canceled the ship's scheduled 4 August sailing and announced that *Kronprinz Wilhelm* would join *Kaiser Wilhelm II, Kronprinzessin Cecilie,* and several other German liners at a Hoboken pier to "await further developments."

But even as NDL spokesmen were assuring the New York press that *Kronprinz Wilhelm* would remain in the United States, very definite plans were being made for her clandestine departure and subsequent use as an auxiliary cruiser. On the evening of 1 August Grahn was summoned to a meeting at NDL's Manhattan office and ordered to get his ship underway at the earliest opportunity.

Grahn was also handed a set of sealed orders—to be opened after *Kronprinz Wilhelm* had safely reached the open sea—that contained detailed instructions regarding the steamer's ultimate destination.

Upon his return to the ship Grahn set his crew to preparing the vessel for both her escape from New York and her transition from liner to warship. Deckhands filled her coal bunkers to overflowing, while teams of engineering personnel checked all of the ship's vital machinery. Workers moved most of the furniture in *Kronprinz Wilhelm*'s passenger accommodations and public rooms into the ship's holds and stacked pillows and mattresses around furnishings and objets d'art that could not be moved. Seamen blacked out the vessel's portholes, nailed sheets of wood over the larger windows and interior decorative glass panels, and set buckets of firefighting sand at strategic points throughout the ship.

All this work was carried out with as much discretion as possible, because any outward sign of impending departure or improvised conversion to naval auxiliary was certain to be quickly relayed to the British warships already gathering just outside U.S. waters. Grahn and his crew carried out most of their preparations unnoticed by the public, though many knowledgeable observers soon realized that the liner was not as dormant as NDL claimed. Among those most interested in the goings-on aboard *Kronprinz Wilhelm* was a team of U.S. Navy intelligence agents and city police detectives tasked with monitoring the movements of German merchant vessels into and out of New York Harbor.

Fortunately for Captain Grahn and his crew, the opportunity to escape New York and the increasingly likely possibility of internment came more quickly than they had dared hope. On the afternoon of 3 August, the same day that the German invasion of Belgium made world war inevitable, a summer thunderstorm blew into New York accompanied by gusty winds and torrential rain. Grahn realized that the dismal weather would help conceal his ship's unannounced departure and ordered his crew to make all preparations for getting the vessel underway.

By eight o'clock that evening all was in readiness, and a few minutes later tugboats eased *Kronprinz Wilhelm* away from her pier and into the main ship channel. As soon as she was pointed in the right direction the tugs cast off and the steamer began to move downriver under her own power. Her departure did not go unnoticed, of course, because British agents had had her under constant surveillance. News of her movement was quickly relayed to the Royal Navy warships offshore. The

Almost as soon as *Kronprinz Wilhelm* made good her 1914 escape from probable internment in New York, her captain ordered her well-known NDL colors to be hidden beneath a coat of dull sea gray. This change, added to the erratic course and high speed the ship maintained, allowed her to reach the rendezvous with SMS *Karlsruhe* unobserved except by a lone British steamer. *Shaum Collection*

British commander expected Grahn to make for Germany by the most direct route, and therefore deployed his ships to the east and north of the New York approaches. But the German master had anticipated the disposition of the enemy flotilla and sought to evade the trap by taking his vessel due south. This unexpected move, combined with the cover provided by the bad weather, allowed *Kronprinz Wilhelm* to reach the open Atlantic undetected.

Once certain that he had evaded the blockade, Grahn opened his sailing orders, which directed him to steam southward and monitor a specific radio frequency for a "message of great importance." This message, received aboard the liner four hours after she cleared Hoboken, was broadcast by the German cruiser SMS *Karlsruhe* and instructed Grahn to rendezvous with the warship on 6 August 300 miles east of Cuba. The signal gave no inkling of what would happen after the rendezvous, and opinion aboard *Kronprinz Wilhelm* was divided as to the ship's ultimate disposition. Some men thought the liner would simply transfer the bulk of its coal, fresh water, and provisions to *Karlsruhe* in order to prolong that vessel's time at sea. Others felt that the warship would supply *Kronprinz Wilhelm* with the guns, ammunition, and naval personnel needed to transform the liner into an AMC.

The cruiser SMS *Karlsruhe*, waiting at the mid-ocean meeting point 300 miles to the east of Cuba, carried weapons, personnel, and equipment vital to *Kronprinz Wilhelm's* success as a ship of war. In return, the liner transferred to *Karlsruhe* much of the additional coal and provisions loaded earlier in New York. *National Archives*

Grahn took no part in most of the discussions about his ship's possible role in the German war effort because he had more pressing matters with which to contend. The most important of these was the question of the liner's immediate survival—scores of Allied ships were scouring the western Atlantic for any sign of the escaped German steamer.

In order to reduce the risk of blundering into the enemy, Grahn doubled the normal number of lookouts and directed the liner's chief radio officer, Lieutenant Brinkmann, to monitor the position reports broadcast by other ships. And though *Kronprinz Wilhelm's* size and silhouette were impossible to disguise completely, Grahn ordered the vessel's distinctive NDL color scheme covered with a coat of sea gray. The German master avoided most other ships by maintaining a high speed, running without lights, and frequently altering course, though early on 4 August the British Ward Line steamer *Sequranca* reported sighting the German liner off Virginia. The sighting report was monitored aboard *Kronprinz Wilhelm*, as were subsequent British Admiralty messages informing those Royal Navy vessels patrolling off the U.S. coast that Britain and Germany were officially at war. This was sobering news for Grahn and his crew because it meant that Allied vessels were now likely to attack the liner on sight rather than attempting to seize her.

Fortunately for *Kronprinz Wilhelm* and the men aboard her, the remainder of the passage to the rendezvous point was uneventful, and *Karlsruhe* hove into sight shortly after 9 A.M. on 6 August. Thirty minutes later the squat and businesslike cruiser and the graceful liner were moored securely to one another, dead in the water but with steam up so that a rapid departure could be made if required.

A hurried meeting with the cruiser's commander soon confirmed what Grahn had anticipated: the orders relayed from Berlin directed the liner's master to turn over to the warship much of the extra coal and provisions loaded aboard *Kronprinz Wilhelm* in New York. In return, *Karlsruhe* would supply the guns and ammunition the liner would need in her new role as commerce raider. Grahn was also ordered to turn over command of his ship to Lieutenant Commander Paul Thierfelder of the German Navy, *Karlsruhe's* 31-year-old navigating officer, who transferred to the liner that afternoon

One of the first people to board *Kronprinz Wilhelm* from *Karlsruhe* was Kapitänleutnant Paul Thierfelder, the liner's new commander. At just 31 years old, *Karlsruhe*'s former navigating officer was the youngest man to command a German auxiliary cruiser in either world war. He returned to German naval service during World War II and died in 1941 while serving as a staff officer in Scandinavia. *Bundesarchiv Koblenz*

accompanied by fifteen senior petty officers. Grahn was instructed to remain with the ship as Thierfelder's senior assistant, while the liner's other officers and crewmen were inducted into naval service for the duration of the cruise. Shortly after Thierfelder and his party came aboard, the Imperial naval ensign was run up the liner's mainmast and *Kronprinz Wilhelm* officially became a ship of war.

The need for *Karlsruhe* and *Kronprinz Wilhelm* to be lashed firmly together, dead in the water, made their mid-ocean rendezvous extremely dangerous. Intercepted British radio traffic indicated that several Allied warships were operating in the vicinity, and the possibility that a British cruiser might appear on the horizon at any moment helped speed the German sailors at their work. Caked with coal dust, teams of men on both vessels worked like demons to transfer the coal and provisions destined for *Karlsruhe*, while at the same time *Kronprinz Wilhelm*'s derricks hoisted aboard the two 8.8 cm rapid-fire guns, 290 rounds of ammunition, thirty rifles, and single water-cooled machine gun that were to constitute the steamer's armament. Over the din of clanging hatch covers, shouted commands, rattling chains, and the whine of cable and rope passing through a dozen winches boomed a medley of patriotic tunes played by the liner's orchestra.

Though this chaos went on until well into the afternoon, barely a third of the equipment and

Elderly yet still dangerous, the British cruiser HMS *Suffolk* surprised *Kronprinz Wilhelm* and *Karlsruhe* during the mid-ocean rendezvous. When the German vessels separated, Admiral Sir Christopher Cradock aboard *Suffolk* chose to pursue the only one he could positively identify as a warship. By following *Karlsruhe,* Craddock allowed *Kronprinz Wilhelm* to slip away to begin her immensely successful career as a commerce raider. *USNHC*

supplies intended to pass between the ships had been put across when, just before three o'clock, the sudden appearance on the horizon of the British cruiser HMS *Suffolk* brought work to a sudden halt. The shriek of *Kronprinz Wilhelm*'s siren, triggered by a lookout in the liner's crow's nest, sent the crews of both German ships into a frenzy as teams of men used axes to sever the lines binding the vessels together and gun crews rushed to their stations aboard *Karlsruhe*. Almost before the lines holding them had been cut, both ships surged forward, their screws churning the water as they began to build up speed. The liner's musicians struck up "Deutschland Uber Alles" and men continued to transfer supplies from one vessel to the other until the gap between the ships grew too wide.

Once up to maneuvering speed, *Kronprinz Wilhelm* turned sharply to port, while *Karlsruhe* began a broad turn to starboard in order to draw the British cruiser away from the vulnerable liner. Aboard *Suffolk* Rear Admiral Sir Christopher Cradock, suddenly confronted with two targets where seconds before only one had been visible, hesitated briefly before deciding to pursue the one target identifiable as a German warship. Cradock's momentary indecision gave Thierfelder the opening he needed, and he ordered *Kronprinz Wilhelm*'s helmsman to steer a course away from the bearing taken by the cruisers. The liner, her engines driving

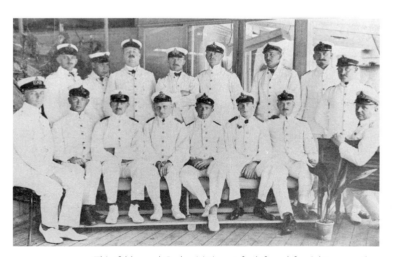

Thierfelder and Grahn (sitting at far left and far right, respectively, in this 1914 group photo) could rely on the talents of a diverse group of junior officers. Drawn from both the Navy and the merchant marine, these men included Count Alfred von Niezychowski (standing far left, behind Thierfelder) whose account of the liner's exploits as a German raider became a postwar bestseller. *Bundesarchiv Koblenz*

her through the water at a speed she had not achieved since her youth, rapidly retired westward as the fast-disappearing warships exchanged their opening volleys.

In the days immediately following the rendezvous with *Karlsruhe*, *Kronprinz Wilhelm* steered a course meant to throw off any pursuing Allied vessels. Thierfelder took his ship north, then west, then southwest, finally settling on a fairly direct course for the Azores where he hoped to meet the small German supply steamer *Walhalla*. Though radio traffic monitored aboard the liner indicated *Karlsruhe* had successfully eluded *Suffolk* and subsequently escaped unscathed from a brief fight with the cruiser HMS *Bristol*, it also quickly became clear that the Allies had redoubled their efforts to locate and neutralize *Kronprinz Wilhelm*. The airwaves were buzzing with messages between enemy warships, and it was only through a combination of skill, intuition, and good fortune that the tireless Thierfelder was able to guide his vessel safely through an increasingly strong cordon of Allied warships.

Kronprinz Wilhelm's crew was kept as busy as her captain during the voyage toward the Azores because there was much still to be done to ready the ship for war. The first order of business, of course, was to mount her weaponry. The two 8.8 cm guns supplied by *Karlsruhe* were manhandled into position and bolted to reinforced deck sections on either side of the liner's forecastle, giving each weapon a 180-degree field of fire. Mounting brackets attached to each bridge wing ensured that the single Maxim machine gun could be moved from one side of the vessel to the other as needed, and positions for riflemen were established at various points on the upper decks.

While the gunners were emplacing their weapons and constructing watertight ready-ammunition lockers, other crewmen were nailing mattresses and carpets over those areas of *Kronprinz Wilhelm*'s superstructure that would be exposed to enemy fire. The padding was intended to add some degree of protection from bullets and shell splinters, and was especially heavy around the bridge and the former Smoking Room. This latter space had been converted into a hospital and was equipped with a makeshift operating theater and twenty beds.

As a final preparation, a team led by the Engineering Officer converted the Grand Salon into a huge reserve coal bin. The men cut holes in

Kronprinz Wilhelm's deck crew was as colorful and capable as her officers. Most of the liner's prewar crew stayed with the ship when she became a raider, as did these two coal-darkened stokers taking a well-earned topside break. The ship's voracious appetite kept the black gang busy around the clock; *Kronprinz Wilhelm*'s prodigious coal consumption ultimately helped bring about the premature end to her AMC career. *Bundesarchiv Koblenz*

bulkheads and deck plates so that coal taken aboard from other vessels could be shoveled quickly off the deck into the Salon or directly down into the liner's bunkers.

The morning of 18 August found *Kronprinz Wilhelm* within sight of the Azores' San Miguel Island, where she was joined by the *Walhalla* shortly after nine o'clock. The two ships traveled in company for the next four days, joined together by ropes while transferring coal and provisions during daylight and cruising a few miles apart during darkness. Though intercepted radio traffic made it clear that numerous Allied vessels were in the North Atlantic, the German replenishment operation was completed without interference. By the time the two vessels parted company, *Kronprinz Wilhelm* had taken aboard several tons of food and fresh water and 2,500 tons of coal. In return the liner had transferred several sacks of mail and 100 older and less fit crew members to *Walhalla* for onward passage to Germany.

The coal *Kronprinz Wilhelm* took aboard from *Walhalla* was sufficient for two weeks of cruising at reduced speed; Thierfelder was optimistic that within that time he would be able to take enough coal from captured enemy vessels to fill the liner's bunkers. But though the German captain positioned his ship in the potentially lucrative shipping lanes leading to South America, southern Africa, and Australia, *Kronprinz Wilhelm* encountered only a neutral Danish schooner and a small and decrepit Russian barque in the two weeks following the rendezvous with *Walhalla*.

Neither of the intercepted ships was carrying coal or other goods of use to the German raider, and both were allowed to go free. Fortunately for Thierfelder and his crew, a 3 September meeting with the German supply ship *Asuncion* off Brazil's Cape San Roque provided enough coal for a few more days' steaming, though the need to locate and capture a coal-laden prize remained.

Kronprinz Wilhelm's luck took a turn for the better on the day following her rendezvous with *Asuncion*. Just after eight o'clock on the evening of 4 September the liner's lookouts spotted the 2,840-ton Princess Line steamer *Indian Prince*. Thierfelder maneuvered his ship close to the British vessel before an alarm was raised, and by ordering lights shined on the commerce raider's guns was able to convince the steamer's master to surrender his ship without resistance.

Darkness and rough seas prevented the Germans from boarding their prize immediately, though at first light the following morning the hapless victim was secured along the raider's port side and searched as both ships moved along at four knots. *Indian Prince* was a fine catch; she carried cocoa, coffee, and preserved food in addition to the several hundred tons of high grade coal in her bunkers.

Thierfelder was anxious to begin stripping his prize immediately, but he wisely ordered the British vessel to follow *Kronprinz Wilhelm* to a less heavily traveled area of ocean well outside the shipping lanes. Once there the steamer was secured alongside and plundered while both vessels moved slowly ahead. Four days after her capture, relieved of coal and cargo and with her small crew and twelve passengers installed in First Class staterooms aboard *Kronprinz Wilhelm*, *Indian Prince* was scuttled.

Though Thierfelder and his crew saw the capture of their first prize as an omen of successes yet to come, it was to be some time before *Kronprinz Wilhelm* took a second victim. Two days after dispatching *Indian Prince* the liner met the German supply vessel *Ebernburg* northwest of Cape San Roque, and for the next three weeks the raider coaled and provisioned from this vessel and two other supply ships that subsequently appeared at the rendezvous point.

The only break from the routine of transferring coal and supplies occurred on 14 September, when *Kronprinz Wilhelm*'s radio operators monitored a transmission indicating that the German

Led by Leutnant zur See Biermann (at right), the crew of one of *Kronprinz Wilhelm*'s two 8.8 cm SK L/45 guns goes through its paces for the camera. These two weapons were provided by *Karlsruhe* and were the largest carried by the commerce raider. They were used to fire warning shots and sink enemy vessels once they had been stripped of everything useful. *Bundesarchiv Koblenz*

commerce raider *Cap Trafalgar* was engaged in a life-and-death fight with the British AMC HMS *Carmania* 150 miles to the south. In a rare display of poor judgment, Thierfelder immediately cast his ship off from the supply vessels and headed at top speed toward *Cap Trafalgar*'s last reported position. This quixotic gesture was understandable given the fact that a comrade was under attack, yet nonetheless violated the German Admiralty's standing orders that Thierfelder avoid enemy detection at all costs. Fortunately for *Kronprinz Wilhelm*'s future career as a raider, *Carmania* sent *Cap Trafalgar* to the bottom before Thierfelder could intercede. He thus had no choice but to return to his rendezvous point and resume the interrupted resupply effort.

Kronprinz Wilhelm's second and most important victory occurred on 7 October when she captured the 8,500-ton British cargo steamer *La Correntina* 200 miles east of Buenos Aires. A new and advanced ship that was the pride of Britain's Houlder Line, *La Correntina* boasted the largest refrigerating capacity of any vessel then afloat and was bound for Liverpool with 7.5 million pounds of frozen Argentine beef. The loss of this cargo was a blow sorely felt in butcher shops and kitchens throughout the United Kingdom, and the steamer's sinking was an excellent example of the type of economic havoc that could be caused by a single well-placed and aggressive commerce raider.

La Correntina was the largest and richest prize *Kronprinz Wilhelm* would take during her military career; it yielded 1,800 tons of coal, several tons of food and fresh water, two brand-new 12 cm cannons and 20 rifles in addition to the frozen beef. The two large cannons were an especially welcome sight because they were of the latest design and much more capable than the liner's existing armament.

Unfortunately, the British steamer had no ammunition for the guns and they were therefore useless as offensive weapons. Thierfelder nonetheless ordered the cannon transferred to *Kronprinz Wilhelm* for use in training gun crews and firing of warning shots using modified saluting cartridges. The guns were emplaced on either side of the raider's aft superstructure by the time the thorough stripping of *La Correntina* was completed on 14 October. That afternoon the hapless steamer's seacocks were opened and demolition charges exploded in her engine room and cargo holds. As her crew and a handful of passengers watched from the German raider's decks, the refrigerator ship capsized and went down by the bow.

Kronprinz Wilhelm's sinking of *La Correntina* produced howls of outrage in England's press and in Parliament, and the furor increased as the converted liner continued to prey on Allied shipping. In the five months following the destruction of the refrigerator ship, Thierfelder and his crew sank no fewer than 13 vessels totaling 49,000 tons.

The fact that most of the raider's prizes were relatively small and of only minimal worth to the Allied war effort in no way lessened the importance of *Kronprinz Wilhelm*'s activities for her attacks had a value far beyond the merely economic. The threat posed by the liner's operations in the South Atlantic shipping lanes forced the Royal Navy to maintain a constant presence in the area—a task that required ships, men, and resources that could have been put to better use elsewhere.

Moreover, the German raider's activities helped disrupt the flow of food and raw materials from South America and southern Africa to Europe. This in turn hindered the Allies' ability to supply their military forces and feed their civilian populations and thereby fanned the flames of national discontent in Britain and France. And, finally, the Royal Navy's continued inability to locate and destroy the converted liner was a propaganda gold mine that the German government exploited at every opportunity.

Kronprinz Wilhelm's career as an AMC was a successful one, but by mid-March 1915 several factors were combining to end that career. First was the ship's increasingly poor mechanical and structural condition; after more than seven months of continuous cruising the liner was simply worn out. Her boilers and machinery had not been cleaned or serviced since the vessel had left Germany on her last commercial passage to the United States, and the repeated banging of hulls with replenishment vessels and prizes had severely damaged her portside plates and adjacent deck areas.

Second, the demands made on the ship by the nature of her work were matched by the hardships endured by her crew. The constant fear and anxiety of the pirate's life, the long hours of backbreaking labor, the infrequent availability of decent food and scarcity of fresh water, and the lack of proper medicines had all combined to steadily reduce the number of men fit for duty. Indeed, by the time *Kronprinz Wilhelm* captured her last prize—the 3,800-ton British freighter *Colby*—on 28 March more than 40 of the raider's officers and crewmen were incapacitated by beriberi and scores of others were in the first stages of the disease.

And, third, by January 1915 the Royal Navy had become increasingly adept at neutralizing the German raiders still at large in the Atlantic. This was done through better protection of Allied merchant ships and better use of available intelligence resources to eliminate the network of small German support vessels upon which many of the raiders relied for fuel, ammunition, and provisions. The increasingly effective British campaign to eliminate Germany's naval supply network in the south Atlantic ultimately proved to be a key factor in ending *Kronprinz Wilhelm*'s raiding career.

After *Colby* had been stripped and scuttled Thierfelder set his ship on a northwesterly course toward a rendezvous with the supply vessel *Macedonia* 200 miles north of the Brazilian coast. Once he had coaled and provisioned the liner, Thierfelder intended to strike north toward neutral Norway and, if the opportunity arose, make a dash through the North Sea to a German port.

This was not to be, however; Allied naval intelligence had pinpointed *Macedonia*'s location and

Seen from directly astern, *Kronprinz Wilhelm* rides quietly at anchor soon after her April 1915 arrival in Newport News. Though her paint shows the effects of many hard days at sea, her Navy ensign still flies proudly, directly above the two 12 cm guns taken from the prize *La Correntina*. These weapons were just for show, however, because there was never any ammunition for them. *Shaum Collection*

the freighter was being captured by two British cruisers even as *Kronprinz Wilhelm* came over the horizon. Fortunately for the raider, a lookout spotted the enemy warships in time and Thierfelder was able to avoid detection and escape by keeping

Obviously relieved to be safely interned in a still-neutral port, members of *Kronprinz Wilhelm*'s crew pose for a group photo soon after the ship's arrival in Virginia. They had good reason to be pleased with themselves and their ship because in the course of her single wartime cruise as a German AMC, *Kronprinz Wilhelm* became the most successful liner-turned-commerce raider in naval history. *National Archives*

his vessel's bow pointed at the cruisers and steaming in reverse until the warships disappeared from sight. Thierfelder kept *Kronprinz Wilhelm* in the vicinity of the rendezvous point for several days, hoping to make contact with another supply ship, but a shortage of coal and a crew decimated by disease soon made it obvious that the liner's freebooting days were over. Internment in the nearest neutral port was now the only alternative to eventual capture or destruction by the Allied naval forces ranged against the German raider.

The haven Thierfelder chose was Newport News, Virginia, and by the night of 10 April *Kronprinz Wilhelm* was 60 miles off the U.S. coast. Proximity to the neutral port did not ensure the ship's survival, however; Thierfelder knew that sev-

eral British cruisers were loitering just outside U.S. waters to prevent German vessels from reaching the safety of Chesapeake Bay. But Thierfelder and his crew had seven months' experience in evading capture and were determined not to be taken. After calling the ship's company to battle stations, the German captain ordered "Full Ahead" and the liner surged forward.

By using the cover of darkness and this last desperate burst of speed, Thierfelder was able to take his ship directly between two British cruisers patrolling off Cape Henry. Just after 10 o'clock on the morning of 11 April 1915, *Kronprinz Wilhelm* entered the harbor to the sound of a salute fired by ships of the U.S. Atlantic Fleet. The dropping of the liner's anchor ended the 72-day cruise during

During much of her internment at the Philadelphia Naval Shipyard, *Kronprinz Wilhelm* lay alongside NDL's 8,797-ton *Prinz Eitel Friedrich* (here between *Kronprinz Wilhelm* and a target raft). The smaller liner had served as an AMC in the Far East until forced into Newport News—and internment—in March 1915. Following the United States' 1917 entry into the war, *Prinz Eitel Friedrich* was commissioned into the U.S. Navy as the troopship USS *De Kalb. USNHC*

which she had sailed more than 37,600 miles and destroyed 60,522 tons of Allied shipping.

Though Thierfelder couldn't have known it, his choice of haven ultimately resulted in a second military career for *Kronprinz Wilhelm*. Within hours of the liner's arrival in the United States, the German embassy in Washington asked the U.S. government's permission to make repairs to the battered vessel in Norfolk and then return her to Germany. This request was promptly denied, and on the morning after her appearance in Virginia the ship was interned for the duration of the war.

She was subsequently moved to the naval shipyard in Philadelphia, where for the next two years she sat tied to a pier with a small staff of workmen her only inhabitants.

This quiet interlude ended, however, upon the United States' entry into World War I. The liner was seized by the U.S. government on 6 April 1917, as were her NDL running mates *Kaiser Wilhelm II* and *Kronprinzessin Cecilie* and dozens of other German vessels interned in U.S. ports. On the morning of 9 June 1917 *Kronprinz Wilhelm* was renamed USS *Von Steuben*[1] and commissioned into the U.S. Navy. The

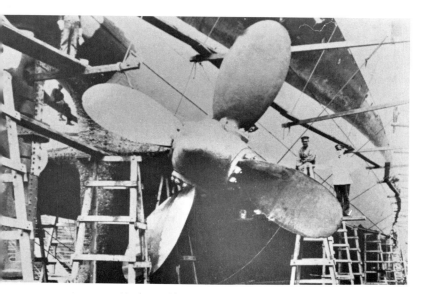

Her long raiding cruise had been hard on *Kronprinz Wilhelm*, and following her 9 June 1917 commissioning as USS *Von Steuben* the tired and somewhat battered liner entered a Philadelphia Naval Shipyard dry dock for a comprehensive overhaul and fitting out as a trooper. Here her starboard screw dwarfs the men working on it and the surrounding hull plates. *USNHC*

extensive repairs needed to return the ship to fighting trim began the following day.

The Navy's renovation of *Von Steuben* lasted nearly four months and was as comprehensive as time and budgetary constraints would allow. After removing the furnishings and accouterments that had been stored in the liner's holds since the outbreak of war, the shipyard work teams turned their attention to the ship herself. Welders and metal workers repaired her battered hull and superstructure while engineers and mechanics completely overhauled the ship's boilers, engines, propeller shafts, and steering gear.

The Navy originally intended to use *Von Steuben* as an AMC and her Philadelphia renovation therefore included the installation of eight 5-inch and four 3-inch guns, two 3-inch anti-aircraft mounts, four 1-pounder cannons, eight machine guns, and two fantail-mounted depth charge rails. These weapons were retained even after the Navy's 21 September 1917 decision to instead use the vessel as a troopship, a change of tasking that necessitated the hurried installation of troop bunks, latrines, a compact sick bay, and additional freshwater tanks. This additional work was completed in just eight days, and *Von Steuben* was ready for service on 29 September 1917. After a month spent working-up off the eastern seaboard, she made for New York's Brooklyn Navy Yard. Upon her 28 October arrival there, the liner joined the New York Division of

Norddeutscher Lloyd's 19,350-ton *Kaiser Wilhelm II*, seen here following her commissioning as the troopship USS *Agamemnon*, was the third of the four units in NDL's "Royal Family" of express liners. *Kaiser Wilhelm II* was both longer and heavier than her older sister *Kronprinz Wilhelm*, attributes that may have helped her avoid serious damage in the November 1917 collision with *Von Steuben*. *National Archives*

Her mangled stem clearly visible, *Von Steuben* (at right) limps toward France under threatening skies following the collision with *Agamemnon* (center); *Mount Vernon* is at left. The damage was partially repaired in Brest and *Von Steuben* was able to set out for Philadelphia under her own power for more complete repairs. *USNHC*

Rear Admiral Albert Gleaves' Atlantic Fleet Cruiser and Transport Force.

Von Steuben began the first of her nine wartime transatlantic trooping voyages on 31 October 1917, departing New York bound for Brest with 1,223 troops aboard. This first crossing was undertaken in familiar company—the other three troopships in the escorted convoy were the former German liners USS *Agamemnon* (ex-*Kaiser Wilhelm II*), USS *Mount Vernon* (ex-*Kronprinzessen Cecilie*), and USS *America* (the former HAPAG *Amerika*).

It also proved to be an eventful crossing; on the evening of 9 November *Von Steuben* collided with *Agamemnon* during a zigzag maneuver. Though sea water flooded in through *Von Steuben*'s mangled stem, she proceeded under her own power while damage-control parties made temporary repairs. The other vessels initially pulled ahead but eventually rejoined the limping *Von Steuben* so that the first convoy of U.S. troops to reach France might arrive as one. This they did on 12 November, pulling into Brest harbor to the sound of bands and the cheering of well-wishers.

The damage *Von Steuben* sustained in her collision with *Agamemnon* could not be repaired completely in Brest's already overworked shipyard, so workmen spent a week shoring up her bow and filling it with concrete ballast to enable the liner to return to the United States for a more comprehen-

Though damage control parties and French engineers saw to *Von Steuben*'s collision damage, it was the members of her black gangs that kept her boilers going after the accident and on the slow voyage home. Here sailors feed her coal on the passage between Brest and Halifax, Nova Scotia. *USNHC*

On her post-collision return voyage to Philadelphia, *Von Steuben* entered Halifax just hours after the explosion of the French ammunition ship *Mont Blanc*. The blast and subsequent fires destroyed much of the harbor area, and *Von Steuben*'s crew spent four days helping with the rescue and firefighting efforts. *National Archives of Canada*

sive refit. The ship departed for Philadelphia on 28 November and the voyage was uneventful until *Von Steuben* reached a point 40 miles east of Halifax, Nova Scotia, on the morning of 6 December.

Shortly after nine o'clock a lookout reported a huge column of black smoke climbing over the Canadian port and almost immediately the ship was buffeted by the shock wave of a tremendous explosion. Speculation as to the cause of the blast was rife aboard *Von Steuben* as the liner headed for Halifax at top speed, but no one was prepared for the scene of total devastation that greeted the troopship when she entered the port that afternoon. The French ammunition ship *Mont Blanc* had collided with a Belgian freighter in the center of the harbor, and the resulting explosion and fire killed more than 1,000 people and virtually demolished the port area and parts of the surrounding city. *Von Steuben*'s commander immediately sent work parties ashore to assist the Canadian authorities. For the next four days the U.S. sailors did what they could to help rescue survivors, bury the dead, and patrol the gutted streets.

Von Steuben left the ruins of Halifax harbor on 10 December and, after a stop in Philadelphia, reached Newport News five days later. The Navy had intended to put the liner into dry dock at this point for comprehensive repairs of her collision damage, but it became apparent that all of the Atlantic coast shipyards capable of handling a vessel of her size were filled to capacity. The commander of the Atlantic Fleet Cruiser and Transport Force, Admiral Gleaves, directed that the liner be repaired at the U.S. Navy dry dock at Balboa on the southern end of the Panama Canal. He further ordered that *Von Steuben* "pay her freight" on the voyage south by transporting to Cuba 2,000 U.S. Marines intended to bolster that island's defenses. This the troopship did, departing Newport News on 20 December and disembarking the Marines at Guantanamo Bay five days later.

By 29 December the liner had transited the Panama Canal and was securely ensconced in the Balboa dry dock. When she reemerged on 20 January 1918, *Von Steuben* sported an entirely new bow and a startling "dazzle-pattern" camouflage paint scheme that incorporated—at least for a short time—the silhouette of a full-sized destroyer painted on the vessel's port side[2].

Von Steuben returned to Philadelphia on 1 February after a stop in Newport News and resumed her transatlantic trooping duties nine days later. The liner made three uneventful round-trips to France during the next three months, transporting 1,500 troops on each outbound voyage. In late May she was withdrawn from service for minor structural modifications intended to increase her passenger capacity by 20 percent.

Fresh from her repairs at Balboa in the Panama Canal Zone, *Von Steuben* sports an experimental paint scheme incorporating the life-size silhouette of a destroyer. Complete with simulated bow wake, the image was thought to be indistinguishable from a real destroyer at ranges of more than a half mile. It was nonetheless quickly replaced by a dazzle-pattern camouflage scheme. *Shaum Collection*

During this revamping of her troop accommodations, *Von Steuben* was provided with several hundred foldaway bunks, known as "pipe berths," which were attached to the walls of passageways and other areas previously considered unsuitable for troop berthing. Additional hammocks were also brought aboard, and together these measures increased the ship's troop capacity to over 3,000. *Von Steuben* first made use of these new accommodations on the voyage that began on 27 May 1918, during which she carried 3,112 troops to Brest.

It was on the return half of this fifth trooping voyage that *Von Steuben* had her closest brush with disaster. The liner was two days out of Brest and traveling unescorted when, shortly after noon on 18 June, a lookout reported wreckage on the horizon. It soon became apparent that the "wreckage" was actually a string of seven lifeboats, each under sail and presumably carrying survivors of a torpedoed Allied ship. When *Von Steuben* was about five miles from the pathetic little flotilla, Captain Yates Sterling Jr., intent on rescuing the survivors yet well aware that a U-boat might still be lurking in the area, ordered reduced speed and directed his helmsman to begin a cautious approach to the lifeboats.

Sterling's caution was well-founded because just minutes after he ordered the approach, lookout Louis Seltzer reported the wake of an incoming torpedo racing toward the liner's bow from a point off the port beam. Sterling immediately ordered the ship's wheel hard to starboard and all engines full astern, while *Von Steuben*'s gun crews opened fire on the torpedo and an object they took to be the periscope of the attacking sub. The maneuvering paid off—the torpedo missed the liner's bow by a matter of feet. A vigorous depth-charging of the submarine's last presumed position produced no visible results, and *Von Steuben* soon resumed her course for Philadelphia. The occupants of the lifeboats, survivors of the torpedoed British steamer *Dwinsk*, were later picked up by a passing freighter. The German submarine that had sunk their ship and then tried to ambush *Von Steuben*, the *U-151*, survived the liner's depth charge attack but was severely rattled and required an extensive refit upon her return to Kiel.

Though *Von Steuben*'s sixth trooping voyage didn't attract the attention of the German Navy, the trip nonetheless proved to be nearly as dangerous as the preceding voyage had been. The liner

45

Like all dazzle schemes, *Von Steuben*'s (seen here soon after its application) used unique combinations of bold shapes over a dull gray base to break up a vessel's silhouette and confuse the enemy as to the true direction, speed, and size of the camouflaged ship. The pattern was different on each side of the trooper. *National Archives*

departed New York on 30 June as part of a Brest-bound convoy that included the troopship USS *Henderson* and several escorts. All went well until just after noon on the third day of the crossing when smoke suddenly belched from *Henderson*'s forward cargo hold. The troopship veered out of position in the convoy and drifted to a stop, her complement of troops milling on deck while her crew attempted to contain the fire and launch the vessel's lifeboats.

Almost as soon as the fire was observed aboard *Henderson,* the convoy commander ordered *Von Steuben* to close with the stricken vessel and act as a rescue ship while the escorting destroyers formed an anti-submarine screen around the two transports. *Von Steuben* moved to within 300 yards of the burning vessel and stayed near at hand, silhouetted by the flames, for the next 10 hours. By the time the rescue effort ended early the following morning, more than 2,200 troops had been safely transferred to *Von Steuben* and the fire aboard *Henderson* had been brought sufficiently under control to allow her crew to bring the vessel about and start slowly for home. *Von Steuben* continued on to France, arriving in Brest on 9 July packed with more than 5,000 troops. Three days later, having coaled, provisioned, and embarked 1,100 wounded troops bound for hospitals in the United States, she departed for New York.

Though dazzle patterns were different for each ship, they could often appear similar on vessels of the same general class. In this July 1918 photo, *Mount Vernon* (ex-*Kronprinzessin Cecilie*, the fourth and final ship of NDL's "Royal Family") shows off a pattern that closely resembles that worn by her older sister *Von Steuben*. *USNHC*

Von Steuben's seventh and eighth round-trip Atlantic crossings took place between 18 August and 10 October 1918. Each involved carrying troops to France on the eastbound leg and ferrying wounded soldiers to stateside hospitals on the westbound voyage. Though unopposed by the enemy, each trip was far from peaceful. While returning from France on the seventh trip, *Von Steuben* was caught up in a hurricane that washed three crewmen overboard, injured hundreds of troops, and battered the ship herself. Worse was yet to come, however; on the eighth voyage the ship was struck by an outbreak of influenza that literally decimated the troop complement and crew.

The great influenza pandemic of 1918–1919, the infamous "Plague of the Spanish Lady," would ultimately kill nearly three times as many people worldwide as would World War I itself[3]. By the time the former German liner began embarking troops on 13 September, the disease had already begun to scourge the dozens of U.S. Army posts used as assembly points for Europe-bound units. It was thus virtually certain that the disease would appear on the crowded U.S. troopships plying the North Atlantic; *Von Steuben*'s chief medical officer was not particularly surprised when the first case appeared aboard his ship two days out of New York. He was shocked, however, by the speed with which the disease

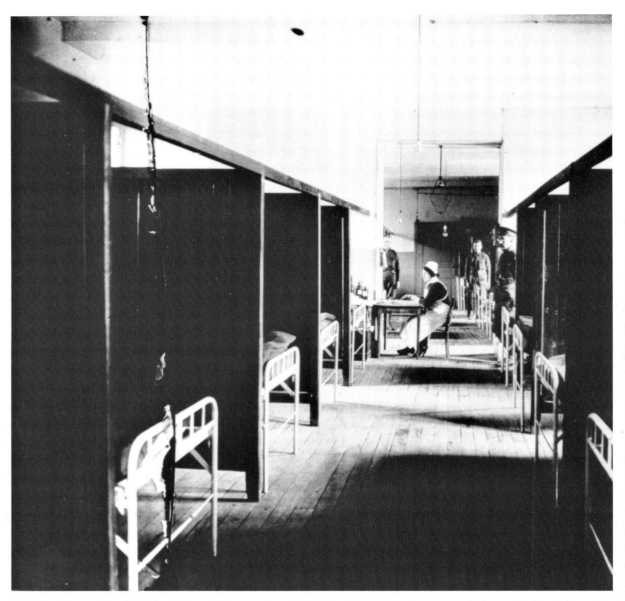

Like virtually every other ship in the Cruiser and Transport Force, *Von Steuben* did not escape the scourge of influenza. On her ninth trooping voyage, 40 of her more than 4,000 embarked troops died of the disease and hundreds of seriously ill soldiers had to be hospitalized in France. Many of those removed from the troopships ended up in influenza isolation wards like this one at Brest's U.S. Army Camp Hospital No. 3. *National Library of Medicine*

spread, the indescribable suffering it inflicted on its victims, and the total ineffectiveness of all known treatments. By the time *Von Steuben* docked in Brest on 24 September, 400 men were critically ill and 40 had died, making the influenza virus the most formidable enemy with which the ship had to contend during her entire military career.

Von Steuben completed her ninth wartime troop crossing on 8 November 1918, and two days later entered dry dock in Brooklyn for a complete

overhaul. This respite was well earned; in twelve months' service the ship had transported to France 14,347 troops and several thousand tons of vital war materiel. The ship's value to the United States did not end with the 11 November signing of the armistice ending World War I because Navy planners had already earmarked the former liner for duty returning U.S. troops from Europe. The ship took up this task immediately after the 2 March 1919 completion of her overhaul, and in the course of eight round-trip voyages made over the next

Clearly battered by her trooping service, *Von Steuben* nonetheless makes a colorful show following the 11 November 1918 armistice that ended World War I. The troopship went on to serve for another eight months, returning thousands of U.S. servicemen from France before her 13 October 1919 decommissioning and transfer to the U.S. Shipping Board. *National Archives*

eight months, *Von Steuben* returned more than 22,000 troops to their homeland.

The end of the colossal national effort to repatriate the American Expeditionary Force from Europe inevitably brought *Von Steuben*'s eventful military career to a close. The battering the ship suffered in four years' duty as both commerce raider and troop transport ruled out any return to civilian service, and Navy plans for using the vessel for peacetime trooping voyages to the Far East didn't survive the massive budget cuts inflicted on the U.S. military services as soon as the war ended. *Von Steuben* was consequently decommissioned on 13 October 1919 and her name was struck from the Navy list the following day. She passed to the control of the United States Shipping Board (USSB) at that time, and in March 1923 the once-proud liner was sold to the Boston Metal Company for scrapping.

Builder: John Brown and
  Company, Clydebank,
  Scotland.
Launched: 1905
Length overall: 678 feet
Width: 72 feet
Gross tonnage (as built):
  19,650 tons
Propulsion: Coal-fired
  steam turbines
  (converted to oil-fired
  in 1923–1924)
Top speed: 20 knots
Capacity:
  Crew: 600–650
  Passengers: 300 First
  Class, 326 Second Class,
  and 2,000 Third Class.
Armament: Eight 4.7-inch
  guns, with secondary
  armament of machine
  guns and small arms.
Disposition: Scrapped at
  Blythe, Scotland, in
  1932.

CHAPTER THREE

CARMANIA

Of all the great passenger steamships that have won renown for their wartime exploits, none has the unique claim to fame of Cunard's elegant *Carmania*. Though built to be a trendsetter of an entirely different sort, the ship holds the distinction of having fought, and won, the only liner-versus-liner battle in history. And though tactically insignificant in itself, that action was to have a far-reaching impact on the way in which passenger liners were subsequently used in wartime.

Carmania's eventual military importance was the last thing on the minds of those who originally conceived her, however. Designed in the first years of the twentieth century, she and her sister ship *Caronia* were intended to be Cunard's answer to the challenge presented by the White Star Line's introduction of the intermediate steamers *Celtic* and *Cedric*.

Launched in 1901 and 1903, respectively, the White Star ships profoundly altered the nature of the transatlantic passenger trade by emphasizing capacity and economical operation over speed. Though five knots slower than the express liners whose exploits were the usual focus of public attention, the new intermediate vessels offered greater cargo capacity, increased stability, and, most importantly, significantly reduced coal consumption. The commercial threat posed by the innovative White Star steamers, coupled with the company's announced intention to add two more ships of

Used as a test ship for the type of turbine engines that ultimately powered the larger *Lusitania* and *Mauretania*, *Carmania* was both faster and easier to maintain than vessels powered by conventional reciprocating engines. She was also attractive, popular, and comparatively economical to operate; the years between her 1905 launching and the outbreak of World War I were busy ones for her. *Shaum Collection*

similar design[1] to its fleet, made Cunard's fielding of comparable vessels an economic necessity.

As advanced as Cunard's two new intermediate steamers were to be, their construction also offered the company a chance to undertake an in-service evaluation of the propulsion systems being considered for the two full-size express liners then on the drawing boards. These vessels, *Lusitania* and *Mauretania*, were intended to be world-class record breakers and there was intense debate within the Cunard Line as to whether they should be driven by traditional quadruple-expansion engines or the more advanced but unproven steam turbines. So it was that when contracts for the intermediate ships were awarded to John Brown and Company of Clydebank, they specified that *Caronia* would incorporate conventional machinery, while *Carmania* would have turbines.

Construction of both liners proceeded without difficulty, and they were launched in 1905. On her builder's trials, *Carmania* attained a top speed of 20.4 knots compared with *Caronia*'s 19.7, though it was the former's reduced coal consumption and much-simplified maintenance requirements as much as her speed that ultimately decided Cunard in favor of adopting turbines for the *Lusitania* pair.

Put to work on the Liverpool-to-New York service—with occasional off-season trips to Italy—*Carmania* and her running mate proved both popular and profitable. Known as the "Pretty Sisters," they each carried 300 First Class, 326 Second Class, and 2,000 Third Class passengers in understated yet obvious style. Though a June 1912 fire took *Carmania* out of service for several months, she was back on duty in time to participate in the October 1913 rescue of survivors from the immigrant ship *Volturno*, which caught fire while en route from Rotterdam to New York. After that it was back to the transatlantic routine, which she maintained right up to the 1914 outbreak of war.

That event found *Carmania* at sea, three days out of Liverpool on the return voyage from New York. Notified by wireless that hostilities had begun, Captain J. C. Barr set extra lookouts and ordered the liner's exterior lights extinguished and her portholes covered over. Knowing that Cunard had pledged *Carmania* to Royal Navy service in wartime as part of the 1903 subsidy agreement that financed construction of *Lusitania* and *Mauretania*, Barr also ordered his senior staff members to take

inventories of all items that would have to be removed from the ship prior to her requisitioning.

Carmania's last commercial voyage before her takeover by the Royal Navy ended at Liverpool on 7 August 1914. The liner arrived at the landing stage shortly after 8 A.M., and over the next few hours disembarked her passengers under the watchful eyes of police and customs officials. Several German passengers were detained for questioning.

Even as people streamed off *Carmania* the Royal Navy officers assigned to take command of her were coming aboard. Captain Noel Grant and Lieutenant Commander E. Lockyer, who would serve as Captain and First Lieutenant, respectively, of the newly requisitioned vessel, were soon closeted with Barr.

The first topic of discussion was *Carmania*'s staffing while in military service. Though Grant would be in overall command, he conceded that he would need to rely heavily on the knowledge and expertise of the liner's civilian crew. Barr was thus offered, and accepted, the rank of commander in the Royal Navy Reserve and agreed to stay with the ship as Grant's navigator and intelligence advisor.

Many other members of *Carmania*'s senior staff also agreed to remain aboard, including her chief officer, most of the engineering department, the ship's surgeon, and the chief steward. All were given temporary commissions. The ship's carpenter was made a temporary chief petty officer and put in charge of the ship's painters, plumbers, blacksmiths, and coopers, all of whom were made temporary petty officers. The remainder of the ship's 420-man crew would consist of Navy officers, ratings, midshipmen, and a contingent of Royal Marines.

With the personnel issues settled, Grant and his crew turned their attention to preparing *Carmania* for war. The liner was to shift to the Huskinson Dock in nearby Sandon, where the conversion work would be done. However, her usual berth was already occupied by Cunard's *Caronia*, herself undergoing conversion into an AMC. *Carmania* was thus forced to remain moored in the harbor basin for two days until pier space became available.

This did not hamper the start of work, however; teams of laborers lightered out to the ship to began her transformation by submerging her well-known Cunard livery beneath a sea of gray paint. Other workmen gathered *Carmania*'s luxury fittings and tagged them for later removal. At the same time, Royal Navy engineers mapped out spaces that could be used as magazines, crew quarters, and gun positions.

On Monday morning a berth became available and *Carmania* was soon alongside the Sandon pier. The conversion work then began in earnest as workers swarmed over the ship. All cargo remaining from the liner's last voyage was taken ashore, the ornamental woodwork was removed from her passenger cabins and public areas, and her better furnishings and objets d' art were carted off to Cunard's warehouses for the duration.

With *Carmania*'s peacetime paraphernalia safely out of the way, workmen began installing the trappings of her new profession. Hinged steel blast shutters appeared over the liner's bridge windows, and sandbags and huge splinter curtains of plaited rope soon festooned her more vulnerable areas. Large searchlights and smaller semaphore lamps were installed on each bridge wing, and a six-foot-wide Barr and Stroud gunnery rangefinder was fixed atop the signal bridge.

The most important change made to *Carmania*, of course, was the addition of armament. The Royal Navy engineers judged her capable of carrying eight 4.7-inch guns, as well as a secondary armament of machine guns and small arms. The cannons were fixed to circular mounts evenly distributed around the ship, though several bulkheads fore and aft on B Deck had to be removed in order to give the weapons sited there the widest possible fields of fire. Once in position the guns were fitted with splinter shields, and weatherproof ready-ammunition lockers were emplaced close at hand.

Safety precautions were not forgotten in the rush to make *Carmania* ready for sea. Buckets of sand were sited in strategic areas around the ship, and the two cargo holds converted into magazines were equipped with high-pressure pipes that could completely flood each space within minutes. Two lifeboats and 18 collapsible Maclean rafts capable of accommodating the entire crew were retained aboard, as were life jackets for every man.

Work on *Carmania*'s conversion advanced so quickly that on Wednesday, 12 August, the Admiralty ordered Grant to make preparations for departure. Coaling was completed that same evening, and fresh water, provisions, and ammunition came aboard the following morning. All was in readiness by Thursday evening, and in the early hours of Friday *Carmania* set out on a day-long

shakedown cruise in the Irish Sea. The liner-turned-warship passed this test with flying colors, and on the morning of Saturday, 15 August, she headed down the Mersey River to the sea.

The Admiralty sailing orders given to Captain Grant just before *Carmania*'s departure directed him to patrol the main convoy routes to Halifax and to monitor merchant shipping in the Irish Sea en route. Within hours of leaving port the liner encountered two neutral ships bound for Britain; each was allowed to go on its way after Grant had verified its nationality and destination. Hardly had the second vessel disappeared from view, however, when Grant received a priority radio message ordering him to set a course southwest toward Bermuda.

This abrupt change in plans was the result of information that had reached the Admiralty only days before. Intercepted radio broadcasts indicated that a number of German warships were active in the South Atlantic and along the northern coast of South America. The vessels were thought to include the cruisers *Karlsruhe* and *Dresden*, and the liners-turned-armed auxiliaries *Kaiser Wilhelm der Grosse* and *Kronprinz Wilhelm*. Such a flotilla, if it existed, could wreak havoc among Allied ships in the south Atlantic, and *Carmania* was being sent to join in the effort to locate and destroy the German vessels.

The voyage south was uneventful, and *Carmania*'s crew spent the time readying themselves and their ship for battle. Damage control and fire-fighting parties practiced their emergency routines, while stretcher-bearers charted the quickest routes between decks. The gun crews spent hours in loading drills and carried out practice firings at every opportunity. Abandon-ship drills also became a regular part of the ship's routine, as did the raising and lowering of her two full-size lifeboats.

Carmania reached St. Georges, Bermuda, on the morning of 23 August. After navigating a channel never before used by a ship of her size, the liner moored alongside the port's single coaling pier. It took five days to fill the ship's bunkers, during which time her supply officer scoured local shops for tropical clothing, insect repellent, and sterile bandages. With the liner fully coaled, Grant took her south toward Trinidad. *Carmania* passed into the Gulf of Paria on September 3, arriving at Port of Spain early that evening.

Once in Trinidad *Carmania* was quickly put to work. On September 10 she joined Admiral Sir Christopher Cradock's 5th Cruiser Squadron,

Carmania's transformation from an express passenger liner into an armed merchant cruiser included the installation of eight 4.7-inch guns, one of which is shown here, as well as a secondary armament of machine guns. The heavy cannons were bolted to reinforced deck sections and fitted with splinter shields. *Cunard Archives, University of Liverpool*

which was searching the coast of northern South America for the German cruisers *Dresden* and *Karlsruhe*. *Carmania* was ordered to search for the enemy vessels in the vicinity of Trinidad Island, an uninhabited outcropping 500 miles off the coast of Brazil.

Well off the beaten track, Trinidad Island had once been a regular stopover for pirates. Cradock's intelligence staff believed it to be equally popular with German raiders, who were thought to be using it as a coaling station. The British were unaware, however, that the island had been the site of an August 28 rendezvous between the gunboat *Eber* and the liner-turned-armed merchant cruiser *Cap Trafalgar,* during which the latter had not only taken on coal, but guns as well.

Built in 1913 for Germany's Hamburg-South America Line, the modern and elegant 18,710-ton *Cap Trafalgar* had avoided capture on the outbreak of war by putting into neutral Buenos Aires. There her master, Captain Hans Langerhansz, was advised by the German naval attaché that the liner was to be commissioned as a naval auxiliary. Langerhansz was ordered to take his ship quietly out of Buenos Aires and make for Trinidad Island,

where he would be met by a supply vessel that would provide him with armament and, more importantly perhaps, with coal.

Cap Trafalgar cleared Buenos Aires on August 22, ostensibly bound for Las Palmas in the Canary Islands. As soon as the ship was in the open sea, however, Langerhansz shaped a roundabout course for Trinidad Island, which hove into view six days later. *Eber* was there already, having arrived two weeks earlier, and the transfer of weapons and coal was soon underway. Over the next three days the gunboat was virtually stripped bare as every useful piece of equipment—including two 10.5-cm SK L/40 guns and four 3.7-cm quick-firing cannons—was passed to *Cap Trafalgar*.

Even as the liner's weapons were being brought aboard, teams of sailors were altering *Cap Trafalgar*'s identity. They first removed the vessel's third funnel—a dummy used mainly to house ventilators—then repainted the two remaining stacks in black-and-red stripes to disguise the ship as the Union Castle Line's somewhat larger *Edinburgh Castle.* When *Eber*'s captain, Korvettenkapitän Julius Wirth, officially took command of *Cap Trafalgar* on August 31, he judged the liner to be ready for battle.

Roughly comparable in size to *Carmania*, *Cap Trafalgar* had been in commercial service on the Europe-to-South America run for barely a year when World War I began. The liner escaped capture by putting into the neutral port of Buenos Aires, then fled to Trinidad Island to rendezvous with the gunboat *Eber* (shown here alongside *Cap Trafalgar*). *Bundesarchiv Koblenz*

Four days later Wirth ordered a skeleton crew to take *Eber* to internment in Brazil, and that afternoon *Cap Trafalgar* sortied from Trinidad Island on her first cruise as an armed auxiliary.

Unfortunately for Wirth and his crew, this first privateering voyage was something of an anticlimax. *Cap Trafalgar* cruised the east coast of South America for a week, sighting neither quarry nor friend. There was, however, every indication that British warships were active in the region; the liner's signal officer intercepted continuous radio traffic among the ships of Cradock's 5th Cruiser Squadron. Wirth, already concerned about *Cap Trafalgar*'s heavy coal consumption and the inadequacy of her armament if faced by a real warship, ultimately decided to take the liner back to Trinidad Island. There he would rendezvous with the colliers *Berwind, Eleonore Wörmann,* and *Pontos* and, after filling *Cap Trafalgar*'s bunkers, reassess his battle plan.

The converted liner reached Trinidad Island without incident on the morning of Sunday, 13 September, to find all three of the colliers waiting on the island's westward side. The grueling task of transferring coal between ships tied precariously together in rolling swells began almost immediately and continued until dark. Just before dawn on Monday, *Pontos* came along *Cap Trafalgar*'s port side, and the rising sun found both vessels wreathed in drifting clouds of coal dust.

The first hint of trouble came just before 7 A.M. Noting a steady increase in the strength and number of British radio transmissions, *Cap Trafalgar*'s

signal officer informed Wirth that a single enemy warship was approaching the island. Though still 50 to 100 miles away, the vessel seemed to be coming on fast. With nothing yet visible on the horizon, however, Wirth decided that he still had time to top off the liner's bunkers. The coaling continued, but the ship's gunners were called to their mounts and the chief engineer was ordered to stand ready to get the ship underway at a moment's notice.

Activity was also increasing aboard the oncoming *Carmania*. Captain Grant had ordered the decks cleared for action soon after dawn, and by the time Trinidad Island appeared on the horizon at 9:30 A.M. the crew was standing by at battle stations. Grant had unknowingly given himself a tactical advantage by approaching from the west-northwest; the anchorage was on the opposite side of the island, and the Germans thus didn't sight *Carmania*'s smoke until shortly after 11 A.M.

Once they detected the British liner, however, the Germans reacted quickly. Alarm bells and bugles brought the coaling to a halt, and crewmen worked frantically to cut the lines binding *Cap Trafalgar* and *Pontos*. Once free, Wirth ordered the colliers to scatter and then took his own vessel away to the southwest until he could decide how to deal with the intruder. Within minutes Wirth determined that the British vessel was a converted passenger steamship like his own, not the cruiser he initially feared, and shortly after 11:30 he ordered *Cap Trafalgar* about.

The vessel's course change was quickly evident to the men on *Carmania*'s bridge, and Grant ordered his helmsman to steer to starboard of the oncoming ship. At 12:10 P.M., still unclear as to his adversary's identity but certain she was German, Grant ordered his portside forward 4.7-inch mount to put two warning shots across the enemy's bow from a range of about 8,500 yards.

The reply, when it came just seconds later, was almost overwhelming. Turning to put *Carmania* off his own starboard side, Wirth commenced a withering fire with his lighter but longer-ranged 10.5-cm guns that peppered the British liner's superstructure with armor-piercing rounds. As the two ships closed, *Cap Trafalgar*'s 3.7-cm cannon joined the battle, raking *Carmania*'s upper works with shrapnel. Shells holed the liner's stacks and carried away ventilators; a fire on the bridge forced Grant to pass control of the ship to the aft steering position.

But *Carmania* was not to be outdone. Maneuvering the liner to put *Cap Trafalgar* off his quarter, Grant was ultimately able to bring five of his 4.7-inch guns to bear. The British gunners pounded the German ship with more than 400 rounds, sweeping her decks but aiming most of their fire at her waterline. This sound tactic had the desired effect; shell after shell tore through *Cap Trafalgar*'s hull to pierce vital bulkheads and open the liner to the sea. Flooding was rapid and widespread; the German liner was soon listing heavily to starboard.

With his crew decimated and his ship battered, burning, and taking on water, Wirth—himself badly injured—broke off the battle and turned *Cap Trafalgar* toward the island. He ordered the lifeboats lowered even though he knew the ship's list would swamp most of them, then directed scuttling charges be set. Even as this was being done, however, two massive explosions rocked the stricken vessel and brought her dead in the water. As sailors scrambled over her sides, *Cap Trafalgar* rolled onto her side. Shrouded in steam, she raised her stern and went down by the bow. It was shortly after 1 P.M.

In this postwar illustration executed for a Cunard Line publication, *Carmania* bears down on the already listing *Cap Trafalgar* during their historic duel. During the course of the one hour and forty minute battle, the two converted liners exchanged nearly a thousand rounds of main-gun ammunition. Though *Cap Trafalgar*'s two 10.5-cm mounts were slightly longer-ranged than *Carmania*'s 4.7-inchers, the British vessel's ability to bring five of her eight cannons to bear ultimately won the day. *Cunard Archives, University of Liverpool*

Cap Trafalgar's Captain Wirth hoped to beach his mortally wounded vessel on Trinidad Island, but huge internal explosions brought her dead in the water before she reached her goal. As the liner rolled on her side, the German collier *Eleonore Wörmann* moved in to help. Her crew ultimately plucked 279 survivors from the shark-infested waters, and the collier, her crew, and the rescued seamen spent the rest of the war in a Brazilian internment camp. *Bundesarchiv Koblenz*

As this picture of *Carmania*'s devastated bridge illustrates, the British AMC was badly damaged in the fight with *Cap Trafalgar*. The ship sustained 80 main-gun hits, as well as countless hits by small arms and extensive shrapnel damage. The ship's surgeon, Edwin Maynard (at right, in dark jacket) and his staff had to cope with a score of wounded. *Illustrated London News*

Grant and his crew could only watch as the collier *Eleonore Wörmann* moved back in and began pulling *Cap Trafalgar*'s 279 survivors[2] from the shark-infested waters because *Carmania* herself was still in danger. Fires raged on several decks and the German AMC *Kronprinz Wilhelm* was approaching rapidly from the north in response to *Cap Trafalgar*'s earlier calls for assistance[3]. It would be decidedly unhealthy for *Carmania* to remain in the area, so Grant took his battered vessel away to the southwest.

Limping away from the battle, Grant and his crew had time to count the cost of their victory. They had suffered nine dead and 26 wounded in the fight with *Cap Trafalgar*, and their ship had sustained nearly 80 hits from the German raider's main guns. Machine-gun rounds and shrapnel had riddled *Carmania*'s superstructure, fire had gutted her bridge and radio room, and all her radio antennas and much of her other rigging had been swept away.

But *Carmania* had survived despite her grievous injuries, and Grant and his crew now turned their attention to getting themselves and their damaged ship to safety. As repair parties struggled to clear the wreckage and bring essential systems back into service, other crew members extinguished the last small fires smoldering on the lower decks. Senior Wireless Officer H. W. St. John jury-rigged a workable transmitter from the wreckage of the radio room and managed to raise the cruiser HMS *Bristol*. A rendezvous was set for the next morning, and Barr was able to plot a rough course to the appointed spot using a damaged sextant and charred compass card salvaged from the gutted bridge.

Carmania and *Bristol* met shortly after eight the next morning, and later in the day were joined by the cruiser HMS *Cornwall*. All three ships made their way toward the Abrolhos Rocks off the Brazilian coast, where the following morning they met the auxiliary cruiser *Macedonia*. Over the next three days, repair parties from the four vessels worked to mend the worst of *Carmania*'s wounds, and on the morning of September 19 the liner got underway for the Brazilian port of Pernambuco[4], which she reached that afternoon. It was a brief stop—after dropping dispatches for the Admiralty with the British consul, Grant got his ship underway for Gibraltar that evening.

The South Atlantic crossing was uneventful, and *Carmania* arrived at Gibraltar on the morning of 28 September. Almost as soon as her lines were secured, her surviving crew members began dispersing to other ships and other assignments, while the liner went into the yards for a comprehensive refit. When she reappeared some months later, all outward signs of her battle with *Cap Trafalgar* were gone.

Though *Carmania* resumed her duties as an AMC following her refurbishment at Gibraltar, the remainder of her military career consisted primarily of uneventful patrolling[5]. In 1916 she was returned to Cunard and, after being restored to something approaching her original civilian appearance, she was put back to work on a reduced Liverpool-to-New York passenger service. The United States' entry into the war prompted a brief return to military duty—the liner carried a total of nearly 10,000 U.S. troops to Europe over the course of three voyages between July and October of 1918—but *Carmania* did not participate in the great repatriation of the American Expeditionary Force following the armistice.

The end of World War I marked a renaissance for *Carmania*. Converted to all-Cabin class accommodations, she joined *Caronia* on a regular Liverpool-to-Quebec service until 1923, when both were withdrawn and converted to oil-fired propulsion. In 1926 they established a London-to-New York shuttle that kept them busy until 1930, when both were retired from service and laid up. The end finally came for Cunard's "Pretty Sisters" two years later; *Caronia* was sold to a Japanese shipbreaker and ultimately scrapped in Osaka, while the gallant *Carmania* met her end at Blythe, Scotland, in 1932.

In the final analysis, *Carmania*'s victory over *Cap Trafalgar*, though noteworthy, was not the vindication of the liner-turned-AMC concept many of

The devastation of *Carmania*'s bridge led Captain Grant to order the temporary conning station seen here to be built on the liner's relatively unscathed aft end. The liner's crew spent most of the voyage toward the rendezvous with HMS *Bristol* extinguishing the dozens of small fires still burning below decks. It took months of repair work at Gibraltar to erase the scars of the gallant Cunarder's battle with *Cap Trafalgar. Illustrated London News*

its supporters claimed it to be at the time. The ships were essentially evenly matched, and it was only Captain Grant's superior tactical skills that allowed him to reduce the younger and faster German liner to smoldering wreckage before Captain Wirth could do the same to *Carmania*.

Indeed, the only clear lesson to emerge from the brutal slug-fest at Trinidad Island was one that many naval experts had long foreseen. No matter how much armor is added to them, and no matter how skillful or fortunate their captains and crews may be, converted passenger liners confronted by modern naval weapons almost always come off second best. In the end, this understanding was to speed the transfer of such vessels to the troop transport and medical evacuation roles for which they were vastly more suited.

Builder: John Brown and Company, Clydebank, Scotland.

Launched: 1907

Length overall: 787 feet

Width: 88 feet

Gross tonnage: 31,550 tons

Propulsion: Steam turbines driving quadruple screws.

Top speed: 24.5 knots

Capacity:

　Crew: 800–950

　Passengers: 560 First Class, 460 Second Class, and 1,138 Third Class.

Armament (as designed): 10 4-inch guns

Disposition: Sank off the south coast of Ireland on 7 May 1915 after being torpedoed by German submarine *U-20*.

CHAPTER FOUR

LUSITANIA

Few stories in maritime history are as dramatic, as tragic, or as enduringly controversial as that of the short life and premature death of the majestic *Lusitania*.

Yet to discuss the ill-fated liner's military significance might at first glance seem pointless. For though the ship was built to be the most capable naval auxiliary the world had yet known—as well as to be the premier transatlantic passenger steamship of her era—what military tasks she ultimately undertook spanned only a few short months, had at best only a nominal impact on the course of the struggle in which her nation was engaged, and were brought to an abrupt and ignominious end by a single torpedo.

But it is the very way in which *Lusitania* met her end that makes her story militarily significant. Though she was not the first express liner to be lost in wartime, her destruction was of historic and lasting importance. *Lusitania*'s sinking shocked the world out of the last vestiges of Edwardian complacency, galvanized the Allied war effort, turned world opinion irreversibly against Germany, and made the ship herself a universally recognized symbol of both the ultimate consequences of military folly and the stark brutality of modern war.

Ironically, the creation of the liner destined to play such a pivotal role in World War I was a direct result of the same political and commercial forces that would ultimately help spark that conflict.

Conceived during the first years of the twentieth century,

With a bone in her teeth *Lusitania* makes a high-speed test run just days before her maiden voyage. The epitome of technological innovation, speed, and luxury when she entered service in September 1907, the liner and her equally capable and attractive running mate *Mauretania* reestablished the Cunard Line as a major player in the North Atlantic passenger trade. *Shaum Collection*

Lusitania was the first of a planned pair of superliners intended to reestablish Britain's dominance of the North Atlantic passenger trade. That dominance had lately come under vigorous attack by Germany's Norddeutscher Lloyd and Hamburg-Amerika lines, and by U.S. financier J. Pierpont Morgan's huge International Mercantile Marine (IMM) shipping conglomerate.

Morgan's firm was of special concern to the British government because in 1901 and 1902, IMM acquired no fewer than four British shipping companies including the renowned White Star Line. The U.S. company's absorption of these firms not only greatly diminished Britain's profits from the transatlantic trade, but also significantly reduced the number of merchant vessels available to the Royal Navy in wartime.

The British government's reaction to the German maritime expansion, and to the equally serious threat posed by the growth of IMM, was simple and direct. The Admiralty proposed to Parliament that the British government underwrite the construction and operation of two new "superliners." These vessels could restore Britain's dominance of the transatlantic passenger trade, blunt the influence of Morgan and his IMM, and give the Royal Navy the fastest and most technologically advanced auxiliaries money could buy.

The Admiralty's proposal was a godsend for the Cunard Line. As Britain's sole remaining independent premier transatlantic passenger steamship company, Cunard was being hard pressed by its competitors. The firm's only hope for survival was to dramatically increase its share of the North Atlantic trade while simultaneously securing the sort of long-term financial backing that would allow it to both modernize its fleet and spurn IMM's advances. Cunard had secretly lobbied for just such a subsidy as the Admiralty was advocating, and therefore welcomed the government's overtures.

It was a measure of the immense importance Cunard placed on obtaining the subsidies that the line willingly accepted the government's stringent requirements for the design, operation, and wartime conscription of the new liners. Moreover, several members of Cunard's board of directors agreed that building the ships to naval specifications would give the liners an unprecedented level of structural strength and watertight integrity, attributes at least as desirable in a transatlantic passenger steamer as they were in a warship.

The Admiralty's design criteria were comprehensive. In addition to extensive watertight compartmentation, each liner's steam plant, engines, and steering gear were to be placed below the waterline to protect them from direct and plunging gunfire. Watertight compartments along both sides of each ship would hold the coal the liners would need during their transatlantic runs, while also providing additional buoyancy and an added layer of protection against mines and torpedoes. Each vessel would have a wartime armament of 10 4-inch guns, which were to be stored ashore until needed and then installed on reinforced deck sections. Finally, the new liners were to be capable of maintaining a fair-weather speed of 24.5 knots.

Signed in July 1903, the subsidy agreement stipulated that Her Majesty's government would underwrite the construction of the two new liners up to a total cost not to exceed £2.6 million, as well as paying yearly per-vessel operating expenses up to £75,000 and granting Cunard annual contracts to carry the Royal Mail. In return, the shipping line pledged to accept the Admiralty's design and construction criteria, agreed that a proportion of each vessel's crew would be drawn from members of the Royal Naval Reserve, and promised to turn the ships over to the Royal Navy immediately upon the outbreak of hostilities.

With the formalities completed, detailed design work began in earnest. Cunard chief designer Leonard Peskett sought to plan for the ships' seemingly divergent commercial and military missions by building passenger liner superstructures on warship's hulls. The new ships—each with a waterline length of 762 feet and displacing 31,000 tons—would be protected by partial double hulls, transverse interior bulkheads and longitudinal watertight compartments running two-thirds of each ship's length. Watertight doors piercing the transverse bulkheads could be closed automatically from the bridge, while key areas of each vessel's main deck were reinforced with extra plating to defeat plunging gunfire.

The new liners' propulsion systems were built around the turbine engines that had proven their worth aboard *Carmania*. Each ship would have four turbines driving quadruple screws, with 25 boilers providing the steam. The boilers were arranged in four sets, with coal for each boiler being shoveled through watertight doors from the longitudinal compartments.

Because the hull of each new ship would be given over almost completely to machinery, the design team had nowhere to go but up when deciding where to place the passenger accommodations. These were spread throughout six decks, with space for 560 First Class, 460 Second Class, and 1,138 Third Class passengers. Each vessel was also provided with the dining rooms, public areas, and amenities expected of premier transatlantic liners, as well as with the vastly less glamorous storerooms, service areas, and work spaces that no grand seagoing hotel can do without.

Cunard accepted the design of the two new liners without major revisions and in early 1905 let the contracts for their construction. The first of the two, *Lusitania*, was awarded to John Brown and Company at Clydebank, Scotland; the second, *Mauretania*, went to Swan Hunter & Whigham Richardson at Wallsend-on-Tyne. *Lusitania*'s keel was laid in February 1905, and *Mauretania*'s a few months later.

Construction of the new superliners went smoothly, and *Lusitania* was launched at Clydebank on 7 June 1906. Her running mate took

So popular was *Lusitania*, and so widely thought of as invulnerable, that even the outbreak of war in August 1914 did not scare away passen The liner was well patronized on each of her wartime Atlantic crossings, including the one that began at New York's pier 54 on the first May 1915. In this photo, taken that day, the ship is being moved into the stream before making her way downriver to the sea. *National A*

60

to the water three months later, and over the next year both vessels were transformed from hollow shells into the largest, most advanced, and most luxurious passenger steamers the world had yet seen. They were striking vessels, with four slightly raked funnels and Cunard's distinctive livery giving the appearance of both speed and elegance. Each incorporated only the best in accommodations and furnishings, and both exuded an aura of grandeur and style without resorting to the bloated opulence that characterized the premier German liners of the day.

But speed was as important as beauty, and both liners proved to be ocean greyhounds. *Lusitania* averaged better than 25 knots during her July 1907 sea trials, and *Mauretania* proved marginally faster on her own trials the following November. Though the Blue Riband (the traditional streamer flown by the ship with the fastest transatlantic crossing time between two set points) eluded *Lusitania* on her maiden voyage to New York in September 1907, she easily captured it the next month on the east-bound leg of her second crossing.

Over the next few years the two liners maintained a friendly rivalry on the North Atlantic, swapping the Blue Riband on several occasions. The liners' ability to maintain a regular transatlantic shuttle reestablished Cunard as a major player, thus easing the pressure of competition from IMM and other national lines. Business became so good, if fact, that in 1910 Cunard contracted with John Brown for a third superliner, *Aquitania*, which joined the company's fleet in May 1914.

Unfortunately, 1914 also brought the outbreak of the European war that was to have such tragic consequences for *Lusitania*. The liner was in New York preparing for an evening departure to Liverpool when hostilities erupted on 4 August. The ship's master, Captain Daniel Dow, was instructed to delay his departure until the early hours of 5 August, at which time he was to discretely make for the open sea.

Lusitania's 1 A.M. sailing attracted little attention, and after reaching the Atlantic she was joined by the cruiser HMS *Essex*. The liner and her escort turned north toward Newfoundland and promptly disappeared.

It was with some surprise and not a little relief the residents of Liverpool greeted the liner as made her way up the Mersey River on the night August. The ship had relied on her speed and

a roundabout course for protection, and many of the 200 hardy passengers who accompanied her on the transatlantic dash commended Dow and his crew for their skill and courage in bringing the liner home.

With *Lusitania* safe, the Royal Navy and Cunard pondered the liner's role in the nation's war effort. She and her two running mates had been designed as auxiliary cruisers, and *Aquitania* was already undergoing conversion for such service. Moreover, in May 1913 *Lusitania* had been withdrawn from service for eight weeks and put into dry dock in Liverpool so that her specifically military features could be enhanced.

According to Cunard records, this work included the addition of extra plating to key areas of her upper and shelter decks; installation of mounting rings for guns on her forecastle, afterdeck, and shelter deck; and the conversion of a coal bunker and one of her mailrooms into magazines. No guns were installed, and the gunrings themselves were apparently set below the level of the ship's decking and covered with deck sections because there was no visible sign of them when the liner reentered service in July 1913.

Despite these preparations, there were other missions for which *Lusitania* and *Mauretania* were ideally suited, and which might keep them out of harm's way until *Aquitania*'s performance as an AMC could be evaluated. In the end, both liners were assigned to carry home the thousands of neutral Americans stranded in Europe by the outbreak of war.

It is at this point that "The Great Lusitania Debate"—the ultimately unanswerable question as to whether the *Lusitania* was a warship or passenger liner at the time of her sinking—begins in earnest. Several sources[1] insist the ship was fitted out as an auxiliary cruiser before her departure for New York on her first repatriation voyage. According to this scenario, the liner was fitted with several 6-inch guns; her F Deck passenger staterooms were converted into cargo spaces or troop accommodations; and much of the shelter deck was enclosed, apparently to house cargo.

Though such a conversion would have been both possible and understandable, little evidence exists to prove that such work was undertaken. Moreover, no guns were evident upon the ship's arrival in New York at the conclusion of her first repatriation voyage, and there is no credible evi-

Lusitania's master on her final voyage, Captain William Turner, was supremely confident in the abilities of himself, his crew, and his ship. He was not a fool, however, and had planned the liner's route with careful attention to the latest intelligence reports on the locations of German submarines and surface ships. *National Archives*

dence suggesting that any knowledgeable observer noticed any conversions to the ship's passenger accommodations or shelter deck. And, finally, *Aquitania*'s poor showing as an armed merchant cruiser—she served in the role for just 17 days before colliding with a merchant vessel and was immediately withdrawn from armed service—proved that Cunard's superliners were not suited for duty as auxiliary cruisers.

In any event, the *Lusitania* that undertook monthly Liverpool-to-New York passages through the fall and winter of 1914 showed no obvious signs of having been "militarized." She was regularly boarded by U.S. officials and any obvious signs of armament or cargo banned by the still-neutral U.S. government would have drawn immediate notice and automatic classification of the liner as a combatant. That no such classification was ever invoked suggests that, whether or not *Lusitania* was covertly transporting munitions or other contraband, her primary role remained that of carrying people.

By the spring of 1915, *Lusitania*'s Atlantic crossings had become almost routine. The widely held perception that the ship's great speed or her status as a passenger ship somehow made her immune to attack induced in both the traveling public and in some members of the Cunard Line itself an almost cavalier disregard for the threats *Lusitania* faced. This despite the fact that the German government had on several occasions publicly announced its determination to attack any and all enemy vessels found within the war zone surrounding the British Isles, and that German submarines were indeed taking an increasingly large toll of merchant shipping in the approaches to Britain's western ports.

This widespread belief in *Lusitania*'s supposed invulnerability was greatly in evidence on 1 May 1915, the day of her last departure from New York. Few of the passengers boarding the liner at Pier 54 had paid attention to a German advertisement placed that morning in several major metropolitan newspapers. The notice, which ran next to Cunard's sailing schedules, reminded travelers that a state of war existed between Germany and Great Britain, and that vessels flying the flag of Britain or of any of her allies were "liable to destruction" and that "travellers sailing in the war zone on ships of Great Britain and her allies do so at their own risk."

The elderly but still potent cruiser HMS *Juno* was to be *Lusitania*'s welcoming committee when the liner arrived off the Irish coast at Queenstown. The warship failed to appear at the rendezvous point, however, and Captain Turner decided to take *Lusitania* closer inshore to avoid U-boats reportedly operating dead ahead. *USNHC*

Though a few passengers canceled their bookings, most seemed to take the threat of attack as nothing more than a German attempt to scare off paying customers. Indeed, the liner's passenger list was the fullest and most cosmopolitan it had been since the outbreak of war. Among the 1,257 people embarked for the passage to Liverpool were 950 holding Australian, British, Canadian, or Irish passports; 189 Americans; 71 Russians; and small groups of travelers from 14 other nations. And as the passenger list carefully noted, the liner's guests included 129 children ranging from infants to adolescents.

Also aboard *Lusitania* that Saturday morning was a variety of cargo bound for Britain. The goods included a considerable amount of comestibles already in great demand in wartime England—tubs of lard and butter, sides of beef and pork, barrels of oysters, and crates of cheese—as well as bales of fur, crates of camping equipment, and boxes of canned goods and miscellaneous sundries.

Not all of the ship's cargo was as mundane, however. The clearance manifests turned over to the New York Collector of Customs also listed 4,200 cases of .303-caliber rifle cartridges, over 1,200 crates of empty casings for shrapnel-producing artillery shells, 189 cases of non-ordnance military equipment, and 18 cases of empty artillery shell fuses. Though of a decidedly military nature, these items were not classed as prohibited munitions by the U.S. Customs authorities, and their shipment did not violate U.S. neutrality.

The loading of these obviously warlike items is yet another key aspect of The Great Lusitania Debate. In the years since the liner's sinking, several authors[2] have contended that the "ammunition" listed on the cargo manifest should more correctly have been labeled "munitions." They cite Cunard records and other documents that came to light after the liner's sinking that indicate the "empty" shrapnel shells were actually filled; that much of what was manifested as cheese and other foodstuffs was, in reality, gun cotton and other high explosives; and that the liner was probably carrying enough contraband war materiel to have warranted both her internment under U.S. neutrality laws and her legitimate targeting by the Germans.

The key point to remember, of course, is that no one can say with certainty whether *Lusitania* was carrying explosives beyond those listed on her manifests. Though compelling, the documents indicating that she was being used to transport considerable amounts of munitions and other war materiels cannot be verified—the ship and all aboard her that day who could have helped solve the mystery are long dead. We shall simply never know for sure.

We are, however, far more certain about the circumstances leading to *Lusitania*'s destruction.

Having taken aboard passengers, coal, cargo, fresh water, and food, the liner slipped her moorings at 10:30 A.M. on 1 May. After dropping the pilot at Sandy Hook, the ship hove to briefly just outside the U.S. territorial limit to drop off several passengers thought to be German sympathizers and to take on mail from the liner-turned-armed auxiliary *Carmania*, which along with HMS *Essex* and HMS *Bristol* was patrolling the approaches to New York in search of German shipping. The rendezvous complete, Captain William Turner shaped a course for Ireland and ordered the liner's engines to flank speed. Because Cunard had ordered six of *Lusitania*'s boilers shut

down as an economy measure, however, she could do no better than 20 knots.

The liner's voyage to Britain was, for the most part, uneventful. The passengers contented themselves with the usual diversions—eating, socializing, and gazing at the passing sea—though German submarines and the possibility of an attack were common topics of discussion. Turner, for his part, seemed unperturbed about possible threats.

Despite his outward calm, Turner was in fact quite anxious about the possibility of an attack on *Lusitania*. He had been briefed on German naval dispositions before leaving New York, and during the voyage received several messages updating him on the possible positions of U-boats that might threaten his ship. The ship's course would take her around southern Ireland past Queenstown, where she was to pick up the escorting cruiser HMS *Juno*, then up the St. George's Channel and into Liverpool. Turner knew that U-boats had been active along his route, but he could not substantially alter his course without Admiralty instructions.

Turner could, however, ensure that *Lusitania* was ready for trouble. As the liner neared the danger zone he set double watches, ordered curtains throughout the ship drawn at night, and had 22

Lusitania's turn inshore took her directly into the path of Kapitänleutnant Walter Schwieger's *U-20*. A week out of Emden, the U-boat had already sunk one British vessel and damaged a second, and the sudden appearance of the huge liner was a golden opportunity. Even Schwieger was stunned, however, at the havoc his single torpedo wreaked. *Bundesarchiv Koblenz*

This artist's impression gives a good idea of what the attack on *Lusitania* must have looked like, despite the fact that the artist has the ship being hit by two torpedoes (note the hole just below the starboard bridge wing). In reality, *U-20*'s single G-type torpedo was enough to doom the liner. *Library of Congress*

lifeboats swung out and their tarpaulins removed. On the evening of Thursday, 6 May, after receiving a message advising him that U-boats were active off southern Ireland, Turner reduced speed so *Lusitania* would round Fastnet in darkness.

Friday, 7 May, dawned foggy and gray, and *Lusitania*'s passengers spent the morning preparing for the ship's arrival in Liverpool. Lunch that day was undoubtedly the most spirited event of the voyage, yet things on the bridge were far less animated; HMS *Juno* had failed to make her rendezvous with the liner and Turner had received yet another message warning him of U-boat activity directly ahead. He altered course to take *Lusitania* closer inshore, and by 2 P.M. the ship was just 17 miles off the Irish coast and only 25 miles from Queenstown.

Turner could not know that his change of course took him directly into the path of the German submarine *U-20*. Commanded by Kapitänleutnant Walter Schwieger, the U-boat

had left Emden a week earlier with orders to locate and sink British ships in the area from Dartmouth on the English Channel to the mouth of the Mersey. Schwieger had had reasonable success, having sunk one sailing vessel and damaged a steamer. By mid-day of 7 May he was off the Old Head of Kinsale, the fog that had blanketed the area for most of the morning was burning off, and his lookouts were eagerly scanning for any sign of a target. At a few minutes past 1 P.M., they found one.

Schwieger ordered his lookouts below and promptly took *U-20* down to periscope depth. He soon identified the oncoming ship as either the *Lusitania* or *Mauretania*, both of which he knew were classified as reserve armed auxiliaries. He maneuvered the submarine to within 700 meters of the liner, set up a solution for a shot from one of the U-boat's four forward tubes, and, when the parameters were right, fired a single G-type torpedo.

Though this 1918 rendering by artist Charles Dixon inaccurately shows *Lusitania* listing to port (she was hit on the starboard side and listed in that direction as she went dead in the water), it nonetheless gives a chilling impression of the pandemonium that reigned for the 18 minutes it took *Lusitania* to die. Looking on through his periscope, Schwieger noted a "terrible panic" aboard the liner as she went down by the bow. *USNHC*

Sixty seconds later that torpedo, traveling at almost 22 knots, slammed into *Lusitania*'s starboard side just aft of the bridge. Within moments the initial explosion was followed by a much larger and more powerful detonation, and the liner immediately lost way and began heeling to starboard. Schwieger, watching through *U-20's* periscope, noted a "terrible panic" on the liner's decks as she settled by the bow.

Despite her extensive watertight compartmentation, *Lusitania* flooded with astonishing speed. Her sharp list to starboard made it difficult to launch the portside lifeboats, for they had swung inward toward the ship's side and would not clear their davits. Thus many passengers could not get away from the rapidly sinking ship, and when she slipped beneath the waves just 18 minutes after being hit, *Lusitania* left behind only floating debris and scattered knots of terrified survivors. Despite the best efforts of rescue craft of all sizes and shapes, only 764 of her 1,959 passengers and crew survived.

Lusitania's destruction sparked outrage in the Allied nations, where the attack was characterized as an unprovoked slaughter of innocents and the ultimate example of German barbarism. Germany,

on the other hand, greeted the news of the liner's demise with exultation. The German government insisted that *Lusitania*'s status as a reserve armed auxiliary made her a legitimate target, and contended that the massive death toll in the sinking was caused by the munitions she was carrying, not by *U-20*'s single torpedo.

In the end, of course, what *Lusitania* was or wasn't carrying didn't doom her. It was, instead, that she was the largest and potentially most capable naval auxiliary the world had yet seen. That capability made her a legitimate target and, coupled with the British government's decision to keep an announced naval auxiliary in commercial service in wartime, ensured that she would be attacked. Any contraband *Lusitania*'s owners or their government might have been foolish and callous enough to transport aboard her on her passenger runs merely facilitated her destruction and ensured the massive loss of innocent lives.

That *Lusitania* was technically a legitimate target does not, of course, absolve the German government or Schwieger and his crew. The sinking of a known passenger vessel on the high seas was then and remains today a war crime, and

Relatives of *Lusitania*'s passengers await news of their loved ones' fate in this photo taken outside Cunard's New York offices the day after the sinking. The liner's destruction was a shock felt throughout the civilized world, and did more than virtually any other single event to swing U.S. public opinion toward the Allied cause. *National Archives*

Germany's adoption of unrestricted submarine warfare was a gross violation of both moral principle and international law. Schwieger and the men who sailed with him committed a calculated act of mass murder, and the responsibility for the deaths of so many innocent people aboard *Lusitania* must ultimately rest with the men who fired the torpedo.

Finally, *Lusitania*'s sinking holds an equally important lesson about the military potential of passenger vessels. The torpedo that sent the steamer to the bottom proved beyond all doubt that "superliners," despite their much-vaunted ability to outrun their enemies, could indeed be sunk if the attacker managed to be in the right place at the right time. Moreover, the sinking was a grim reminder of the passenger steamship's inherent fragility when subjected to the effects of modern weapons. It was a lesson that would be reinforced throughout World War I.

CHAPTER FIVE

VATERLAND

Builder: Blohm & Voss, Hamburg, Germany

Launched: 3 April 1913

Length overall: 907.5 feet

Width: 100.3 feet

Gross tonnage: 54,282 tons

Propulsion: Direct-acting steam turbines geared to quadruple screws.

Top speed: 22.5 knots

Capacity:

   Commercial crew: 1,120

   Military crew: 2,200 (1917); 1,165 (1919)

   Passengers: 750 First Class, 535 Second Class, 850 Third Class, 1,536 Fourth Class.

Troops: 7,250 (1917); 8,250; 8,900; 10,500; 12,000 (1918)

Armament: Eight 6-inch guns, two 1-pounder cannons, two .30-caliber machine guns.

Disposition: Scrapped at Rosyth, Scotland, 1938.

In May 1913 Germany's Hamburg-Amerika Line hosted a reception aboard its huge new express steamer, *Vaterland,* which had just arrived in New York on its maiden voyage. One of the guests, a U.S. Navy captain named Albert M. Gleaves, asked a member of the ship's staff how many troops the liner could carry in wartime. "Seven thousand," the German replied, "and we built her to bring them over here." Gleaves, not missing a beat, smilingly answered, "And when they come we shall be happy to meet them.[1]"

Neither of the men involved in this exchange had any idea how prophetic their words would prove to be. Just over four years later, *Vaterland* would indeed carry 7,000 troops to a distant battlefield, but they would be U.S. soldiers, not German. The great vessel sitting at a New York pier that bright spring day three months before the outbreak of World War I was destined to become—with Gleaves' help—the most capable and successful troopship of that conflict.

Martial glory was not, of course, the destiny *Vaterland*'s designers had in mind for the huge liner. Indeed, Albert Ballin, the prewar director of the Hamburg-Amerika Line, was a dedicated anti-militarist who believed that the only conflicts in which Germany should be involved were commercial ones. He also believed that the best way to ensure a HAPAG victory in the economic battle then being waged on

Interned in New York following the 1914 outbreak of World War I, HAPAG's *Vaterland* sat idle for the next three years manned by only a skeleton crew. The U.S. government seized the liner on 7 April 1917, and she is seen the following day with a newly raised U.S. flag flying at her stern. *National Archives*

the North Atlantic was to build a trio of large, fast, and luxurious express steamers that would outshine in every respect the British vessels then coming into service, most notably the White Star Line's *Olympic* and *Titanic*.

Under Ballin's leadership, HAPAG contracted with two Hamburg shipyards for construction of the three new superships. The first, *Imperator*, was launched by Vulkan AG in 1912. At 882 feet and 51,969 tons she was a stupendous vessel by any measure, yet she was soon surpassed by *Vaterland*. Built by Blohm & Voss of Hamburg and launched in April 1913, the latter vessel was 25 feet longer and 3,000 tons heavier than *Imperator*, making her the largest ship afloat until the 1914 launching of the third member of the HAPAG triumvirate, the 56,551-ton *Bismarck*.

Though they differed in size and detail, all three of HAPAG's new superliners shared a number of common traits. The most obvious of these was a similar profile: each vessel had three funnels (the farthest aft of which was a dummy), tall masts fore and aft, four huge screws, and a clipper stern. The liners also boasted richly appointed passenger accommodations and public rooms, as well as such innovations as hot and cold running water in all First Class cabins. More importantly, they were the first large German passenger vessels to be powered by direct-acting steam turbine engines. Far more economical to operate and easier to maintain than conventional reciprocating engines, the turbines were intended to make the ships fast enough and dependable enough to conduct the weekly, three-ship Germany-to-New York service for which they were built.

The dream of that transatlantic shuttle was brought a step closer to reality when *Vaterland* joined *Imperator* in commercial service in May 1914. On her maiden Hamburg-to-New York crossing that month *Vaterland* maintained a steady 22 knots, displaying none of the vibration or other mechanical teething troubles that had plagued her older sister's first voyage. *Vaterland*'s reception in New York was a warm one, and her next two crossings were well subscribed in both directions.

Justifiably proud of both *Imperator* and *Vaterland*, Ballin and HAPAG's board of directors eagerly anticipated the scheduled late-1914 commercial introduction of *Bismarck* to complete the supership trio and allow the long-awaited introduction of the weekly transatlantic shuttle. Their anticipation was tempered, however, by the knowl-edge that the ominous clouds gathering over Europe since the 28 June assassination of Austrian Archduke Franz Ferdinand might well bring forth a European war. Knowing that the sudden outbreak of such a conflict could lead to the destruction or confiscation of many of their vessels, the Line's directors ordered the captains of all HAPAG ships to keep their crews at the highest levels of readiness and be prepared at any time to evade enemy warships should war erupt.

As if the threat of war was not enough for *Vaterland*'s crew to worry about, on her fourth crossing the ship was bedeviled by a host of mechanical problems that mocked the liner's youth and the newness of her machinery. En route for New York one of the ship's four driving turbines failed, forcing her master, Captain Ruser, to shut down one of the ship's four propellers. To add insult to injury, the almost simultaneous failure of all four of her backing turbines reduced *Vaterland*'s low-speed maneuverability to almost nothing. The liner thus had to rely on tugs to bring her into the harbor and help with even the simplest docking movements.

It was during the liner's slow entry into New York on 29 July that the U.S. harbor pilot guiding the vessel witnessed an extraordinary scene. The pilot had just come aboard and was passing through *Vaterland*'s smoking room when he came upon Ruser and several of his senior officers gathered about a large portrait of Kaiser Wilhelm II. The seamen, so distressed about the increasing likelihood of war and the potential danger to their ship, angrily pulled the portrait from the wall and slashed it to pieces[2].

The Germans' anger was well placed; *Vaterland* was interned by the U.S. government within days of the 4 August outbreak of war between Britain and Germany. This action saved the liner from possible destruction by British warships patrolling off the U.S. coast, but it also signaled the end of her career as a German vessel. The ship spent the next three years tied to her pier, manned by a small skeleton crew. The United States' entry into World War I on 6 April 1917 sealed the liner's fate; the following day federal agents backed by troops seized her.

Though the United States' seizure of *Vaterland* removed the ship from the German war effort, the action led to friction between the navies of Britain and the United States. Albert Gleaves, now an admiral and commander of the U.S. Atlantic Fleet's Cruiser and Transport Force, realized that

Admiral Albert M. Gleaves, World War I commander of the U.S. Navy's Cruiser and Transport Force, had first been introduced to *Vaterland* and her capabilities during the liner's 1913 maiden visit to New York. After her seizure in 1917 he was instrumental in having the ship assigned to vital troop transport work, rather than to the hospital ship role envisioned for her by the British. *USNHC*

the liner would make an ideal troop transport and was stunned when the British Admiralty proved unwilling to allow the huge vessel into Liverpool or Southampton. The Admiralty felt that *Vaterland* would overtax existing facilities, and that if she were sunk or damaged during arrival or departure, she could completely close the ports to other ships. His Majesty's government therefore suggested the liner serve as a hospital ship, sailing between some unspecified European port and the United States.

Gleaves overcame these British misgivings, however, by arguing that hospital ship duty would be an almost criminal misuse of the largest ship afloat. The liner, he pointed out, could carry 7,000 troops at speeds of more than 22 knots, abilities that would significantly enhance the United States' effort to transport vital reinforcements to the battlefields of Europe. The Admiralty's ultimate agreement that *Vaterland* would be best used as a troopship prompted the U.S. Shipping Board to pass the vessel to the Navy's control in June 1917.

The Navy evaluation team that boarded *Vaterland* soon afterward found the ship to be structurally sound, but the mechanical problems that plagued her on her last prewar crossing had not disappeared during her forced idleness. Though the steamer's propulsion machinery had not been purposely sabotaged by her crew, improper maintenance and operation during her first years of commercial service and neglect during her internment had taken their toll. *Vaterland*'s turbines were in bad shape, as were her boilers, auxiliary machinery, and piping. Moreover, the ship's hull was encrusted with several years' growth of barnacles, and silt buildup anchored her to the muddy bottom of her slip.

As daunting a task as *Vaterland*'s reconditioning promised to be, it was one the Navy could not postpone. The ship had a vital role to play in the United States' war effort, and the sooner she was reborn as a troop transport the better. Accordingly, the first teams of workers went aboard the liner within days of the survey crew's visit.

The first step in *Vaterland*'s rebirth was to recondition her propulsion gear. Though working without detailed engineering drawings, Navy repair teams were able to bring the liner's boilers and turbines back on line. Replacing her damaged piping and rerouting much of her electric cabling was a more challenging task, but this too was accomplished with surprising speed.

As the engineers worked below, other workers set about modifying *Vaterland*'s interior. Most of her civilian furnishings and fittings were moved ashore, and in their place carpenters and pipefitters installed thousands of troop bunks. Her original kitchens and food storage areas were enlarged and her medical spaces were fitted with additional folding beds. To conserve fresh water during trooping voyages, the water faucets were removed from all accommodations except the staterooms assigned to the captain, executive officer, and commander of embarked troops[3]. Finally, the ship's interior spaces were scrubbed, fumigated, and disinfected.

As work was going on aboard *Vaterland*, Navy salvage experts were exploring ways to release the liner from her silted-in berth. Divers reported that she was fast in the mud, so the Army Transport Service brought in dredges to shift the silt. Guided by the divers, the dredges were able to free the steamer after four days of nonstop work.

Vaterland was now ready to be dry-docked. Unfortunately, no structure large enough to accommodate her existed in the United States, and plans to send the liner to Balboa, on the Pacific end of the Panama Canal, fell through when a rock slide closed the waterway to ships of *Vaterland*'s width. The solution was a compromise: Divers were sent down to clean as much of the hull and screws as they could, and *Vaterland* was scheduled for a thorough cleaning in Liverpool's huge dry dock at the end of her first eastbound crossing.

By midsummer of 1917 *Vaterland*'s conversion had reached an advanced stage, and on 25 July the vessel was commissioned into the Navy under the command of Captain J. W. Oman. Over the next five weeks he welcomed aboard the nearly 2,000 men

Leviathan's armament included 1-pounder light cannons. Though their range was not as great as the ship's 6-inch main guns, the smaller mounts were ideal for use against close-in raiders or surfaced submarines. The vessel's air defense was left up to the two .30-caliber machine guns installed on her bridge wings. *National Archives*

that would crew the ship, which was renamed USS *Leviathan*[4] on 6 September. By October Oman judged his ship and crew ready for a shakedown cruise, and in the middle of that month the troopship left Hoboken for Cuba. *Leviathan*'s performance on this brief outing was outstanding; she was able to maintain a steady 23 knots throughout the voyage.

Back in Hoboken, *Leviathan* underwent the final preparations for her trooping debut. These included the installation of eight 6-inch guns, two 1-pounder cannons, and two .30-caliber machine

Though slightly different than the color scheme actually applied, this dazzle camouflage pattern planned for *Leviathan* well illustrates how such a design disrupted the huge ship's outline and confused observers as to her true course and speed. That it also made her possibly the world's largest example of abstract art was completely unintentional. *USNHC*

guns, as well as a central magazine in one of her cargo holds and weatherproof ready-ammunition lockers near each weapon. The ship's most obvious modification also took place during this period: She received a dazzle paint scheme like those being applied to most Allied warships.

By early December 1917, *Leviathan* was judged ready to take her place in the Cruiser and Transport Force. Coaling and provisioning began on the 11th, and the first of 7,250 troops began boarding three days later. All preparations were completed by the afternoon of the 15th, and that evening tugs pushed the ship away from her pier. The slow journey to the sea that followed was something of a test for all concerned because *Leviathan*'s size and immense draft restricted her to narrow channels and any error would have resulted in instant grounding. Fortunately, Captain William S. McLaughlin, the master pilot who would guide the vessel on most of her wartime departures, skillfully orchestrated the efforts of the liner's crew, and the tugs and the heavily loaded *Leviathan* made it to the open sea without incident.

Once in open water Captain Oman ordered his ship's engines to full ahead and shaped a course that would take *Leviathan* along the northern circle route to Britain. The trooper's turbines pushed her to 22 knots and held her there for most of the pas-

sage. Though Oman wasn't expecting trouble—the briefing he'd received in New York indicated no enemy activity along his planned route—he took no chances. Lookouts stood double watches and gun crews stayed at their weapons for hours at a time. The soldiers, for their part, were subjected to safety briefings and lectures on what to do if the ship was attacked. Fortunately for all, the crossing was uneventful and *Leviathan* pulled into Liverpool on the morning of Christmas Day.

After disembarking her troops, *Leviathan* was prepared for the dry-docking she'd been unable to undergo in the United States. This did not occur for several days, however, because only the highest tides would allow the huge ship to float over the dry dock's sill and she thus had to wait for the full moon. Once the vessel was safely ensconced, workers cleaned her hull and screws, while carpenters installed an additional 1,000 bunks. Work was completed during the last days of January 1918, and the troopship sailed for New York on 9 February.

Preparations for *Leviathan*'s second trooping voyage began immediately upon her 19 February arrival in New York. After disembarking the more than 1,000 injured soldiers and U.S. and British diplomats brought from Liverpool, the ship was cleaned and fumigated, her refrigerators and fresh water tanks were filled, and coal barges begin fill-

During her 1917 conversion, *Leviathan* was fitted with accommodations for 7,250 troops, most of whom slept in row upon row of four-tier bunks. This photo, taken near the end of the conversion, shows just how claustrophobically close the bunks had to be to accommodate the ship's allocated number of troops. *USNHC*

Leviathan's passageways and decks were almost as crowded as her troop berthing areas. This 1917 view of the ship's aft end—already strewn with ventilators, hatch covers, and winches—depicts the array of cargo and equipment carried on each voyage. This included lifeboats, cardboard-like flotation devices, cargo-handling equipment, and boxes of miscellaneous supplies. *National Archives*

Men of a deploying infantry regiment board *Leviathan* in 1917. The troop embarkation process normally took about 24 hours, with coaling and provisioning undertaken either before or during the loading. Note that each of the these soldiers is carrying a full load of personal-issue equipment, including entrenching tool, bayonet, and canvas-wrapped Model 1903 rifle. *National Archives*

ing her bunkers. Workers installed 650 additional bunks, increasing the steamer's troop capacity to 8,900. The first soldiers arrived from New Jersey staging camps on the first day of March, and the rest came aboard over the next two days. *Leviathan* sailed on the evening of 4 March, arrived in Liverpool eight days later, and returned to Hoboken on 17 April.

Though successful, *Leviathan*'s first two round-trip crossings pointed out one glaring problem. The ship's deep draft allowed her to enter Liverpool only during the high tides of the new or full moon, and she was therefore able to make only one round-trip voyage every two lunar months. This restricted the number of troops the vessel could contribute to the war effort and kept idle the Allies' largest and most capable troop transport.

In an effort to remedy the situation, Gleaves suggested in April that *Leviathan* be routed to Brest rather than Liverpool. The deep-water French port was not affected by tides, which would allow the huge troopship to speed up her transatlantic shuttle and dramatically increase the number of U.S. troops reaching the battlefields. In addition, sailing directly to Brest would eliminate the time-consuming step of transporting U.S. troops off-loaded in the United Kingdom onward to France. Finally, the need to coal in Liverpool could be eliminated simply by shipping the coal to Brest. The off-loading of troops and coaling could then be carried out simultaneously, further shortening *Leviathan*'s turnaround time.

The Navy Department agreed with Gleaves' suggestions and, with British concurrence, subsequently shifted *Leviathan*'s port of debarkation to Brest. The trooper's first passage to the French port began on 24 April, and she was back in New York by 12 May. From that point on, *Leviathan*'s average turnaround time dropped from 54 days to 26. This change, coupled with the increase of her troop capacity to 10,500, resulted in an annual increase of 30,000 troops carried by the ship to France.

The steady growth of *Leviathan*'s troop capacity and the increased frequency of her sailings would have been meaningless, of course, if the ship's crew had been unable to cope with the numbers of people involved. As it was, a complex yet efficient system evolved to govern the care and feeding of the embarked troops. This system controlled every aspect of shipboard life, dictating when and where soldiers and crew members slept, where and when they relieved themselves, where they could smoke and, most important, when and how much they ate.

Because early experiences had shown that adequate food was one of the most important factors governing the morale—and thus the discipline—of embarked troops, much thought and effort went into feeding them. It was no small task, of course; preparing three meals a day at sea for more than 10,000 bored and hungry people requires detailed planning and preparation. The usual list of provisions loaded aboard *Leviathan* in New York before

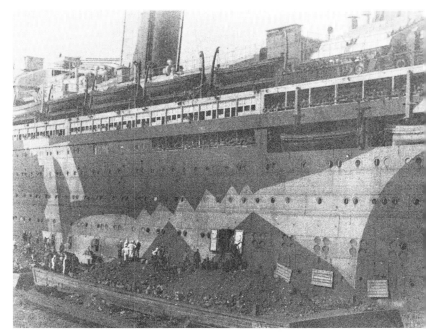

When done concurrently with the troop embarkation, coaling of *Leviathan* was undertaken with an interested audience of Doughboys. These barges have just been brought alongside, and the coal will be transferred both by hand and by mechanical lifts that have not yet been put in place. The process was arguably the dirtiest job aboard ship. *National Archives*

Leviathan departs for France, cheered on by troops and nurses packed aboard a smaller vessel. *Leviathan*'s first transatlantic trooping voyage began in New York on 15 December 1917, and ended in Liverpool on the morning of Christmas Day. Contrary to the apprehensions of British and U.S. naval planners, the crossing was blissfully uneventful. *National Archives*

In this staged photo, three soldiers take exaggerated notice of a cautionary sign on *Leviathan*'s C Deck. The warning was deadly serious, however, because German submarines were known to have trailed the liner several times by collecting various articles thrown overboard by both the ship's company and embarked troops. The articles ranged from garbage bags to flotation devices and, on at least one occasion, a dozen half-empty 55-gallon oil drums mistakenly tossed over the side during an overzealous cleanup operation. *National Archives*

Lifeboat drills were a fact of life aboard *Leviathan* and the other U.S. troopers plying the North Atlantic during World War I, both when the ships were outbound with troops or, as here, returning to New York relatively empty. Whether the crews could actually have launched the boats in a real emergency was a question that, fortunately, never had to be answered. *National Archives*

each eastbound voyage reflects the extent of the task:

260,000 pounds of fresh and canned meats;
25,000 pounds of fresh poultry;
360,000 eggs;
200,000 pounds of flour; and
595,000 pounds of fresh fruits and vegetables.

Added to this pile of provisions were several thousand gallons of fresh water, milk, coffee, tea, and fruit juice. These provisions would feed 10,000 troops for up to 25 days and 1,800 crew members for 125 days.

Transporting the provisions wasn't enough, of course; they also had to be stored and prepared. During her trooping conversion, *Leviathan* was equipped with additional walk-in freezers and more than a dozen large pantries. She was also provided with large electric ovens, automatic dough mixers, heavy-duty steam kettles, and other high-quality appliances. All cooking was done in the former First and Second Class galleys, with much of the preparation done by working parties drawn from among the embarked troops.

Serving the food required just as much planning. While officers sat at tables on the upper level of the First Class dining room and were served by waiters, enlisted personnel aboard *Leviathan* ate standing up as they filed slowly through the dining room's lower level. Troops and crew members entered the area via the grand staircase, at the base of which were 12 serving stations, and cleaned their trays and utensils at stations set up just inside the exit doors. They then returned to their assigned work stations or berthing areas. This system allowed *Leviathan*'s catering staff to feed nearly 11,000 people in one hour and fifteen minutes.

Packing such tremendous numbers of troops aboard *Leviathan* and the other large ex-liners was a calculated risk because a single well-placed German torpedo could have resulted in the deaths of several times the number of people lost aboard *Titanic* or *Lusitania*. Navy planners took the risk in order to move desperately needed troops to Europe, and they managed to beat the odds—not one large troopship was sunk when fully loaded. Unfortunately, their gamble also virtually ensured the deaths of hundreds of people at the hands of an enemy far more implacable than the Germans—the Spanish influenza.

As noted in Chapter 2, the great Spanish influenza pandemic of 1918–1919 killed far more people than did World War I. The disease ravaged

Doughboys and bluejackets shelter from the wind on *Leviathan's* fo'c'sle during a winter crossing. Note the profusion of rigging foundations, the 6-inch gun mount (at right), the bell engraved with the name *Vaterland* (center), and the ever-present stacks of lifeboats and rafts. The chain leads to the ship's huge starboard anchor. *USNHC*

the globe, and was especially active in the staging areas in which U.S. troops were marshaled before being sent overseas. The illness ultimately scourged every ship of the Cruiser and Transport Force, and hit *Leviathan* during her ninth trooping voyage.

The vessel left New York for Brest on 29 September 1918, carrying 9,320 troops and a ship's company of nearly 2,500. The disease was apparently brought aboard by the troops because by the morning of the ship's second day at sea, stricken soldiers filled every bunk in *Leviathan's* small hospital. By 2 October 615 additional bunks had been filled by the sick. The first death occurred that day despite the efforts of the troopship's medical staff, and by the time *Leviathan* reached Brest on 7 October 93 more soldiers had died. A further 15

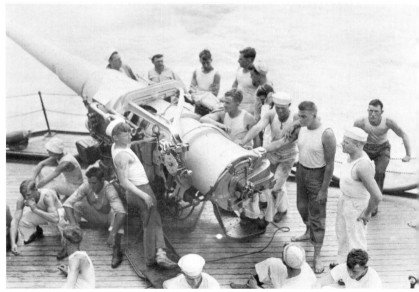

The crew of one of *Leviathan's* 6-inch guns takes a break near their weapon, surrounded by fellow bluejackets. The ship was armed with eight of these weapons: four forward, two aft, and two amidships. Only the forward and aft mounts had splinter shields, though all eight guns had ready-ammunition lockers fixed to the deck close at hand. *USNHC*

In April 1917 *Leviathan* began off-loading her troops in Brest rather than Liverpool. Coupled with an increase in her troop complement from 7,250 to 10,500, this change allowed the ship to make faster and more "profitable" crossings. She is seen here (with the cruiser USS *New Orleans* alongside) just before leaving New York with nearly 14,500 persons aboard in July 1918. *USNHC*

Seen from the deck of an escorting British destroyer, *Leviathan* plows her way around England's southern coast on the way to Brest in the spring or summer of 1918. The ship's average crossing time was six days in either direction, and she spent between a week and 10 days in port on each end before resuming her shuttle service. *USNHC*

victims died after being taken ashore, and the ship's medical officer estimated that more than 3,000 of the 11,800 men aboard were seriously ill[5].

Horrific as the influenza's toll was, it was not allowed to interfere with *Leviathan*'s vital trooping duties. The ship stayed in Brest just long enough to coal, provision, and have her troop spaces fumigated and disinfected, and then set out on the return voyage to New York. She arrived in Hoboken on 16 October, and by the 26th had been turned around and made ready for what turned out to be her last wartime crossing. She departed for France on the

Troops and sailors look on from every possible vantage point as *Leviathan* is warped alongside her Brest pier in May 1918. The debarkation process actually started before the troopship reached the French harbor; cleanup operations and the marshaling of personal equipment began while she was still a day out. Once ashore, the troops were mustered at the pier and then moved on to nearby collection and processing centers. *USNHC*

Each soldier embarked aboard *Leviathan* and the other troopers of the Cruiser and Transport Force for an eastbound crossing was given a "safe passage" card during the boarding process. The cards were collected as the troops disembarked in France and were mailed to the United States to let anxious relatives know the voyage had ended safely. *National Archives*

27th with 7,570 troops, and arrived in Brest on 3 November. Fortunately, there were only a few isolated cases of influenza on this voyage, and no deaths.

The 11 November Armistice found *Leviathan* still in Brest. Though originally scheduled to sail for the United States a few days later, her departure was postponed as Army and Navy planners organized the repatriation of two million U.S. soldiers, sailors, and Marines. Virtually all the foreign-flagged vessels that had carried the bulk of U.S. forces to Europe were withdrawn from trooping soon after the Armistice, meaning that the job of transporting the American Expeditionary Force home would fall almost completely to the men and

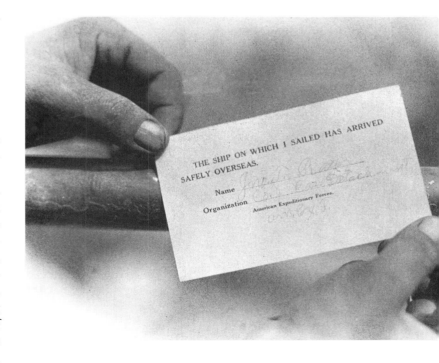

Shifted to repatriation duty following the Armistice, *Leviathan* routinely carried between 8,000 and 12,000 troops on each westbound crossing. Here she moves toward her New York pier on 16 December 1918, loaded with 9,000 returning servicemen. Note that the dazzle camouflage scheme has been removed from her hull but she still carries her full complement of 6-inch guns. *USNHC*

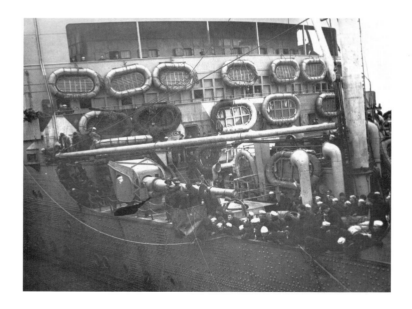

In this view of the same 16 December arrival, some of the 4,000 sailors *Leviathan* was returning from duty in France crowd around one of the starboard forward 6-inch mounts for a better view of the docking. Note that several of the life rafts suspended from the ship's forward superstructure had been painted as part of the overall dazzle scheme. Though the majority of the ship's hull was by now overall gray, parts of her upper works retained traces of the dazzle scheme. *USNHC*

ships of the Cruiser and Transport Force. As the largest ship in that fleet, *Leviathan* was destined to play a major role in the repatriation effort[6].

That role began within a week of the Armistice, when hundreds of French workers boarded *Leviathan* in Brest. They installed more standee bunks, ventilators, and toilets throughout the ship, increasing her troop capacity to 12,000. Nor was the increase unique to *Leviathan*: Freed from the threat of enemy attack, every ship of the Cruiser and Transport Force—warship and trooper alike—could now be packed with homeward-bound soldiers.

Members of *Leviathan*'s crew stand opposite one of the many mounds of life jackets discarded by disembarking troops. Even after the Armistice, embarked personnel were sometimes ordered into life jackets as the ship approached port, primarily as a precaution in case the troopship collided with another vessel or hit a rogue mine. *National Archives*

Joining *Leviathan* in the postwar troop repatriation effort was her older sister, the 51,950-ton *Imperator*. The liner had sat out the war at her Bremen pier, and following the cessation of hostilities was drafted into U.S. service. As USS *Imperator*, she is seen here carrying U.S. troops in 1919. *USNHC*

Clad in dress whites, *Imperator*'s crew mans her railings on the day of her decommissioning. Sister ships and fellow wartime members of the Cruiser and Transport Force, *Leviathan* and *Imperator* became commercial rivals after leaving military service. *Imperator* became the Cunard Line's *Berengaria*, while *Leviathan* joined the United States Line. *National Archives*

Leviathan's first postwar voyage began on 9 December 1918, when she left for New York with 14,000 souls aboard. The crossing was plagued by bad weather but was otherwise routine, and the trooper reached Hoboken on 16 December. The ship made eight more round-trip voyages to France over the next 10 months, carrying an average of 10,500 troops per voyage in addition to her crew. Despite this massive overloading, *Leviathan* proved herself almost as stable and nearly as fast as she had been in commercial service, routinely plowing through moderately rough seas at speeds approaching 20 knots.

By the time she was withdrawn from military service on 8 September 1919, *Leviathan* had compiled a record of achievement unmatched by any other vessel in the Cruiser and Transport Force or, indeed, by any other troopship up to that time. During her 19 transatlantic crossings as a naval vessel the ship transported 192,753 people to and from Europe, a figure more than twice

that carried by *America*, the Force's second most active vessel. *Leviathan*'s size was the most important factor in her success, and her maximum per-crossing troop capacity during the postwar repatriation effort remained unsurpassed until the World War II voyages of Cunard's *Queen Mary* and *Queen Elizabeth*. Most important, perhaps, *Leviathan* lost not a single passenger or crew member to enemy action.

Struck from the Navy List on 29 October 1919, *Leviathan* was laid up in Hoboken for two years as various shipping companies wrangled over her disposition. Though the International Mercantile Marine Co. at first seemed to have the best chance of winning ownership of the vessel, she was ultimately transferred to the United States Line (USL). In April 1922 the ship was moved to Newport News, Virginia, for a reconditioning meant to make her worthy of her planned position as USL's flagship. Her yearlong, $8 million refurbishment saw her converted to oil fuel

Struck from the Navy list in October 1919, *Leviathan* ultimately underwent a comprehensive refit in Newport News, Virginia. In this damaged but revealing photo, shipyard workers pour from the vessel in response to the noon whistle. During her yearlong, $8 million refurbishment, *Leviathan* was converted to oil fuel and returned to her full prewar splendor. *USNHC*

and returned to her prewar splendor. She undertook her first postwar commercial Atlantic crossing in July 1923.

Leviathan remained with USL throughout the firm's many incarnations, and her popularity rivaled that of the newer and faster vessels that appeared on the Atlantic following the end of World War I. Periodic modifications to her passenger accommodations kept *Leviathan* profitable for some time, and she was one of the first of the larger express steamers to cater to significant numbers of Tourist Class travelers. However, by 1933 USL's

seemingly endless financial problems, coupled with the effects of the worldwide depression, made the huge liner too expensive to operate and she was laid up at Hoboken.

Though returned to service for five voyages during the summer of 1934, *Leviathan*'s days were numbered. In September she was again laid up in New York. There the ship sat until January 1938, when she undertook her final Atlantic crossing. That voyage ended at Rosyth, Scotland, where in mid-1938 the proud and justly famous *Leviathan* was broken up for scrap.

Resplendent in her USL colors, the restored *Leviathan* steams out of New York in the late 1920s. A popular and capable ship, she remained a moneymaker into the 1930s. She ultimately became too expensive to operate in those recessionary times, however, and was withdrawn from service in 1934 and scrapped four years later. *National Archives*

Builder: John Brown and Company, Clydebank, Scotland.
Launched: 21 April 1913
Length overall: 901 feet
Width: 97 feet
Gross tonnage: 45,647 tons
Propulsion: Steam turbines geared to quadruple screws
Top speed: 23 knots
Capacity:
  Commercial crew: 1,300
  Military crew: 1,200 (WWI); 875 (WWII)
  Passengers: 597 First Class, 614 Second Class, 2,052 Third Class.
Troops: 5,000 (1914); 6,500 (1917); 6,000 (1940); 6,700 (1942).
Armament: 10 6-inch guns (WWI); one 6-inch gun, five 3-inch guns, plus various combinations of 20 mm and 40 mm cannons and machine guns (WWII).
Disposition: Scrapped at Faslane, Scotland, in 1950.

CHAPTER SIX

AQUITANIA

Widely regarded as one of the most elegant steamers ever to ply the North Atlantic, Cunard's *Aquitania* holds another, less widely known distinction. The last of the great four-funnel liners, the stately vessel was the only major pre-1914 passenger ship to see military duty in both world wars. And what duty it was: As armed merchant cruiser, hospital ship, and troop transport, *Aquitania* circled the globe, playing key roles in both conflicts and eluding the enemy at every turn.

As important as her military abilities would prove to be, *Aquitania* was first and foremost a commercial venture. Conceived as the third member of Cunard's "superliner trio," the ship was intended to join *Lusitania* and *Mauretania* in conducting a weekly Liverpool-to-New York service. Together, the three would challenge similar multi-vessel operations being put together by both the White Star and Hamburg-Amerika lines. And though reasonably high speed was to be a factor in *Aquitania*'s design, Cunard's board of directors decreed that her primary attribute—and selling point—would be a level of luxury and comfort thus far unattained by any passenger steamer.

The contract for *Aquitania*'s construction was let in December 1910 to John Brown and Company of Clydebank. The liner's keel

The third ship of Cunard's "superliner trio" takes shape in the cradle of so many famous passenger liners: John Brown and Company's Clydebank shipyard. Unlike her consorts *Lusitania* and *Mauretania*, the 45,647-ton *Aquitania* was funded entirely from Cunard's own resources. Laid down in June 1911, she was launched 22 months later. *Shaum Collection*

was laid in June 1911, and over the next two years workers fulfilled in steel, wood, and glass the vision the ship's designers had captured on paper. It was an immense task, for at an overall length of 901 feet and tipping the scales at 45,647 tons she was among the largest vessels then in existence.

Of conventional construction, *Aquitania* was powered by triple-expansion steam turbine engines driving quadruple screws. Her long and relatively slender hull was the result of extensive preconstruction research, and her ruggedness belied her lithe appearance. Though Cunard built the liner without the government subsidies that had helped finance *Lusitania* and *Mauretania*, *Aquitania*'s design nonetheless included features meant to simplify her conversion into an armed naval auxiliary should she be required to join her stablemates in military service. These included extensive watertight compartmentation, deck areas strengthened to support gun mounts, and redundant electrical systems.

As advanced as *Aquitania*'s structure may have been, it was upon the splendor, luxury, and sophistication of her accommodations that Cunard intended her fame to rest. Following her 21 April 1913 launching, the liner was configured to carry 597 First Class, 614 Second Class, and 2,052 Third Class passengers in a unique style blending the best of Louis XVI, Christopher Wren, and what might be described as English country house opulence. Her furnishings complemented her design and layout with a subtle charm her German competitors lacked, and she conveyed a sense of both warmth and elegance that captivated the public from the moment her maiden Atlantic crossing began on 30 May 1914.

Travelers did not have long to enjoy *Aquitania*'s comforts, however, because the liner made only three round-trip voyages to New York before the outbreak of World War I. When hostilities between Britain and Germany commenced on 4 August 1914, *Aquitania* was moored at Cunard's Liverpool pier, her conversion to AMC already underway. His Majesty's government had requisitioned the huge liner two days earlier, and most of her furnishings and nonessential fittings had already been moved ashore. The declaration of war added an increased sense of urgency to the conversion work, and by 8 August *Aquitania*'s transformation was complete.

Though her famous profile remained unchanged, the ship was now quite obviously a man o' war. Her house colors had disappeared beneath drab camouflage paint, hinged blast shutters covered her bridge windows, and plaited-rope splinter curtains shielded her exterior passageways. In recognition of her size and status, *Aquitania* was equipped with 10 6-inch guns rather than the 4.7-inch weapons supplied to vessels of lesser potential.

The size of *Aquitania*'s guns was to prove irrelevant, however, because the liner's career as an AMC was brief. The ship set out from Liverpool on 8 August bound for patrol duty in the Irish Sea and the North Atlantic. But sometime during her third week at sea, *Aquitania* collided with the 9,000-ton steamer *Canadian* off the Irish coast, severely damaging the smaller vessel and crumpling her own stem. The liner-turned-AMC returned to Liverpool for repairs. While she was indisposed, two events occurred that hastened the end of her career as an armed auxiliary.

The first, on 27 August, was the sinking of the converted German liner *Kaiser Wilhelm der Grosse* by HMS *Highflyer*. The German raider was caught in neutral Spanish waters and, despite heroic resistance, was quickly dispatched by the aging British light cruiser. This

The August 1914 sinking of *Kaiser Wilhelm der Grosse* by HMS *Highflyer*, depicted here in a photo from the October 1914 *Illustrated London News*, helped bring a quick end to *Aquitania*'s career as an armed auxiliary cruiser. The converted German liner's destruction clearly pointed out the passenger steamer's inherent vulnerability in direct combat, and helped convince the Admiralty to withdraw *Aquitania* from service until a more suitable—and safer—role could be found for her. *Illustrated London News*

engagement clearly pointed out the innate vulnerability of converted passenger vessels, and the ease with which an immensely costly national symbol could be destroyed if put in harm's way.

This first lesson was reinforced on 14 September, when Cunard's *Carmania* and Hamburg-Amerika's *Cap Trafalgar*—both serving as armed auxiliaries—battled it out in the South Atlantic. *Carmania* won the engagement by sinking her opponent, but was herself so badly damaged she had to be withdrawn from service for months. The British government, reflecting on the results of these two actions, decided not to squander as expensive and potentially valuable a national asset as *Aquitania* in the AMC role. The liner, along with *Mauretania*, was withdrawn from military service, stripped of her armament, and laid up in reserve until a more suitable task could be found.

Aquitania's furlough ended in May 1915, when she and *Mauretania* were tapped for troopship duty in support of Britain's campaign in the Dardanelles. Allied forces had bogged down soon after landing at Gallipoli in late April, and it had quickly become obvious that large numbers of reinforcements would be needed if the campaign was to succeed. The liners were ideal choices; each could transport six or seven battalions of troops to the combat zone, as *Mauretania* had proven earlier by carrying a brigade of the British 52nd Division to the island of Lemnos. Fitted with additional bunks, the ships were rushed into service in late May.

Over the next three months the two liners carried thousands of vital reinforcements to Mudros. The ships usually traveled alone until they reached the Sea of Crete, where each was joined by one or two escorts for the dash north to Mudros.

The huge troopers were at great risk in the Aegean's confined waters, vulnerable to both mines and the Austrian and German submarines that so zealously sought them. Indeed, one U-boat nearly bagged *Mauretania* as she approached Mudros, but the liner evaded the torpedo and escaped unharmed. And other parts of the voyage could be equally hazardous, as *Aquitania*'s crew discovered on 5 July. Outward bound from Southampton with six battalions of troops, a U-boat attacked the liner off the French coast. An alert lookout spotted an incoming torpedo in time and *Aquitania* was able to elude it and continue the voyage to Lemnos.

Between May and August 1915 *Aquitania* carried 30,000 British, Australian, and New Zealand troops to staging areas throughout the Aegean, a contribution that helped the Allies maintain their toehold on the beaches of Gallipoli. Unfortunately, by mid-August the enormous numbers of casualties being sustained by the Allies on those beaches led to yet another change of career for *Aquitania*, this time from troop transport to hospital ship.

The liner's change in missions was the work of Sir James Porter, Britain's senior medical transport officer in the Dardanelles. In late July, Porter announced to the Allied staff that the rear-area hospitals to which casualties were evacuated—on Lemnos, Malta, and in Egypt—were packed to overflowing and that immediate evacuation to England was the only hope for many of the wounded. When told that the few small and slow hospital ships then available in the region were already overworked, Porter immediately requisitioned *Aquitania*, then at Mudros discharging troops, and ordered her fitted out as an ambulance transport[1].

Hastily equipped with additional beds and staffed by medical personnel drawn from units throughout the Aegean, *Aquitania* soon departed Mudros with 2,400 seriously wounded troops. The liner's size and speed ideally suited her to the evacuation role, and upon her arrival in England the Admiralty ordered her fitted out as a full-fledged military hospital ship[2].

During her subsequent conversion, *Aquitania* was given the most extensive patient accommodations of any World War I hospital vessel. She was equipped with 4,182 beds, with separate wards for different categories of wounds. The ship was also fitted with several well-equipped operating theaters, various types of treatment rooms and exercise areas, and specialized food preparation equipment. Several of her larger public rooms were converted into storage areas for medical supplies and equipment and, in recognition of war's grim realities, one of her cold storage rooms became a morgue. Finally, *Aquitania* was painted white and given the buff-colored funnels, horizontal green hull bands, and large crosses used to distinguish hospital ships from combatants.

Aquitania's conversion into a hospital ship was completed in late August 1915, and she immediately sailed for the Dardanelles. She was joined in late October by the similarly converted *Mauretania*, and in mid-November by White Star's *Britannic*. All

After initial service carrying troops to the Dardanelles in the spring and summer of 1915, *Aquitania* was shifted to the ambulance transport role. She proved so adept at medical evacuation that in August 1915 she was converted into a full-fledged military hospital ship. Seen here after returning a load of wounded to Britain in early 1916, the ship sports the hull band and crosses required of hospital ships by the Geneva Convention. *Shaum Collection*

three liners were dedicated solely to evacuating casualties from the Dardanelles. Sailing from Mudros and Imbros, the ships carried their cargoes of maimed and shattered men to hospitals on Malta and in Egypt, and from there to Great Britain. *Aquitania* made several heavily laden passages to Southampton, once carrying nearly 5,000 ambulatory and litter patients.

Operated under the provisions of the Geneva Convention, *Aquitania* and her consorts could not be armed, nor could they carry military equipment or able-bodied combat troops. Observance of these rules theoretically meant that the vessels were safe from direct attack, though the protection offered by their noncombatant status was often problematical. Mines were a particular threat, and it was such a weapon that ultimately claimed one of the ships. On 21 November 1916 *Britannic* struck a mine while approaching Mudros to pick up a load of wounded; she flooded quickly and sank with the loss of 34 lives.

Britannic's loss was a sobering reminder of the danger facing *Aquitania* during her own medical

evacuation voyages, but it was not allowed to interfere with the converted liner's vital work. Though the Allies had completely withdrawn from Gallipoli in January 1916, the many casualties generated by the ill-fated assault jammed hospitals throughout the Aegean and Mediterranean for a year afterward. The Admiralty's decision to withdraw *Mauretania* from service in March 1916 and lay her up[3] left *Aquitania* to carry on the evacuation effort alone. She soldiered on, and by the time she herself was withdrawn from service in mid-1917, she had transported more than 25,000 ill and injured soldiers to the United Kingdom.

As capable as they had proved themselves to be in both the trooping and medical-evacuation roles, *Aquitania* and *Mauretania* were ultimately judged too valuable to risk in further military operations and were kept tied up throughout 1917. The Admiralty briefly considered using the vessels to evacuate British wounded from France, but wisely concluded that the huge liners would be terribly vulnerable in the confined waters of the English

Channel and Bay of Biscay. Germany had begun attacking hospital ships operating in those areas in an attempt to force the Royal Navy to tie up its valuable destroyers on escort duty, and the two liners would have been hunted without respite.

Aquitania and *Mauretania* might well have spent the remainder of World War I tied up in Liverpool had it not been for General Frank T. Hines of the U.S. Army. As his nation's chief of embarkation, Hines was tasked with moving the American Expeditionary Force to Europe following the United States' April 1917 entry into the war. It was a daunting task; the United States joined the conflict with virtually no modern troop transports. Though the seizure of all German vessels interned in U.S. ports had improved the situation somewhat, Hines believed that the large British passenger liners then idle in U.K. ports could considerably boost the number of U.S. soldiers reaching France. In late November 1917 he requested that *Aquitania*, *Mauretania*, and *Olympic* be made available for U.S. trooping service.

After careful consideration, Britain's Ministry of Shipping granted Hines' request in return for U.S. agreement to several preconditions. These were that the United States assume full risk for the vessels, that the ships be operated by British crews, and that His Majesty's government retain control of the steamers' cargo holds. The U.S. government agreed to these provisions, and all three liners sailed for New York in late December 1917.

In Hoboken *Aquitania* was quickly repainted in dazzle camouflage and made ready for her first voyage with U.S. troops. This took place in mid-January 1918, and over the next 10 months the liner made nine round-trip crossings to Southampton. On each voyage *Aquitania* carried an average of 6,000 soldiers in addition to her crew; she did not lose any passengers to enemy action. This U.S. phase of the liner's World War I career was not entirely free of tragedy, however; on her eighth crossing the ship was involved in one of the most spectacular collisions of the war.

The accident occurred near the end of a rough voyage. *Aquitania* had departed Hoboken on 2 October 1918 with 5,387 troops and a crew of over 1,000. She had been battered by atrocious weather for most of the trip, and on the morning of 8 October was fighting her way through a squall line southwest of Ireland. Shortly after 5 A.M. the liner was met by her escorts, the U.S. destroyers *Conyngham*, *Downes*, *Duncan*, *Kimberley*, and *Shaw*. The Queenstown-based warships took up positions around the trooper, and for the next 24 hours the flotilla battled its way east through mountainous waves and high winds.

Following the United States' 1917 entry into World War I, *Aquitania* was made available for U.S. trooping service. The ship, shown here in her dazzle camouflage and with a smaller troop-transfer vessel alongside during a turnaround in Britain, carried an average of 6,000 troops on each eastbound crossing. *USNHC*

Mauretania, seen here in her own distinctive dazzle scheme, joined *Aquitania* in carrying U.S. troops to Europe. Though 14,000 tons lighter and 100 feet shorter than her running mate, *Mauretania* built a solid reputation of her own as a stable and capable trooper, routinely hauling from 4,500 to 5,800 troops on each passage from New York to Britain. *USNHC*

At daybreak on 9 October *Shaw* moved into her daylight escort position on *Aquitania*'s port bow and began zigzagging at 27 knots. Without warning, the destroyer's steering gear jammed, swinging her toward *Aquitania*. *Shaw*'s captain, Commander William A. Glassford, had to instantly decide whether to ram the trooper amidships or let his own vessel be struck. He made his bitter but inevitable choice in seconds: Ordering the destroyer's engines full astern to cut her speed and check the swing of her bow, he and his crew braced for the collision.

The immediate impact was tremendous. Racing along at 22 knots, *Aquitania* cut through *Shaw* just forward of the bridge and drove the two sections apart. Flames erupted from the warship's ruptured oil tanks, and the bow section sank almost immediately, killing two officers and 14 men. *Aquitania*'s master, Captain J. T. Charles, could do nothing to help. Under orders not to stop for any reason, lest his ship and her embarked troops become a U-boat's trophy, he took his vessel on toward Southampton.

Aboard what remained of *Shaw*, Glassford ordered his crew to abandon ship and make for the circling *Duncan* and *Kimberley*. Glassford and 19 others stayed aboard to try to save the destroyer, and over the next two hours they were able to stop the flooding and put out the fires. Amazingly, they were also able to bring the destroyer's engines back on line, and shortly after 8 A.M. Glassford asked *Kimberley* to lead the way toward Portland, 40 miles to the north. Six hours later the bow-less *Shaw* limped into port to the cheers of those aboard *Duncan* and *Kimberley*[4].

Aquitania, for her part, suffered no appreciable damage in the collision with *Shaw* and returned to New York during the third week of October. By 2 November she was again underway for Southampton, carrying 5,717 troops on what proved to be her last wartime crossing. The liner reached port just days before the Armistice and, after disembarking her passengers, remained at her pier while the Admiralty and Cunard pondered her postwar employment.

For the short term, at least, that employment would simply be to reverse the direction of her trooping shuttle. Acceding to a U.S. government request for assistance in repatriating the American

With her mangled hull stark evidence of her collision with *Aquitania*, the destroyer USS *Shaw* rests in a British dry dock. The warship's steering gear jammed during a zigzag maneuver, putting her dead in front of the onrushing *Aquitania*. Sixteen men were killed when the liner sliced into the destroyer at 22 knots. *USNHC*

Expeditionary Force, the Admiralty and Cunard agreed to make *Aquitania* available for three voyages from Liverpool to New York via Brest. The first trip began in early February 1919, and all were completed by the end of March. On each crossing *Aquitania* embarked between 5,500 and 7,500 U.S. troops, in addition to carrying several hundred paying passengers on each westbound passage.

The conclusion of the third repatriation voyage marked the end of *Aquitania*'s World War I military service and she was subsequently returned to Cunard. The firm put the liner through a partial refit meant to return her to civilian service as quick-

ly as possible, and she was back on commercial duty by June 1919. She sailed on the Southampton-Halifax-New York service until December 1919, when she was withdrawn from service for a comprehensive refurbishment. During this yard period her interior was completely renovated and her propulsion system was converted from coal to oil. She was also fitted with the first gyrocompass ever to be permanently installed on a merchant ship.

Aquitania resumed her regular transatlantic passenger service in July 1920, and for the next two decades she maintained her reputation as the grande dame of express liners despite the appear-

Her World War I duty over, *Aquitania* underwent a comprehensive refurbishment before returning to commercial service in July 1920. For the next two decades she remained popular with passengers despite her advancing years and maintained her reputation as one of the most elegant liners ever to ply the North Atlantic. *Shaum Collection*

ance of newer, larger, and faster competitors. Working in concert with *Berengaria, Mauretania,* and, after 1936, with *Queen Mary, Aquitania* remained the vessel of choice for many of the entertainers, artists, and politicians of the day. She was also popular as a cruise ship, and regular modifications to her passenger accommodations put increasing emphasis on Cabin and Tourist class rooms. In keeping with her past military history, the ship also ferried at least one load of British troops to Palestine.

Despite her continuing popularity, by 1939 *Aquitania* was growing long in the tooth and Cunard had begun planning her withdrawal from service. The outbreak of World War II in September of that year put an immediate end to such plans,

however, for she had much to offer the Allied cause despite her age. The ship made one last commercial voyage following Britain's declaration of war against Germany, and was then requisitioned for military service. She was subjected to much of the same type of conversion that had prepared her for war in 1914, though this time she was intended from the start to serve as a troopship rather than an armed auxiliary.

Once again *Aquitania*'s elaborate furnishings and artwork were removed, her carpets and brass fittings were hauled away, and the paraphernalia of war was brought aboard. Gun mounts and rangefinders appeared along her upper decks and superstructure, and a coat of battleship gray masked her company colors. Sandbags and splin-

Recalled for military duty after the outbreak of World War II, *Aquitania* initially carried Canadian troops to Britain before shifting to Australia in March 1940. For the next 22 months she carried ANZACs to the Middle East, usually by way of South Africa. She is seen here (at right rear) at Cape Town in company with *Queen Mary*, with the South African training ship *General Botha* in the foreground. *South African Defense Forces*

ter shields replaced plush draperies and etched glass, and her passageways soon echoed to the sound of the same type of boots that had ravaged her decks a quarter of a century earlier.

Aquitania's conversion was again completed in record time, and by November 1939 she was ready for sea. Her first task, begun that month, was the transportation of Canadian troops from Halifax to Southampton. She remained on that service until March 1940, when she was shifted to Australia. For the next 22 months, *Aquitania* carried Australian and New Zealand troops to England via Cape Town and the Middle East by way of the Indian Ocean and the Red Sea. On her return voyages to Sydney and Freemantle, Western Australia, the ship carried both wounded ANZACs and Axis prisoners destined for POW camps in the Australian outback.

During her Australian service, *Aquitania* played a small but key role in solving one of World War II's first great mysteries—the disappearance of the Royal Australian Navy cruiser HMAS *Sydney*. The warship had departed Freemantle on 11 November

Aquitania rests at anchor in the background as ANZAC troops watch the tanker *Scalarba* refuel *Queen Elizabeth* in this July 1941 drawing by an Australian war artist. *Aquitania* often operated in concert with the larger Cunarder during the Middle East shuttle days, and the two liners frequently encountered each other while later carrying U.S. troops to Britain. *Shaum Collection*

1941 on a routine escort mission and, after signaling completion of the task eight days later, had subsequently vanished without a trace. On 24 November *Aquitania* was en route from Singapore to Australia to pick up yet another load of troops when, at a point about 100 miles west of Carnarvon on Australia's west coast, a lookout spotted a rubber raft heavily loaded with people. Deciding that the risk of attack was slim, *Aquitania*'s master slowed his ship almost to a stop and took aboard 26 exhausted and dehydrated survivors.

Much to the surprise of everyone aboard the huge troopship, the bedraggled seamen plucked from the raft turned out to be German sailors from the commerce raider *Kormoran*[5]. Even more surprising, the Germans claimed that their 3,287-ton raider had engaged an unknown Allied cruiser on 19 November and, by pretending to be a Dutch merchantman, had managed to draw the unwary man o' war in quite close. Then, through a combination of good luck and excellent gunnery, the Germans had raked the warship with cannon fire and hit her with at least two torpedoes. Though *Kormoran* was herself mortally wounded in the encounter, the Germans were able to inflict incredible damage on the cruiser, which had limped from the scene on fire and wracked by secondary explosions.

In keeping with standing orders, *Aquitania*'s captain did not break radio silence to report either the recovery of the survivors or their tale of combat with the unknown Allied warship. It was thus not until the troopship reached Sydney on 27 November that the full story of *Sydney*'s encounter with *Kormoran* came out. The effect of the news was only slightly dampened by the cloak of secrecy the government immediately imposed. The knowledge that *Sydney*, a veteran of combat in the Mediterranean manned by 645 experienced and highly capable crewmen, had been sunk by a converted cargo ship was almost too much for Australians to bear. No survivors from the cruiser were found, and a shrapnel-riddled life ring was the only vestige of the ship ever recovered.

Tragic though it was, *Sydney*'s loss was soon overshadowed by Japan's December attacks against Allied forces throughout the Pacific, and by the United States' subsequent entry into the war. The U.S.'s decision to join the Allied cause also had an immediate effect on *Aquitania*; the liner stopped in Hawaii to refuel just weeks after the Japanese attack and was quickly chartered to evacuate U.S. civilians to the mainland.

Packed with women, children, and the elderly, *Aquitania* left Honolulu in early February 1942 in company with the Matson Line's similarly loaded *Lurline* and several other ships. The mini-flotilla took a roundabout route to San Francisco, turning what was normally a weeklong passage into a four-week odyssey. Most of the trip was made through heavy seas and dense fog, and at one point the murky conditions contributed to a near-collision between *Aquitania* and *Lurline*. Sharp-eyed lookouts and a break in the fog averted disaster, however, and the liners arrived in San Francisco on 1 March.

Aquitania's appearance in California was a stroke of good luck for the U.S. government. Fearing a Japanese invasion of Hawaii but lacking the large troop transports necessary to effect a rapid buildup of forces in the islands, the Roosevelt administration "borrowed" *Aquitania* from Britain to supplement the efforts of the smaller and slower Army and Navy transports that had been carrying men and equipment to Hawaii since late December. *Aquitania* made two trips to the islands between 12 March and 5 April, carrying approximately 6,000 troops on each westbound passage and several hundred civilian evacuees on each return to San Francisco.

The end of her second voyage to Honolulu brought *Aquitania* only a brief respite; within days of her arrival she was again underway. Though her captain and crew did not realize it, the ship's departure from Hawaii marked the beginning of a world-circling odyssey that would ultimately take *Aquitania* back to Australia.

The first stop on that marathon voyage was New York, where the troopship embarked U.S. soldiers bound for Britain. Arriving in Liverpool on 12 May, she exchanged her Yanks for Tommies and departed for Suez via Madagascar and Aden. Soon after her 8 July arrival in Egypt *Aquitania* sailed for the United States, stopping in Madagascar and Cape Town. The trooper docked in Boston on 14 August and, after taking aboard U.S. soldiers and airmen bound for the Middle East, Australia, and New Zealand, returned to Suez via Cape Town and Aden. Arriving in Egypt on 31 October, *Aquitania* embarked Axis POWs bound for camps in Australia, as well as ANZAC soldiers returning home to bolster their nations' defenses against the Japanese. She sailed for Sydney soon after, and completed her round-the-world voyage in early November.

Shifted to the "GI Shuttle" service during Operation Bolero—the buildup of U.S. forces in Britain prior to the Allied invasion of Europe—*Aquitania* made regular passages between New York and Gourock. Seen here in Scotland at the end of an eastbound voyage in 1944, the liner looks surprisingly fit given her age and hectic schedule. *Shaum Collection*

The conclusion of *Aquitania*'s great globe-circling voyage did not bring a respite from the rigors of wartime trooping; the ship had barely finished off-loading Australian and U.S. troops in Sydney when she moved on to New Zealand. Reaching Wellington on 27 November, *Aquitania* disembarked the remaining Americans and the New Zealanders she had brought from Suez, and within days began taking aboard Royal New Zealand Air Force personnel destined for Egypt. The trooper sailed for the Middle East in early December, stopping briefly in Australia, and arrived in Suez on 5 January 1943.

During the course of her voyages between Australasia and the Middle East, *Aquitania* some-

times traveled in convoy with ships of similar size and performance, and at other times voyaged alone with only her speed and the diligence of her crew to protect her. It was difficult, demanding, and dangerous work, though the heat of the southern hemisphere proved to be the deadliest enemy. *Aquitania* was never attacked by enemy forces, but heatstroke and dehydration claimed several lives during the liner's transits of the South Pacific and Indian oceans.

In mid-1943 *Aquitania* was ordered back to the United Kingdom to take part in the buildup of U.S. forces in Britain in preparation for the invasion of Europe. The ship operated on the U.S.-U.K. shut-

Canadian naval personnel pass the time in a traditional way as *Aquitania* carries them home from Europe. The liner began repatriating Canadians following the surrender of Japan, and carried an average of 6,000 troops on each westbound passage from Southampton to Halifax. On her return trips to Britain she carried home children evacuated to Canada during the early days of the Blitz. *National Archives of Canada*

tle for the next 18 months, working in concert with *Queen Mary, Queen Elizabeth, Mauretania*[6], *Nieuw Amsterdam,* and *Ile de France.* All six liners, known collectively as "The Monsters" because of their size and capacity, sailed from New York literally packed with U.S. troops. The vessels' contribution to the success of the Normandy landings and, ultimately, to the Allied victory in Europe, was both vital and irrefutable.

The end of the war against Germany freed *Aquitania* for duty elsewhere, and in the summer of 1945 the Admiralty allocated her for trooping use in the Pacific during the buildup for the planned Allied invasion of Japan. The atomic bombing of Hiroshima and Nagasaki and Japan's resultant surrender made such duty unnecessary, and in late 1945 the troopship began repatriating Canadian soldiers from Europe. *Aquitania* carried 6,000 troops on each

westbound passage between Southampton and Halifax, and on the return voyages carried home to Britain thousands of children evacuated to Canada early in the war.

The final phase of *Aquitania*'s World War II service began in late 1946. During a brief yard period the ship was relieved of most of her standee bunks and the other trooping paraphernalia, and many of her staterooms were refurbished to a semblance of their prewar condition. These changes were made to accommodate a decidedly different class of passenger than the soldiers *Aquitania* had transported for the past six years: With the end of the war and the winding down of the troop repatriation effort, the ship was now free to carry the British wives and children of Canadian servicemen to their new homes in North America.

Though officially listed as military voyages, the "war bride" trips *Aquitania* undertook through March 1948 were a definite change from her earlier trooping work. The thumping of combat boots on her decks was replaced by the laughter of children at play; the anxiety of young men facing combat gave way to the uncertainty of young women facing new lives in a new land. Each time the liner approached Halifax, young mothers and their children lined the rails, eagerly anticipating both their first glimpse of Canada and their imminent reunion with loved ones.

Aquitania's World War II service ended in March 1948 when the Admiralty returned her to Cunard. It was the conclusion of a magnificent military career because during her second war the venerable liner traveled over 526,000 miles and transported close to 400,000 people. She had sailed around the world, visiting virtually every theater of war and contributing immeasurably to the Allied victory. More important, perhaps, *Aquitania* was never attacked and did not lose a single passenger to enemy action. And, in poignant counterpoint to the martial nature of her first voyages, during her war bride period she witnessed the births of more than a dozen children.

Though Cunard was widely expected to retire the elderly and worn *Aquitania* after her withdrawal from military duty, the firm decided instead to put the liner back to work on a limit-

Her World War II service over, *Aquitania* sits tied to her Southampton pier as *Queen Mary* settles in nearby. The only major pre-1914 passenger ship to see military duty in both world wars, *Aquitania* served ably as armed merchant cruiser, ambulance transport, hospital ship, and trooper. The proud liner circled the globe, playing key roles in both conflicts and eluding the enemy at every turn. *Shaum Collection*

ed commercial service carrying British immigrants to Canada. A brief refit during April 1948 made her somewhat more presentable, and the following month she began sailing between Southampton and Halifax. She proved so successful in her new role that she continued it through late 1949, carrying more than 22,000 people to new lives in North America.

Aquitania's final passage on the immigrant service began in Halifax on 24 November 1949 and ended in Southampton six days later. She was subsequently laid up and ultimately purchased by the British Iron and Steel Company. "The Ship Beautiful," heroine of two world wars, undertook the last voyage of her long and eventful life on 19 February 1950. Manned by a skeleton crew of Cunard veterans and scores of reporters, she sailed to the breaker's yard in Faslane, Scotland, where she was scrapped over the following 18 months.

Builder: John Brown and Company, Clydebank, Scotland.

Launched: 26 September 1934

Length overall: 1,018 feet

Width: 118 feet

Gross tonnage: 80,774 tons

Propulsion: Single-reduction steam turbines driving quadruple screws.

Top speed: 29 knots

Capacity:

  Commercial crew: 1,280

  Military crew: Approximately 875

  Passengers: 776 Cabin, 784 Tourist, 579 Third (1934); 711 First, 708 Cabin, 577 Tourist (1947).

  Troops: 5,000 (1940); 7,500 (1941); 8,500 (1942); 15,000 (1942).

Armament: One four-inch gun, 5–10 Lewis and Vickers machine guns (1940); 24 20 mm cannon, 10 40 mm cannon, six 3-inch cannons, four 2-inch anti-aircraft rocket launchers (1942).

Disposition: Permanently moored hotel and entertainment complex in Long Beach, California.

CHAPTER SEVEN

QUEEN MARY

Arguably the most elegant, capable, and successful North Atlantic passenger steamship, the Royal Mail Ship *Queen Mary* is also one of history's most important troopships. Born in the years just before World War II, she formed the backbone of the Allied trooping effort in that conflict and introduced innovations that revolutionized the seaborne transportation of military forces. Moreover, during her six-and-a-half-year trooping career she set endurance and capacity records that will never be surpassed.

The most successful liner-turned-troopship of all time was born out of the worldwide economic crisis that followed World War I. Britain was especially hard hit by the Depression, and by the early 1920s unemployment and commercial decline were rampant throughout the United Kingdom. The nation's maritime industries were particularly vulnerable, and the shipping lines of France, Italy, Germany, and the United States soon began to erode Britain's traditional dominance of the world's seaborne passenger trade.

The birth of a monarch: RMS *Queen Mary* under construction at John Brown and Company's Clydebank yard in 1934. Cunard's agreement to merge with the White-Star Line, and the British government's subsequent passage of the North Atlantic Shipping (Advances) Bill, ensured Hull 534's completion. *John Brown Engineering, Ltd.*

For the Cunard Steamship Company, long Britain's foremost passenger line, the nation's maritime decline was most apparent on the North Atlantic. Cunard's premier liners—*Aquitania*, *Mauretania,* and *Berengaria*—were too old to compete with the new generation of vessels being built in Europe and the United States. The firm was thus being edged out of its most profitable market, a situation that if not reversed would lead to economic disaster.

Cunard's directors found a two-fold solution to the firm's problem. First, to remain competitive the company would acquire ships that could surpass the performance of the latest European and U.S. designs. And second, Cunard would avoid the cost of building several huge and expensive vessels by instituting a Southampton-Cherbourg-New York service built around just two liners. Ships of comparable size and speed could maintain a weekly shuttle service, doubling revenues and reducing costs by eliminating the need for additional liners.

Design work on the first of the new ships began early in 1926. It was an awesome task, because in order to be economically feasible the liner would have to carry at least 1,700 passengers as well as 1,200 crew members at a minimum speed of 27 knots. She would have to maintain that speed for six days and would require absolute mechanical reliability and excellent fuel economy. The ship would also have to be stable in all sea and weather conditions to maintain her schedule and, lastly, would have to boast the luxury and style that were Cunard's hallmarks.

The liner's design, finished in the spring of 1930, depicted an awesome vessel. She was to be the largest merchant ship yet built, with an overall length of 1,018 feet and a gross weight of 81,000 tons. Her 12 decks would accommodate 776 Cabin, 784 Tourist, and 579 Third Class passengers, as well as 1,280 crew members and 45,000 cubic feet of cargo. Twenty-four oil-fired watertube boilers would produce 160,000 shaft horsepower through four sets of single-reduction geared turbines, turning four 35-ton screws at three revolutions per second for a projected top speed of 28.5 knots. Cunard's engineers estimated the liner would burn 1,000 tons of fuel oil every 24 hours at sea, and allocated space for 8,600 tons of the fluid.

In May 1930 Cunard selected John Brown and Company to build the liner; construction of what the press was already calling the "ultimate ship"

began in Clydebank on 1 December. Work progressed rapidly over the next 11 months, and by November 1931 the nearly completed hull towered over the shipyard.

But as winter wore on, it became obvious the new Cunarder was in trouble. British earnings in the maritime passenger trade had dropped 50 percent between 1928 and 1931; Cunard was finding it increasingly difficult to support the costs of the liner's construction. Faced with bankruptcy, on 11 December 1931 Cunard ordered John Brown to halt work on Hull 534.

For the next two-and-a-half years the Clydebank shipyard resembled a ghost town, with the superliner's hull the only reminder of prosperous times. However, in November 1932 hope appeared on the horizon in the form of Neville Chamberlain, Britain's Chancellor of the Exchequer. Chamberlain had long advocated the creation of a consolidated British shipping line that could, with government support, compete with Europe's nationally subsidized fleets. Cunard's financial difficulties were matched by those of Britain's White Star Line, and the Chancellor saw Hull 534 as a lever that could force the two companies to merge and thereby establish a strong British firm in the North Atlantic passenger trade.

At Chamberlain's urging the British government offered the companies £9 million in low-interest subsidies—including those for carrying the Royal Mail—if they merged. Cunard would retain a controlling interest in the new Cunard-White Star Line, and the subsidies would guarantee completion of Hull 534 and her sister. The two firms accepted the proposal, and Parliament approved the North Atlantic Shipping (Advances) Bill on 27 March 1934.

Work on Hull 534 resumed almost immediately, and *Queen Mary* was launched at Clydebank on 26 September 1934. For the next 18 months the ship lay in Brown's fitting-out basin as workers installed the engines, fittings, and furnishings intended to make her the ultimate express liner. By March 1936 *Queen Mary* could rightfully claim that title; with five dining areas, five lounges, two bars, two swimming pools, a ballroom, and a small but well-equipped hospital, she was as much a posh resort as she was a ship.

Queen Mary embarked on her maiden voyage on 27 May 1936, surrounded by the pomp and circumstance befitting a national icon. She did not,

Queen Mary receives a tumultuous welcome in New York at the end of her maiden voyage in May 1936. From Cunard's point of view the celebration was premature, however, because the vaunted new liner exhibited a host of serious deficiencies during her first transatlantic crossing. Once these were corrected, the liner proved herself as capable as her designers had intended. *The Cunard Line*

however, end that first Southampton-New York passage with the return of the Blue Riband to England. In fact, on her first Atlantic crossing, Britain's expensive symbol of maritime supremacy revealed several serious deficiencies. Among them were severe screw vibrations, funnels that showered passengers and crew with soot, problems with her plumbing and electrical systems, and groans from her hull that indicated critical structural flaws. Though Cunard-White Star attempted to correct these problems with stop-gap measures, it soon became obvious that only a comprehensive refit would suffice. So, less than a year after her maiden voyage, *Queen Mary* was sent to Southampton for a complete overhaul.

This refit transformed the liner into a stable and dependable mount, and in August 1936 *Queen Mary* vindicated herself by winning the Blue Riband with an Atlantic crossing of less than four days. The ship's luxury and elegance quickly made her a favorite of the traveling public, and the elite of several continents soon considered her the only civilized way to travel. Though not as advanced or as stylish as her arch-rival, the French Line's *Normandie*, *Queen Mary* was far more successful economically, and by 1939 had established herself as the undisputed queen of the express liners.

That title lost all meaning, however, with the coming of World War II. The outbreak of hostilities on 3 September 1939 found *Queen Mary* at sea, nearing the end of her 143rd Atlantic crossing. She had sailed from Southampton four days earlier with 2,332 passengers, most of them Americans hoping to escape the European war that suddenly seemed inevitable. Under normal circumstances the liner's bridge crew would already have sighted the approaches to New York harbor. But, sailing under Admiralty orders to avoid regular trade routes, *Queen Mary* was almost 100 miles south of her usual track.

Other precautions were also in force; the same coded radio message that had directed the liner's course change on the night of 2 September ordered her master to put his ship on war alert. Work crews had immediately begun blacking out *Queen Mary*'s 2,000 portholes and windows, and the surrounding sea had gone dark as all the ship's exterior lights were extinguished. Additional lookouts had been posted, and the helmsman had been ordered to steer a zigzag course.

Now, with war a reality, *Queen Mary* raced west across a sea quite possibly teeming with enemies. Few of the passengers aboard that night could forget *Lusitania*'s tragic sinking during World War I; it was a grim reminder of the fate that awaited any passenger vessel attacked without warning on the high seas. And as the most prestigious and visible symbol of Britain's maritime might, *Queen Mary* would undoubtedly be a prime target for every German warship on the North Atlantic.

But the remainder of the liner's voyage was uneventful, and she arrived in New York on the morning of 5 September. Because the Admiralty had directed that all British liners remain in whatever friendly or neutral ports they found themselves upon the outbreak of war, on 6 September Cunard-White Star's New York office canceled all of *Queen Mary*'s scheduled sailings "for the foreseeable future." The ship thus went into forced hibernation at Pier 90 on the Hudson River, moored near the similarly marooned *Normandie*. Most of the Cunarder's crew immediately returned to vital war jobs in Britain, and by 10 September only a small maintenance party remained aboard.

A few weeks after her arrival, however, *Queen Mary*'s ranks began to swell with the members of a special British Intelligence security team. The huge liner was a tempting target for Axis saboteurs, and a joint British-U.S. effort had been organized to protect her. The FBI and the New York Police, as well as the U.S. Army, Navy, and Coast Guard, joined forces with the British agents to ensure *Queen Mary*'s safety. Floodlights were set up to sweep the ship after dark, and armed guards began patrolling the liner and her pier around the clock.

Inactive *Queen Mary* might be, but her guardians were determined that her forced stay in New York would be a quiet one.

And so it was. Indeed, the only excitement around Pier 90 during the first six months of *Queen Mary*'s stay was the 7 March 1940 arrival in New York of Cunard-White Star's other superliner. RMS *Queen Elizabeth* had been launched at Clydebank in 1938, but the outbreak of war had interrupted her fitting out. She had never entered commercial service, and had lain uncompleted in the River Clyde until the Admiralty ordered her to the United States. She had left Scotland on 2 March, and upon her arrival in New York was tied up only a stone's throw from her elder sister.

Queen Elizabeth's appearance in New York marked the first time the two liners had been in the same port at the same time, and they made quite a sight. *Queen Mary,* still resplendent in her peacetime livery of red, white, and black, contrasted sharply with her sister's coat of camouflage gray. And though she was just a few years older, her vast array of topside louvers and exhaust ventilators marked her as being of a different generation than the more streamlined and modern-looking *Queen Elizabeth*[1].

While Cunard's queens sat idle in New York the debate over their ultimate fate raged in London[2]. Britain's increasingly dismal military fortunes made the need for troopships obvious, yet key members of the British government argued that the Cunarders were not suited to the dangers of wartime service. The ships' critics charged that the liners' size would make them the objects of constant enemy attention, and complained that Britain could not spare the men and warships necessary to protect the queens at sea. Moreover, the argument ran, the vessels could not carry enough cargo to make them useful as materiel transports, and the 1,000 tons of fuel oil each would burn every 24 hours could be better used for warships of the Royal Navy. Finally, the liners' critics suggested that the Cunard queens might better serve the war effort as sources of scrap metal than as troopships.

But the liners had their supporters as well, and the arguments in favor of requisitioning the queens for trooping duty received increasingly favorable attention as the months passed. Britain's more realistic leaders realized that the "phony war" that had enveloped Europe after the German invasion of Poland was just the calm before the storm, and argued that *Queen Mary* and her sister would

Having reached safety in New York following the September 1939 outbreak of war, *Queen Mary* sat idle until officially requisitioned by the British government in March 1940. She is seen here soon after her call up—already wearing her coat of camouflage gray—moored next to her prewar arch-rival, the French Line's 83,423-ton *Normandie*. *Library of Congress*

be essential for transporting badly needed reinforcements from the far-flung nations of the Commonwealth to the Home Islands.

In addition, the queens' advocates pointed out that the size of the liners was a plus, in that each ship would be able to carry large numbers of troops over vast distances, using routes that smaller and less sturdy vessels could not safely navigate. More importantly, the Cunarders were much faster than any other troopship then in use and, if operated on the sort of shuttle service for which they had originally been designed, would prove more economically practical than a larger fleet of smaller, slower ships. The queens' speed would also allow them to outrun virtually any existing Axis warship, eliminating the need for escorts and freeing the hard-

pressed Royal Navy for service elsewhere. And, finally, the more pragmatic members of the British government reasoned that the money used to operate the liners as troopships would be better spent than that used to maintain them idle in New York.

Those in favor of using the Cunard queens as troopships eventually won, and the Admiralty decided that the already proven *Queen Mary* would be the first to be called up. The requisition note was delivered to Cunard-White Star in March 1940[3], and for the remainder of that month workmen in New York labored nonstop to prepare the liner for her first military voyage. Her well-known Cunard colors disappeared beneath a coat of camouflage gray, and the huge letters spelling out her name on bow and stern were obscured to disguise her identity. Most of her furniture, artworks, and better fittings were taken ashore for storage, thus clearing her decks for the comprehensive trooping conversion she was to undergo in Australia.

Despite her supporters' claims that *Queen Mary* could outrun any Axis submarine, the Admiralty insisted that the liner be equipped with an ASDIC underwater sound-detection system. And though her speed would be her best defense against enemy surface vessels, London ordered that a single 4-inch gun be mounted on the ship's fan-tail. The weapon would prove inadequate against the 11-inchers of a German battleship, but might offer some protection from lesser vessels. The Cunarder was also provided with a score of vintage Lewis and Maxim machine guns for air defense, and with a waterline-level degaussing girdle meant to neutralize magnetic mines.

On the morning of 19 March 1940 *Queen Mary*'s master was summoned to Cunard-White Star's offices in midtown Manhattan. There Captain R. B. Irving was informed that his ship must be ready to sail within 48 hours, and that he was to take her to Sydney via Trinidad, Cape Town, and Freemantle. Upon returning to his vessel, Irving fleshed out his skeleton crew with 470 officers and men drawn from the Cunarder *Antonia*, and that afternoon the task of preparing *Queen Mary* for sea began. Harbor workers noticed increased activity around the supposedly dormant vessel that evening, with lifeboats being tested and stronger security patrols on the pier.

Public speculation about *Queen Mary*'s status intensified on 20 March following the unannounced evening sailing of the Cunarder *Mauretania*. That vessel, also destined for trooping conversion in Australia, slipped down the Hudson hidden by fog and rain. British intelligence agents in New York hoped the city's resident community of Axis spies would assume the activity aboard *Queen Mary* had been only a cover for the departure of *Mauretania*. If this double deception worked as planned, German warships lurking off the U.S. coast would concentrate their attentions on the smaller liner, making *Queen Mary* safe from all but a chance encounter with enemy units.

Just after eight o'clock on the morning of 21 March, tugs edged *Queen Mary* out into the Hudson and pointed her downstream. She moved slowly toward the open sea, an escort of Coast Guard cutters and New York Police launches lead-ing the way. Once at sea she increased speed and quickly disappeared from view. Thirty-seven days later *Queen Mary* arrived off Sydney Head after a voyage of more than 14,000 miles made at an average speed of 27.2 knots. On 18 April she was moved to the Cockatoo Docks and Engineering Company's pier, where her metamorphosis from luxury liner to troopship began under the watchful eyes of Cunard engineers dispatched from London.

The liner's conversion was a Herculean task. Most of her remaining furnishings and 2,000 of her stateroom doors were packed off to local warehouses. Tiers of wooden bunks and rows of canvas hammocks soon appeared throughout the ship, her galleys and heads were enlarged and most of the shops in her Main Hall were converted into military offices. Workers welded blast shutters over the liner's bridge windows, and hundreds of sandbags were brought aboard to protect vital areas of her superstructure. In two weeks *Queen Mary* was transformed into the largest and fastest troopship the world had yet seen, capable of hauling 5,000 men and much of their equipment around the globe at a speed of nearly 30 knots.

Her conversion complete, the liner was ready to begin her trooping career. On the morning of 4 May 1940 *Queen Mary* left Sydney with the converted Cunarders *Aquitania* and *Mauretania*, the Canadian Pacific liners *Empress of Japan*, *Empress of Britain,* and *Empress of Canada*, and the RMS *Andes*. The group, escorted by the cruisers HMAS *Australia* and HMAS *Canberra*, called at Freemantle to take on provisions and additional troops and, on 10 May, set out on the 6,000-mile journey across the Indian Ocean to Cape Town.

The convoy dropped anchor in Table Bay 16 days later. Though uneventful this first major trooping convoy had been nerve-racking for all concerned, and the crews of the seven troopships hoped for a few days of rest. But early that same evening the Royal Navy representative in Cape Town informed the convoy's senior officers that the liners must be ready to sail again within 24 hours. They would be joined at Simonstown by the escorting cruiser HMS *Cumberland*—*Australia* and *Canberra* being needed elsewhere—and were to make for Britain "with all possible speed."

The Admiralty's plea for a rapid passage was understandable given the bleak situation in Europe. Germany had conquered Denmark and invaded Norway the previous month, and on 10

High and dry for a much-needed overhaul, *Queen Mary* sits in Singapore's Royal Navy dry dock in August 1940. During this yard period her hull was scraped and her machinery was overhauled. She was also fitted with a minesweeping paravane system. The Italian invasion of Egypt cut short her stay in Singapore, however, and she soon headed for Australia to pick up ANZACs needed to reinforce the Middle East. *The Wrather Corporation*

May the Wehrmacht had smashed into Holland, Belgium, and Luxembourg. Three days later German units struck through the supposedly impenetrable Ardennes forests to drive a wedge between the Allied armies and trap the British Expeditionary Force in Belgium and northern France. The successful Dunkirk evacuation saved the BEF from destruction, but the retreating British had to abandon most of their equipment and heavy weapons. The units returning to Britain would be hard-pressed to repel the German invasion that now seemed certain, and the 14,000 Australian and New Zealand troops aboard the seven converted liners were desperately needed to bolster the United Kingdom's sagging defenses.

Queen Mary and her companions stayed in Cape Town only long enough to take on fuel and provisions, setting sail for Scotland on 28 May. But the situation in Europe continued to deteriorate even as the ships raced for the Clyde. On 8 June all Allied troops were evacuated from Norway. Two days later, Italy declared war on Britain and France, and Italian troops crossed the French frontier on a front stretching from Switzerland to the Mediterranean. Paris fell to the Wehrmacht on 14 June, and the following day Premier Paul Reynaud

informed the British government that France could no longer honor her pledge to refuse a separate peace with Germany. On 16 June, the same day *Queen Mary* dropped anchor at Clydebank, Marshal Philippe Petain replaced Reynaud as French premier and appealed to Berlin for an immediate armistice.

Queen Mary's welcome in Scotland was a warm one; the people of the Clyde had a proprietary interest in "their" liner and her safe return was cause for celebration. But the festive atmosphere was dampened by the knowledge that Great Britain faced one of the most dangerous periods in her long history. The fall of France assured Germany's virtual mastery of Europe, and Adolf Hitler could now unleash the full fury of the Nazi blitzkrieg against the United Kingdom.

The British government realized that the nation's only hope for survival lay in the swift arrival of reinforcements from the Commonwealth nations. The speed and capacity of *Queen Mary* and her fellow liners thus increased their value to the war effort after the French capitulation, but also guaranteed they would be relentlessly hunted by every means at Hitler's command. Indeed, the frequency of German attacks on Allied troopships had already increased, with six large troopers having been sunk during the French and Norwegian campaigns. Still, the remaining troopships would have to soldier on no matter what the cost; it was imperative their human cargoes reach the battlefields.

Captain Irving was well aware of the hazards that would face his ship. Yet there was danger, too, even in the relative safety of port. Luftwaffe reconnaissance aircraft had begun to show increasing interest in ships plying the Firth of Clyde, and German spies in Scotland were known to be particularly interested in *Queen Mary*'s activities.

But British Intelligence was working equally hard to protect the great liner. Crew members who spoke too freely about the ship while relaxing at local pubs quickly found themselves transferred ashore. Newspapers were informed that stiff penalties would follow the publication of any information concerning *Queen Mary*'s movements, and photographers who found the ship an interesting subject were detained and their film confiscated. Armed troops maintained round-the-clock patrols of the ship and her pier, and even routine maintenance was performed under the eyes of security personnel. Though seen as excessive by some, such stringent precautions were necessary for the nation's security as well as the liner's: Great Britain's troopship capacity would be reduced by almost 20 percent should the giant Cunarder be sunk or severely damaged.

Fortunately, no harm came to the ship during her sojourn on the Clyde and on the morning of 29 June 1940 Irving took his vessel to sea. His sealed orders, opened only after the liner cleared the Firth of Clyde, directed him to make for Singapore. After a much-needed dry-docking at Britain's huge Asian naval base, the ship would head for Sydney to resume her trooping duties.

The 14,000-mile voyage to Singapore was uneventful, and *Queen Mary* entered the port's Royal Navy dry dock on 5 August. Over the next 41 days workmen relieved her hull of its crust of barnacles, overhauled her engines and steering gear, and touched up her coat of camouflage gray. The liner was also fitted with a minesweeping paravane system which, when towed underwater on either side of the ship, would cut the mooring cables of submerged mines so they could float to the surface and be destroyed by gunfire.

Queen Mary's stay in Singapore ended abruptly following Italy's 14 September invasion of Egypt. The attack posed an enormous threat to Britain, because an Italian seizure of the Suez Canal would sever the United Kingdom's vital supply lines to Australia and India, while at the same time paving the way for an Axis conquest of the Middle East. Almost overnight the Mediterranean became the principal theater of war, and the Admiralty ordered *Queen Mary* to proceed immediately to Sydney to begin carrying urgently needed troops to Egypt. The liner arrived in Australia on 25 September and, after a three-week yard period that increased her trooping capacity to 7,500, was underway for Suez on 20 October.

For the next seven months *Queen Mary* crisscrossed the Indian Ocean, sometimes alone and sometimes in convoy with other fast liners. Too vulnerable in the confines of the Red Sea, the liner traveled only as far as Bombay or Trincomalee, where she off-loaded her troops into smaller vessels. In early April *Queen Elizabeth* joined her in this vital work, and by November 1941 Cunard's queens had carried 80,000 troops from Australia to the Middle East. This contribution allowed Britain to stabilize her defense lines in North Africa and, though the situation in the Middle East was by no means secure, some war planners had begun to predict that 1942 would be the decisive year in the struggle against Nazi Germany and her allies.

But any hopes of a quick end to the war were shattered by the December 1941 Japanese attack on Pearl Harbor. Japan's entry into the war radically altered Britain's strategic planning because in one stroke it put at risk the United Kingdom's vital supply line to Australia and India, endangered Hong Kong and Singapore, and pointed a dagger at Australia. The shipment of ANZAC troops to the Middle East had drastically weakened the island continent's defenses. Should Australia fall, the Axis would dominate the Indian and Pacific oceans, threaten India and East Africa, and halt the flow of oil and rubber so essential to the Allied war effort.

The outbreak of war with Japan found *Queen Mary* in Trincomalee. The liner had been en route to Singapore for a refit meant to further increase her troop capacity, but the Japanese offensive that followed the Pearl Harbor attack made that journey impossible. Japanese troops were advancing down the Malay Peninsula, and the 10 December sinking of the British battleships *Prince of Wales* and *Repulse* by Japanese aircraft showed that no Allied vessel was safe in the South Pacific or Indian Ocean. The Admiralty therefore ordered the Cunarder to New York, and she sailed on 19 December.

Queen Mary dropped anchor in the Hudson River on 12 January 1942 after a 12,000-mile voyage via Cape Town. Her stay in New York was not a long one, however, for 10 days later she sailed for Boston to begin a yard period meant to increase her troop capacity to 8,500. The upgrade was part of a joint British-U.S. plan to use the Cunard queens as the mainstays of a North America-to-Australia troop shuttle intended to reinforce Australia's defenses. The United States agreed to supply the bulk of the men and materiel needed to halt the Japanese advance across the Pacific, while Britain would provide the ships needed to carry the troops to Australia.

The gates of Boston Navy Yard's dry dock closed behind *Queen Mary* on 27 January, and over the next 13 days the ship underwent a comprehensive facelift. Her troop capacity was boosted to 8,500 and her toilet facilities and food and water storage areas were enlarged. Workers also upgraded her armament, installing 10 40 mm cannons in five double mounts sited fore and aft and 24 20 mm cannons in single mounts along her upper works.

Six 3-inch guns were also fitted, two forward of the bridge near the well deck and four on the aft superstructure forward of the fantail. Finally, four sets of primitive 2-inch anti-aircraft rocket launchers were grouped around her aft funnel.

With her refit completed, *Queen Mary* was ready to begin her first voyage with U.S. troops aboard. Late on the night of 17 February, 8,398 soldiers boarded the liner. Fueling and provisioning continued well into the next day, however, and the ship did not get underway until just after noon on the 18th. She headed northeast until out of sight of land, then altered course due south on the first leg of her passage to Sydney.

Increased U-boat activity near Trinidad forced the liner to make a brief stop at Key West, Florida, to reprovision. Fuel and fresh water were not all *Queen Mary* took aboard, however; she also acquired a new master. Captain James Bisset, a 35-year Cunard veteran, replaced Irving, who had reached mandatory retirement age. As soon as provisioning was completed, Bisset took the vessel to sea, setting her on a course around the western end of Cuba and into the Atlantic through the Anegada Passage south of Puerto Rico.

The liner's new master had no way of knowing that two German submarines, *U-161* and *U-129*, were taking the same route. The presence of the

enemy raiders didn't stay a secret for long, however; a few minutes after *Queen Mary* cleared the Anegada Passage her radio operator picked up a distress call from an Allied tanker torpedoed just 10 miles astern of the liner. It wasn't the only close call the ship would experience during her passage to Australia.

The second brush with danger came in Rio de Janeiro, where *Queen Mary* called for fuel and supplies on 6 March. A group of Axis spies led by the Italian count Edmondo Di Robilant had somehow gotten a copy of the liner's sailing schedule and broadcast it to U-boats lurking off Brazil's coast. Di Robilant's message was fortunately intercepted by Allied intelligence agents, and Bisset was ordered to get his ship out of Rio several hours ahead of schedule. This he did, and the Cunarder set out on the 3,300-mile journey to Cape Town on 8 March.

The remainder of *Queen Mary*'s voyage to Australia was routine, and the liner disembarked her load of U.S. troops in Sydney on 28 March. Workmen spent eight days preparing the liner for the return passage to New York, and she sailed on the morning of 6 April. As she was leaving Sydney Harbor she passed the *Queen Elizabeth*, inbound from San Francisco with 8,000 U.S. troops. It was the first time Cunard's queens met at sea, and the liners saluted each other with a chorus of siren blasts.

Queen Mary dropped anchor in New York on 7 May 1942, safely ending a 78-day voyage that had covered nearly 35,000 miles. The liner had navigated some of the world's most challenging sea lanes and her crew had outwitted the Axis' combined military and naval forces. It was a complete vindication of the faith placed in the ship and her crew by Allied war planners, and the success of this first voyage with U.S. troops erased any remaining doubts of the Cunard queens' value to the Allied war effort.

Even as *Queen Mary* was being eased alongside Pier 90 on the Hudson, U.S. military planners were sketching out an even larger role for her and *Queen Elizabeth*. In late 1941 British and U.S. experts had determined that each liner was capable of carrying up to 15,000 troops and, once operational control of both vessels passed to the United States following the country's entry into the war, plans were set in motion to expand each ship's troop capacity.

But developments in the Middle East forced a delay in the plans to upgrade Cunard's queens. The

The first U.S. Army troops transported to Britain aboard *Queen Mary* left New York on 11 May 1942. One of the embarked units on that voyage was the headquarters staff of the U.S. 5th Army, whose administrative staff is seen here at work in an improvised office. *U.S. Army Transportation Corps Museum*

German-Italian invasion of Libya at the end of March 1942 forced London to shift large numbers of troops from Britain to the Mediterranean, and the United Kingdom's defenses were again stretched thin. Allied war planners decided to reinforce the Home Islands with U.S. troops, and *Queen Mary* was needed to transport the soldiers to Scotland. She would embark British troops, carry them to Suez, and then return to New York for the belated renovation that would enable her to carry division-size units.

The Cunarder sailed on 11 May, bound for the Clyde with 9,880 U.S. troops and 875 crew members. It was the first time *Queen Mary* carried U.S. soldiers to the British Isles. The liner arrived in Scotland on 16 May, traded her cargo of GIs for 9,537 British troops and set out for Suez on 22 May. Her route took her first to Freetown, Sierra Leone, then on to Cape Town. The liner arrived in Egypt on 22 June, disembarked her passengers, and began the return passage to the United States the following day.

Queen Mary reached New York on 21 July, having called at both Cape Town and Rio. It had been a fast and hectic trip, covering 31,000 miles in 71 days, but any hopes the crew might have had for some time off were dashed by the need to complete the ship's troop-capacity expansion. Work began immediately, and over the next 12 days standee bunks were installed in virtually every inch of free space. The First Class Smoking Room was converted into a small but well-equipped troop hospital, the ship's galleys and toilets were upgraded yet again, and the vacant Austin Reed's men's shop in the Main Hall was turned into a stockade.

By 1 August *Queen Mary* was ready to embark on her first 15,000-troop voyage. The *entire* U.S. 1st Armored Division—15,125 men—boarded the liner during the night. As the Cunarder moved downriver the next morning, the troops were under strict orders to stand absolutely still so the ship would not list to either side as it passed over the Hudson Tunnel. They obeyed perfectly: The Cunarder cleared the tunnel with ease and soon disappeared into the open sea.

Five days later the people of Gourock woke to find *Queen Mary* riding at anchor in the Clyde. The initial 15,000-man crossing had gone off without a hitch and, upon the liner's 16 August return to the United States, two further New York-Gourock-New York runs were scheduled. The first of these

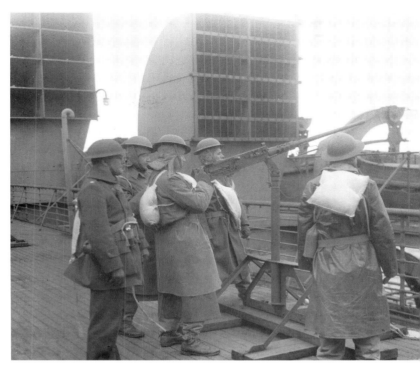

A U.S. Army gun crew mans one of *Queen Mary*'s .50-caliber anti-aircraft mounts during the May 1942 voyage to Scotland. Note that the GIs wear cold weather gear, life jackets, World War I vintage helmets, and that (in this staged photo, at least) it takes four enlisted men and an officer to operate the weapon. *U.S. Army Transportation Corps Museum*

A sergeant inspects the cramped quarters assigned to Battery C, 68th Field Artillery, during *Queen Mary*'s first U.S. trooping voyage. The hammocks (seen here in the stowed position) did not make the best use of the liner's vast amount of space, and were ultimately replaced by tiers of folding bunks. *U.S. Army Transportation Corps Museum*

The elderly British anti-aircraft cruiser HMS *Curacao* as she appeared shortly before her fatal encounter with *Queen Mary* on 2 October 1942. Veering in front of the onrushing trooper, the warship was cut in half and sank in minutes with the loss of 338 officers and men. *The Wrather Corporation*

voyages went well, but the second brought *Queen Mary* the greatest tragedy of her long career.

The crossing started out normally on 27 September 1942, when the Cunarder left New York for the Clyde. By the morning of 2 October *Queen Mary* was 40 miles off the north coast of Ireland, and voyage WW#18E was nearing its end. Just after 7 A.M. the liner's bridge watch sighted the cruiser HMS *Curacao*, a 4,200-ton World War I veteran serving as an anti-aircraft escort vessel. The cruiser's skipper, Captain Wilfred Boutwood, signaled *Queen Mary* that he would take up station five miles ahead, while six destroyers would assume flanking positions on either side of the liner's track.

For the next five hours the convoy moved steadily toward Scotland, all hands scanning the clear skies for German aircraft. A stiff wind was making life difficult for the destroyers, but *Queen Mary* steamed on majestically through the choppy seas. Though the Cunarder was sailing a routine zigzag course, her great speed had allowed her to slowly overtake the slower *Curacao*, and by 2 P.M. the cruiser was only a few hundred yards off the liner's starboard bow.

Queen Mary's Senior First Officer, a Mr. Robinson, became increasingly concerned about *Curacao*'s proximity and ordered his helmsman to turn slightly away from the nearing cruiser. But, incredibly, the warship turned even further toward the liner, and Robinson ordered *Queen Mary*'s helm hard-a-port in a last-ditch effort to avoid disaster. For a moment it looked as though the maneuver would work as *Curacao* veered slightly away. But then, inexorably, the cruiser slid across *Queen Mary*'s path and was sliced in half by the Cunarder's stem.

Queen Mary struck *Curacao* 11 feet forward of her stern, spinning the warship around and driving the two sections of the ship apart. Within seconds both were on fire and beginning to settle; screaming sailors leaped into the oil-covered sea. U.S. troops aboard the liner threw life jackets and anything else that would float over the side, and on the bridge Captain Gordon Illingsworth[4] ordered the Radio Officer to call the escorts in to pick up survivors. *Queen Mary* was under strict orders not to stop for any reason, and she moved on through the carnage seemingly undamaged by the collision. The destroyers were on the scene in minutes, but only 101 of the cruiser's 439 officers and men were saved.

Damage-control parties aboard *Queen Mary* soon reported that the liner had not escaped the accident unscathed. The collision had torn an 11-foot-tall gash in the Cunarder's stem below the waterline, and the vessel's speed was forcing water into the forepeak. *Queen Mary*'s keel-to-main deck collision bulkhead kept the water, which was coming through the buckled stem, from flooding the hull, but the bulkhead might well give way if the entire forward section of the liner flooded. The weight of the water combined with the ship's speed would then drive her bow beneath the waves and rapid submergence would follow.

As soon as the extent of the damage was clear, Illingsworth reduced the liner's speed to 10 knots. The flood of water through the crushed stem slowed enough to allow damage control parties to block the hole with collision mats reinforced with timber shoring. Pumps were brought in to deal with the seawater, and *Queen Mary* was able to limp toward Scotland at 13 knots.

The liner arrived safely in Gourock on the morning of 3 October, and shortly afterward Royal Navy and Cunard Line engineers came aboard to conduct a complete damage survey[5]. The examination showed *Queen Mary* was repairable, but the threat of an Axis attack on the ship should she remain in Scotland prompted a recommendation that repairs be made in Boston rather than Clydebank. With the collision mats replaced by a concrete plug for the journey west, the Cunarder set sail for the United States on 8 October.

Queen Mary entered the Boston Naval Shipyard dry dock on 14 October. By the time she emerged 19 days later, all outward signs of the collision with *Curacao* had disappeared. The urgent need to return the liner to trooping duty left no time for the installation of a completely new stem, so workmen straightened the damaged area and solidly reinforced the ship's forepeak and collision bulkhead. On 3 November Coast Guard inspectors judged the vessel ready to rejoin the war effort, and two days later she sailed for Gourock with 10,389 U.S. troops.

After off-loading the GIs in Gourock, *Queen Mary* embarked 10,669 British and ANZAC troops in preparation for one of her most remarkable voyages. On 23 December she left Gourock bound for Massawa, Ethiopia, by way of Freetown, Cape Town, Aden, and Suez. At Massawa she exchanged her original passengers for 9,995 British soldiers needed in Australia; once in Freemantle she traded these troops for 8,326 ANZACs bound for Scotland. The odyssey lasted four months, and by

Captain Gordon Illingsworth's log entry concerning the Curacao disaster, marked with an "X" in the upper left of the photo, stated simply that "at 2:12 P.M., 2nd October 1942, this vessel was in collision with H.M.S. 'Curacao' in Lat. 55 51'N, Long. 8 38'W." The entry is signed by Illingsworth and the ship's chief purser. *Author's Collection*

The ramming of *Curacao* badly crumpled *Queen Mary*'s stem, flooding the liner's forepeak and threatening to breach her forward keel-to-main-deck collision bulkhead. Damage-control teams managed to avert disaster, and the damage was later repaired at the Boston Naval Yard (where this photo was taken). *USNHC*

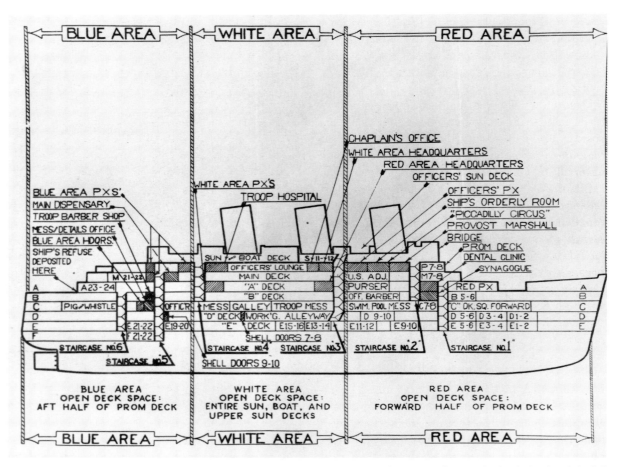

BLUE AREA · WHITE AREA · RED AREA

CHAPLAIN'S OFFICE
WHITE AREA HEADQUARTERS
RED AREA HEADQUARTERS
OFFICERS' SUN DECK
OFFICERS' PX
SHIP'S ORDERLY ROOM
"PICCADILLY CIRCUS"
PROVOST MARSHALL
BRIDGE
PROM DECK
DENTAL CLINIC
SYNAGOGUE

BLUE AREA PXS'
MAIN DISPENSARY
TROOP BARBER SHOP
MESS/DETAILS OFFICE
BLUE AREA HDQRS.'
SHIP'S REFUSE DEPOSITED HERE

WHITE AREA PX'S
TROOP HOSPITAL

SUN DECK · BOAT DECK · S 11-12
OFFICERS' LOUNGE
MAIN DECK
"A" DECK
"B" DECK
MESS GALLEY TROOP MESS
"D" DECK WORK'G. ALLEYWAY
"E" DECK E15-16 E13-14
SHELL DOORS 7-8

U.S. ADJ.
PURSER
OFF. BARBER
SWIM. POOL MESS C7-8
D 9-10
E 11-12 · E 9-10

P 7-8
M7-8
RED PX
B 5-6
"C" DK. SQ. FORWARD
D 5-6 D3-4 D1-2
E 5-6 E3-4 E1-2

M 21-22
A23-24
PIG/WHISTLE
OFFICRS
E 21-22 · E19-20
F 21-22

STAIRCASE NO.6
STAIRCASE NO.5
STAIRCASE NO.4 · STAIRCASE NO.3
SHELL DOORS 9-10
STAIRCASE NO.2
STAIRCASE NO.1

BLUE AREA
OPEN DECK SPACE:
AFT HALF OF PROM DECK

WHITE AREA
OPEN DECK SPACE:
ENTIRE SUN, BOAT, AND
UPPER SUN DECKS

RED AREA
OPEN DECK SPACE:
FORWARD HALF OF PROM DECK

BLUE AREA · WHITE AREA · RED AREA

The decision to carry division-sized units aboard *Queen Mary* meant that, in the interests of order and efficiency, the ship had to be subdivided into separate troop accommodation zones. The "red, white, and blue plan" was a source of great confusion for embarking troops, each of whom was given a copy of this explanatory diagram on boarding. *Author's Collection*

the time *Queen Mary* returned to Gourock on 22 April 1943 she had carried 28,990 men and voyaged almost 38,000 miles.

On 5 May the liner left Gourock for the United States, and eight days later entered dry dock in Bayonne, New Jersey, for a much-needed refit. Even as work began on the Cunarder, however, planners in Washington were undertaking a similar overhaul of the strategy that governed her military career.

Since the outbreak of World War II that strategy had been defensive: *Queen Mary* and the other premier passenger liners converted for trooping had been used to shift Allied forces from one theater to another in response to Axis offensives. But by the spring of 1943 the Allies had managed to halt the enemy's advances in Europe and the Pacific, and the time had come to go on the offensive. In keeping with earlier agreements between President Franklin Roosevelt and Prime Minister

Winston Churchill, the Allies would concentrate first on achieving victory in Europe.

The cornerstone for that victory was Operation Overlord, the Allied invasion of Europe. Because U.S. forces were to play a leading role in the assault, getting the necessary men and equipment from the United States to the battle zone was a prerequisite for success. This movement of troops and materiel to staging areas in Great Britain was dubbed Operation Bolero, and it was a task in which *Queen Mary* and her fellow superliners were chosen to play a major role.

Originally developed to speed large numbers of people between Europe and the United States, *Queen Mary* and her compatriots were ideally suited to bear the brunt of Operation Bolero. Cunard's queens themselves were each able to carry 15,000 troops to Great Britain in less than six days, and *Aquitania*, *Mauretania*, *Nieuw Amsterdam*, and *Ile de*

France were nearly as capable. The Operation Bolero plan called for the six ships to maintain a transatlantic shuttle service until Germany was defeated. They could then be shifted back to the Pacific, if needed.

Queen Mary debuted as a GI shuttle on the first day of June 1943, and for the next 23 months she crossed the Atlantic on a schedule almost as regular as that of her prewar days. The liner usually carried her maximum of 15,000 troops on each eastbound leg, and returned to New York with an average of 2,000 passengers. These normally consisted of wounded troops, Allied military personnel and diplomats assigned to duty in the United States or Canada, Axis POWs being shipped to camps in North America, and civilians traveling on war-related business.

To ease the inevitable problems caused by over-crowding, *Queen Mary* was divided into three roughly equal, completely segregated troop accommodation areas designated Red (forward), White (midships), and Blue (aft). Each soldier boarding the liner was given a colored button corresponding to his unit's assigned area; troops were not permitted outside their designated part of the ship. The allure of their particular section of the liner normally disappeared after the first full day at sea, leaving soldiers to pass the time reading, writing letters home or, in many cases, gambling around the clock.

Food was often the only diversion for embarked troops, and the two daily meals served aboard *Queen Mary* were always well attended. Each meal was served in six staggered sittings, with breakfast available from 6:30 to 11:00 A.M. and dinner from 3:00 to 7:30 P.M. Enlisted troops were fed in the former First Class dining room; the Officer's Mess was the former Tourist Class lounge. Meal times were chaotic; each sitting was only allowed 45 minutes to enter, eat, and make room for the next group. At the end of each sitting one phalanx of troops came in as the previous group was ushered out the opposite end of the dining hall.

The rotational system that governed meal schedules aboard *Queen Mary* was also applied to sleeping arrangements. Only two-thirds of the embarked troops could be accommodated in the liner's 12,500 standee bunks, so an average of 2,500 men were assigned sleeping areas on the ship's decks. A regular rotation ensured that no one spent more than two nights topside, though many soldiers actually preferred it to the crowded spaces below.

Queen Mary's prewar First Class dining room served as the enlisted personnel mess hall and was always a scene of barely controlled chaos during mealtimes. Here, Army Air Force troops queue up in the food line while other soldiers rush to finish their meal. The wall map at upper right used a small model of the ship to show peacetime diners the ship's course and position. *U.S Army Transportation Corps Museum*

As a precaution against attack, *Queen Mary* never followed the same route twice, and her master did not know her exact course until after leaving port. A group of four or five destroyers escorted the liner for 150 miles when Navy patrol planes or blimps relieved them. The aircraft watched over *Queen Mary* as long as their fuel allowed, then turned for home. The Cunarder was on her own until joined by her British escorts off the Irish coast.

The appearance of those escorts was always the most anxiously awaited event of every shuttle crossing because it meant the dangerous transatlantic journey was nearing an end. RAF seaplanes or long-range patrol bombers were usually the first to appear, and were eventually joined by from three to six Royal Navy destroyers. The warships maintained wide-ranging anti-submarine search patterns for the remainder of the voyage because any U-boat lurking along *Queen Mary's* path would have a clear shot as she stopped zigzagging and reduced speed to navigate the River Clyde approaches.

Queen Mary's human cargo began going ashore almost as soon as the liner was safely tied to her Gourock pier. Gangways on A, B, and D decks were normally used to off-load the troops, and the

The ship's 12,500 standee bunks took up nearly every inch of free space including, as seen here, *Queen Mary*'s swimming pool. Given the crowded conditions, many soldiers actually preferred to sleep on deck as part of the rotational "hotbunking" system. *U.S Army Transportation Corps Museum*

debarkation process rarely took more than 36 hours. Once on the pier the soldiers formed up in assembly areas, were mustered again, and boarded waiting British Army trucks. The vehicles, forming a convoy that often stretched for miles, wound through the streets of Gourock toward staging areas outside Glasgow. From there the Americans were sent to other camps throughout Britain and, ultimately, to the battlefronts.

Queen Mary kept up her hectic transatlantic schedule from June 1943 to April 1945, during which time she sailed over 180,000 miles and carried nearly 340,000 U.S. and Canadian troops to the United Kingdom. Her contribution, coupled with that of the equally hardworking *Queen Elizabeth*, was decisive: Soldiering on through the darkest months of the Battle of the Atlantic, the Cunard queens carried the majority of men marshaled in Great Britain during Operation Bolero.

The end of World War II in Europe did not spell the end of the Queens' contribution to the Allied cause, however; they still had a vital role to play in the war against Japan. Allied plans for victory in the Pacific relied on great numbers of troops being shifted from Europe and the Middle East, with Commonwealth forces going directly to Australia and India, and U.S. troops stopping over in the United States to reorganize and reequip before deploying to the Pacific. *Queen Mary*, *Queen Elizabeth*, and *Aquitania* were tapped to carry the majority of U.S. forces back to the United States from Europe because the liners had the speed and passenger capacity to move the greatest number of troops in the shortest possible time.

Queen Mary began this latest military task on 5 June 1945, when she left New York bound for Gourock. Though her course took her over the same route she had traveled for the past two years, this voyage was different from her wartime crossings. Peacetime conditions once again prevailed on the North Atlantic, and for the first time since 1939 the great liner was able to sail without the need to zigzag. No U-boats lay in wait for her, no surface raiders stalked her, and the only aircraft overhead were friends. The Cunarder sped on with all lights blazing, arriving in Gourock on 10 June to an ecstatic welcome.

But if the liner was warmly received in Scotland, her return to New York on 20 June was tumultuous. The 14,777 U.S. troops she had embarked five days earlier in Scotland were the first to be returned to the United States as brigad-

The most eagerly awaited sight on any trooping voyage: the arrival of an RAF Coastal Command Catalina patrol plane off the coast of Northern Ireland. The aircraft's arrival meant the passage was nearly over. The last day of the trip was always the most dangerous because German aircraft and patrol boats often tried to intercept *Queen Mary* as she reduced speed to navigate the River Clyde approaches. *U.S Army Transportation Corps Museum*

The end of the war in Europe brought *Queen Mary*'s New York-to-Gourock trooping shuttle to a close, and she is seen here in April 1945 awaiting the next phase of her military career—the troop repatriation effort. Note that the liner's guns and degaussing girdle have not yet been removed. *U.S Army Transportation Corps Museum*

ed units, and New York's welcome was unbounded. Blimps and other aircraft flew low overhead as the liner eased her way into port. Scores of watercraft steamed alongside with pennants waving and sirens wailing. Fireboats shot streams of water into the sky, and the cheers from the troops lining *Queen Mary*'s rails were answered by the roar of tens of thousands of New Yorkers.

The welcome accorded the liner in New York was no less boisterous on her next three arrivals from Scotland, and by mid-August 1945 31,900 returning U.S. soldiers had witnessed the same scene from the liner's decks. But GIs were not the only ones to receive a warm welcome home; the men, women, and children *Queen Mary* carried

home to the United Kingdom on her return passages received the same sort of reception at Gourock. The majority of these returning Britons had been evacuated to North America during the first months of the war and had not seen family, friends, or homeland for more than five years. The people of the Clyde turned out in force to welcome them home.

On 11 August *Queen Mary* arrived in Southampton for the first time since 1939. The huge port had been heavily damaged by German air attacks, but nothing could dampen the enthusiastic welcome the ship received. This greeting was perhaps even more frenzied than those in New York and Gourock because the scent of a final Allied victory was in the

U.S. troops bound for home aboard *Queen Mary* in June 1945 pass the voyage in time-honored fashion. While still as crowded as the trooping voyages, the repatriation trips were more enjoyable for the troops because the vessel did not zigzag, ran with all her lights on, and most importantly, was not being stalked by unseen enemies. *U.S Army Transportation Corps Museum*

air. Hiroshima and Nagasaki had both been attacked with atomic weapons while the liner was en route from New York, and rumors of a Japanese capitulation had been circulating in Britain for several days. On 14 August, as the Cunarder was preparing to embark 15,000 Americans bound for New York, Japan surrendered unconditionally.

In the United States the Japanese collapse sparked an immediate and vocal public demand for the rapid repatriation of all overseas U.S. forces not absolutely required for occupation duty. The Truman administration reacted to the increasing pressure by assigning every possible vessel to repatriation work. Some 178 Army and Navy assault transports, 11 surface combatants, 8 hospital ships, and a variety of cargo transports, cruise ships, and captured Axis freighters were eventually pressed into service in what became the largest sealift operation in history. *Queen Mary, Queen Elizabeth,* and *Aquitania* played a major role in the redeployment effort, together transporting nearly a quarter of the 500,000 U.S. troops returned to the United States by October 1945.

The success of the repatriation effort soon mollified U.S. public opinion but, ironically, fueled widespread public calls in Britain for the return of the three Cunarders. The liners had been loaned to the U.S. government after Germany's surrender solely to speed the redeployment of Europe-based GIs to the Pacific. But Tokyo's surrender had terminated that agreement in August, and many Britons wondered why the ships were still repatriating U.S. rather than British troops. Pressed for action by their respective governments, Prime Minister Clement Atlee and President Harry Truman announced in mid-October that while *Queen Mary* would remain in U.S. service "for the present," *Queen Elizabeth* and *Aquitania* would immediately return to British service.

Dressed for the occasion, *Queen Mary* is escorted into New York harbor by small boats and a Navy blimp on the 20 June 1945 end of her first troop-repatriation voyage. The liner's welcome was ecstatic; thousands of well-wishers along the shore cheered her progress up the river. *U.S Army Transportation Corps Museum*

As it turned out, the loss of the two Cunard liners did not seriously affect the U.S. repatriation effort. *Queen Mary* and the U.S. ships assigned to the Atlantic Theater were more than able to cope with the number of troops remaining in Europe, and by January 1946 the bulk of U.S. forces had been returned to the United States. That month the War Department designated the repatriation effort "essentially completed," freeing *Queen Mary* for one final important task before her return to British control.

Though dubbed "Operation Diaper" by the U.S. Army Transportation Corps, that remaining task was more widely known as the "bride and baby shuttle." Its goal was to bring to the United States the foreign-born wives and children of U.S. servicemen—60,000 of them from Europe and another 6,000 from Australia and New Zealand. Thirty ships were assigned to the project, and the British government agreed that *Queen Mary* would remain in U.S. service at least until May 1946 to serve as the nucleus of the Atlantic theater dependent-transport program.

But the liner would require extensive modifications before she could assume her new role, and on 14 January she entered Southampton's George V graving dock to undergo another in her long series of conversions. For the next 16 days workmen labored around the clock to prepare *Queen Mary* for her debut as flagship of the bride and baby fleet, with most of the work aimed at stripping her of the military hardware accumulated during six years of war.

Tons of armor that had protected the liner were removed, as were the splinter shields over her bridge windows and the hundreds of sandbags stacked throughout the ship. The barbed-wire barricades remaining from her POW-transport voyages were dismantled and carted away, and the standee bunks that filled every available inch of space were broken down and laid in seemingly endless rows on the Southampton docks. Most of the ship's armament had been removed in New York the previous June, but the few weapons that remained were carted off to local armories. Cunard and the Royal Navy agreed, however, that *Queen Mary*'s degaussing girdle should remain in place for the time being as a precaution against the many German magnetic mines still drifting free in the North Atlantic.

Once the liner had been demilitarized, the workmen set about equipping her for her new role.

Because she was to carry up to 1,200 adult passengers on each crossing—in addition to a large staff of Red Cross workers, doctors, nurses, and stewards—the Army directed that conditions aboard *Queen Mary* be as close to prewar standards as possible. Each of the liner's staterooms was thus equipped with six relatively comfortable beds; those cabins slated to house expectant mothers were fitted with call bells connected to the ship's hospital. The liner's long-stored furniture was brought back aboard, the troop mess halls were reconverted into dining rooms, and some of the shops in the Main Deck arcade were reopened. Finally, the ship was also given a quick but comprehensive overhaul and hull cleaning.

On 5 February 1946 *Queen Mary* left for New York with 2,451 women and children aboard, arriving in New York five days later. A week later she was on her way back to Southampton with 1,720 passengers. For the next three months her transatlantic routine hardly varied. By the time the Cunarder arrived in New York with her final load of dependents on 22 April, she had made five round-trip crossings, steamed more than 31,800 miles, and carried more than 12,200 people. *Queen Mary* maintained her demanding schedule despite fuel shortages in Britain, unusually rough seas, and tug boat strikes in New York; she safely transported more than a quarter of all U.S. dependents brought from Europe in the 12 months following the end of World War II. It was an outstanding performance, but one the liner would soon surpass.

The United States and Great Britain had agreed that *Queen Mary* would be returned to British control and shifted to the Canadian bride and baby effort on 1 May 1946. Four days later she left Southampton for Halifax, Nova Scotia, with 2,495 dependents of Canadian servicemen. Over the next four months the Cunarder kept up a UK-Halifax-New York-UK shuttle service, ferrying 2,200 war brides and children to Canada on each westbound passage and returning to Southampton with 2,000 passengers on each eastbound crossing. By the time the liner's Canadian bride and baby service ended in mid-September, she had transported more than 18,900 dependents, carried 10,000 paying passengers to Britain, and steamed an additional 50,600 miles.

The British government saw no need to retain *Queen Mary* in military service once she had completed her dependent transport duties, and upon her 27 September return to Southampton from

Shifted to "bride and baby" duty following her repatriation service, *Queen Mary* made five round-trips to New York carrying English war brides and their children to new lives in the United States. In this photo some of those brides get their first glimpse of the Statue of Liberty from the liner's deck in March 1946. *U.S Army Transportation Corps Museum*

and structural scars left on the Cunarder by her wartime experiences. By the time *Queen Mary* emerged from the refit in July 1947, she had been thoroughly refurbished and could once again rightfully claim the title of "Stateliest Ship Afloat."

The Cunard queens inaugurated their long-awaited Southampton-New York shuttle service in the summer of 1947, and for the next 20 years they remained the undisputed monarchs of the North Atlantic passenger trade. Their speed, elegance, and luxury made them the standard by which all other express liners had to be measured and, despite the appearance of newer and larger competitors, *Queen Mary* and *Queen Elizabeth* seemed destined for long and profitable careers.

But by the mid-1960s the increasing popularity of international air travel sounded the death knell for the great transatlantic passenger steamships. One after another the world's merchant fleets, faced by spiraling costs and plummeting revenues, dropped out of the maritime passenger trade and retired their liners. Cunard was not immune to this sad trend, and by 1966 was losing $2 million a year on the queens. In 1967, confronted by the specter of financial ruin, the company put both its superliners up for sale.

For several months it seemed as though *Queen Mary* and *Queen Elizabeth* were destined to end their lives as just so much scrap metal. They were far too large to be of any practical use in the burgeoning cruise ship trade, and the only other alternative seemed to be the breaker's yard. But, fortunately, both were eventually bought by organizations dedicated to saving them from the cutter's torch. *Queen Mary*, for her part, was purchased by the city of Long Beach, California, for use as a floating hotel and entertainment complex.

The story of *Queen Mary*'s up-and-down career as a southern California landmark is a fascinating tale in itself, and has been well told elsewhere. Suffice it to say that the liner has hosted nearly 20 million visitors since her 1971 debut in Long Beach and, despite several changes of ownership and stretches of rough economic sailing, shows every sign of remaining a popular attraction for many years to come. It is indeed a fitting retirement for the ship that in peacetime had became famous as the Queen of the North Atlantic, and in time of war became legendary as the Gray Ghost.

Halifax she was demobilized. The ceremony brought to a close nearly six and a half years of danger, privation, hardship, and faithful service to King and country. During that period the liner had traveled more than 600,000 miles, transported nearly 800,000 human beings, and played a major role in virtually every Allied campaign of World War II. In the course of her duties *Queen Mary* became the first ship to transport an entire U.S. military division on one crossing and the *only* ship ever to embark more than 16,500 persons on a single voyage. Though hunted by the combined forces of Germany, Italy, and Japan, the liner was never attacked, never fired her guns in anger and, most importantly, never lost a single passenger to enemy action.

With her military service at an end, *Queen Mary* was free to return to the North Atlantic as a ship of peace. But nearly 79 months of hard and constant use had wreaked havoc on the once immaculate liner and, like *Queen Elizabeth*, she required a complete renovation prior to resuming regular service. This refurbishment began in Southampton within 10 days of the liner's demobilization, and over the next 10 months 4,000 workers erased the cosmetic

Anchored in Long Beach following her retirement from service, *Queen Mary* became a hotel and entertainment complex that since 1971 has hosted 20 million visitors. Though her retirement has not been without its difficulties, the last of the pre-World War II great liners seems set to welcome guests well into the twenty-first century. *The Wrather Corporation*

The end of a distinguished military career: His Majesty's Transport *Queen Mary* returns to Southampton at the end of her final military voyage, 27 September 1946. The ship passes the already "civilianized" *Queen Elizabeth* as tugs move her toward her pier. *Southampton City Council*

Builder: John Brown and
Company, Clydebank,
Scotland.
Launched: 27 September
1938
Length overall: 1,031 feet
Width: 118 feet
Gross tonnage: 83,673 tons
Propulsion: Steam turbines
driving quadruple
screws.
Top speed: 29 knots
Capacity:
　Commercial crew:
　1,100
　Military crew: 865
　Passengers: 823 First
　Class, 662 Cabin Class,
　798 Tourist Class.
　Troops: 5,000 (1941);
　8,000; 10,000; 15,000
　(1942).
Armament: One 6-inch gun,
three 3-inch guns, two
20 mm cannons, and 10
.303-caliber machine
guns (1940); one 6-inch
gun, five 3-inch guns, 24
20 mm cannons, 10 40
mm cannons, four
2-inch anti-aircraft
rocket launchers (1942).
Disposition: Burned out
during 1972 conversion
in Hong Kong; scrapped
in place.

CHAPTER EIGHT

QUEEN ELIZABETH

If *Queen Mary* was the foremost liner-turned-troopship of all time, her consort *Queen Elizabeth* was surely a close second. Built to join her sister on Cunard's two-ship transatlantic express service, *Queen Elizabeth* brought to her wartime duties the same qualities that made her running mate so militarily successful: speed, capacity, and reliability. Yet the younger vessel did not bask in reflected glory; *Queen Elizabeth* made her own immeasurably important contribution to the Allied victory in World War II and was in no way beholden to her companion for the fame such service brought her.

The conflict that ultimately proved *Queen Elizabeth*'s mettle was years in the future when the liner's keel was laid at John Brown and Company's Clydebank yards in December 1936. Though intended to complement *Queen Mary* in size and capability, the new steamer was not a duplicate of the older vessel; at 1,031 feet overall and 83,673

Queen Elizabeth was launched at Clydebank in 1938, but the outbreak of war interrupted her fitting out. Cunard's second superliner lay uncompleted in the River Clyde until ordered to New York in March 1940. In this photo taken by A. C. McNaught, the liner moves slowly down the Clyde at the start of that first Atlantic crossing. *Author's Collection*

gross tons *Queen Elizabeth* was both longer and heavier than her predecessor. Though she kept her older sister's quadruple screws, cruiser stern, and stepped-aft superstructure, the more modern *Queen Elizabeth* had 12 boilers rather than 24, a sharply raked stem incorporating a third anchor, a streamlined silhouette, and two funnels in place of *Queen Mary*'s three. The new steamer was designed to accommodate 823 First Class, 662 Cabin Class, and 798 Tourist Class passengers and was to be operated by a crew of about 1,100.

The British Parliament's 1934 passage of the North Atlantic Shipping (Advances) Bill, which subsidized the construction and operation of Cunard's two superliners, ensured that work on *Queen Elizabeth* progressed swiftly. On 27 September 1938 she was launched by the monarch for whom she was named. Nearly 500,000 onlookers cheered their approval as Queen Elizabeth, flanked by the princesses Elizabeth[1] and Margaret Rose, smashed a bottle of champagne against the liner's stem to both christen her and send her down the ways.

Though few of those present at the launching ceremony could have predicted it, events then unfolding in Germany would have an immense effect on both their nation and the ship they had gathered to see. Even as *Queen Elizabeth* slid into the River Clyde, British Prime Minister Neville Chamberlain was preparing to meet with Adolf Hitler in a last-ditch effort to avoid war over Germany's claims on the Czech Sudetenland. And though the situation eased somewhat following Chamberlain's 30 September return to Britain bearing an Anglo-German "friendship pledge" he claimed ensured "peace in our time," perceptive observers realized that conflict had only been postponed, not prevented.

Though a tragedy for Czechoslovakia, Chamberlain's appeasement of Hitler at the Munich Conference proved a boon for the Cunard Line and its newest superliner. Had war erupted over the Sudetenland in the fall of 1938 the fitting out of the still-uncompleted *Queen Elizabeth* would have come to an immediate halt as John Brown shifted to the production of warships. The new steamer would thus have been trapped in Clydebank, incapable of moving under her own power and therefore an easy target for the German bombers that would surely have been sent to sink her.

As it was, however, the temporary reprieve from war Chamberlain purchased with Czechoslovakia's sovereignty allowed *Queen Elizabeth*'s fitting out to reach a point that greatly enhanced her chances of survival[2]. Though her passenger accommodations were unfinished and her electrical and plumbing systems incomplete, installation of her powerplant was well advanced by the time Germany invaded Poland on 1 September 1939. All work on the ship ceased following Britain's declaration of war two days later, but on 2 November the Ministry of Shipping issued the licenses necessary for John Brown to complete work on the engines. On 29 December the firm was able to test the liner's entire propulsion system, and within a week Cunard's on-site engineer pronounced the ship capable of putting to sea.

Queen Elizabeth's departure from Clydebank was delayed, however, by the British government's indecision about the Cunard queens' value to the war effort. The debate—whether to use the ships as naval auxiliaries, trade them to the Americans for urgently needed weapons, or scrap them for vital raw materials—immobilized *Queen Mary* in neutral New York and kept *Queen Elizabeth* tied to her Clydebank pier well into the new year. Fortunately, First Lord of the Admiralty Winston Churchill realized how vulnerable the newer vessel was in Scotland, and on 6 February 1940 he ordered Cunard to move the liner to safety outside Britain even though her ultimate fate remained undecided.

Churchill's directive sparked a flurry of activity around *Queen Elizabeth* because the high tides needed to float a vessel of her size out of the fitting-out basin and down to the open sea occurred only twice a year. The next tide was due at the end of February, and if the liner missed it she could be trapped in the Clyde for months. Workers labored nonstop to prepare her in time. Fuel, provisions, and fresh water were brought aboard, the ship was given a coat of gray paint, and a degaussing girdle—a series of electrically charged cables meant to neutralize magnetic mines—was wrapped around her hull above the waterline. Her crew members pitched in following their 22 February arrival, and four days later *Queen Elizabeth* was ready to leave the basin that had been her home for five months.

Though watched by virtually everyone in the immediate area, the liner's departure from Clydebank was decidedly low-key. No bands played as *Queen Elizabeth*, aided by tugs, moved slowly out into the river. Her stern was caught briefly by the incoming tides, and it took nearly an hour for the

Racing west toward the safety of New York, *Queen Elizabeth* is captured by the cameras aboard a U.S. Navy patrol plane sent to meet her. Captain John Townley and his crew of 398 volunteers pushed the ship hard on this first crossing, and she maintained nearly 26 knots for virtually the entire passage. *USNHC*

tugs to get her turned toward the sea. Once pointed the right way, *Queen Elizabeth* moved slowly downriver, appearing five hours later off the Tail-of-the-Bank, a deep, broad anchorage near the mouth of the River Clyde.

Over the next four days the liner's crew members prepared her for sea. Final tests were conducted on her propulsion, navigation, and communication systems, additional fuel and water were brought aboard, and her remaining lifeboats—24 had been off-loaded at Clydebank before her departure—were inspected and their davits tested. Told the ship would be making a sea voyage to an undisclosed location, *Queen Elizabeth*'s crew members also used this time to decide whether or not to make the journey. Those few who chose to leave the ship were put ashore, and by the evening of 1 March the liner and her 398 crewmen were ready for sea.

Captain John Townley, *Queen Elizabeth*'s master, received his sealed sailing orders early the following morning. The huge liner was underway shortly before 8 A.M., escorted by four destroyers

and several RAF patrol bombers. Once into the Firth of Clyde, Townley opened the orders to find that his ship's ultimate destination was New York. He immediately set a course westward, taking *Queen Elizabeth* into the North Channel separating Scotland and Northern Ireland. After clearing Rathlin Island to port Townley rang up FULL AHEAD on the engine telegraphs and the liner leapt ahead, quickly reaching 26 knots as she headed into the open Atlantic. Some 150 miles northwest of the Donegal coast the escorting destroyers and aircraft turned back, leaving *Queen Elizabeth* to rely solely on speed and stealth for protection.

Townley and his crew pushed the untested ship hard, using the transatlantic voyage to test her limits. They found only minor problems, and for most of those aboard the passage soon became something of a boredom-endurance contest. There was no heat, and the liner's unfinished and deserted public spaces offered no diversions. Though an abundance of good food and the nightly performance of crew-produced theatricals helped pass the time, the members of the ship's company were vastly relieved when the U.S. coast hove into view on 7 March.

Queen Elizabeth's sudden appearance in U.S. waters caused an immediate sensation. Her subsequent welcome in New York was jubilant, with thousands of people cheering her stately progress up the Hudson River. As tugs nudged her into place on the north side of Pier 90, her crew dipped the ship's Red Ensign in salute to *Queen Mary*, which returned the greeting from her berth on the pier's south side. It was the first time Cunard's queens had been in the same port at the same time, and the presence of the French Line's *Normandie* at Pier 88 meant that New York was also witnessing the first meeting of the world's three largest passenger vessels.

The pomp and circumstance that accompanied *Queen Elizabeth*'s arrival in the United States soon gave way to the peculiar demands of British wartime security. Even as newspapers up and down the eastern seaboard continued to run front-page articles about the liner's daring transatlantic dash, the ship herself was quickly put off limits to visitors and closely guarded by New York Police. And though press speculation about *Queen Elizabeth*'s fate increased significantly following the sudden departure of Cunard's *Mauretania* on 20 March and of *Queen Mary* the following day, the media's famously short attention span ensured that *Queen Elizabeth* figured ever less prominently in the news as the weeks wore on and she remained securely moored to her pier.

Unknown to the press was the fact that the same Admiralty requisition order that sent *Queen Mary* off to Pacific trooping duty in mid-March would apply equally to *Queen Elizabeth* once the liner had undergone preliminary work in New York. That work included the rough completion of her public rooms, the installation of heating, venti-

Queen Elizabeth (foreground) is moved alongside Cunard's Pier 90 shortly after her 7 March 1940 arrival in New York. *Queen Mary* is moored on the other side of the pier, and the uncamouflaged *Normandie* stands out sharply just beyond. The smaller, two-funneled ship to starboard of the French liner is Cunard's second *Mauretania*. *Library of Congress*

lation, and interior communication systems, and the addition of expanded toilet and kitchen facilities. Though most of the liner's crew went home to Britain within weeks of the ship's arrival in the United States, senior officers and key seamen stayed aboard to supervise the effort. Cunard contracted the strictly non-military work out to Todd Shipyards of nearby Hoboken, and shifts of workers toiled throughout the summer of 1940 to finish the task.

Queen Elizabeth's belated fitting-out was completed by the end of October, and during the first two weeks of November the liner was prepared for the next leg of her journey. Neither the preparations nor the arrival in New York of 400 British merchant seamen went unnoticed, and local newspapers revived their speculation on the liner's fate. Though the possibilities suggested by the press included such exotic concepts as the liner's conversion into an aircraft carrier, the reality was more practical. The Admiralty had decided to send the ship to Singapore for dry-docking, and from there to Australia for conversion into a fast trooper. In keeping with that decision the ship raised anchor early on the morning of 13 November and by noon had disappeared into the open Atlantic.

The voyage took Queen Elizabeth south into the Caribbean, and she made her first stop at Trinidad to take on 6,000 tons of fuel and 4,000 tons of fresh water. The liner headed for Cape Town, arriving in Table Bay on 27 November. She stayed in South Africa until early December, then set out for Singapore via India and Ceylon.

Queen Elizabeth's arrival at Singapore's Naval Docks was greeted with little enthusiasm by the locals because Queen Mary's visit to the sprawling port several months earlier had been marked by extreme rowdiness on the part of many crew members. As a result, most of Queen Elizabeth's seamen were restricted to the ship during the course of her much-needed refurbishment. During this time the liner's engines were overhauled, her hull was scraped and painted black, and her superstructure received another coat of battleship gray. In addition, the Cunarder was fitted with an antiquated 6-inch gun aft and three equally outmoded 3-inch anti-aircraft weapons.

Her brief overhaul completed, Queen Elizabeth departed for Australia on 11 February 1941. For the first part of her voyage, the four-day passage to the western port of Freemantle, the Cunarder was

escorted by the cruiser HMS Durban. The trip was uneventful, and after pausing for two days to refuel and reprovision the liner sailed alone for Sydney. She averaged 25 knots on the trip, which took her across the Great Australian Bight and around the southern coast of Tasmania. Her 21 February arrival off Sydney Head sparked widespread public celebration, and progress toward her anchorage off Bradley's Head was slowed by the scores of small craft that came out to meet her.

The quality of the overhaul work done on Queen Elizabeth in Singapore was less than sterling, and much of it was redone during the liner's stay in the Cockatoo Docks and Engineering Company's Sydney yards. More importantly, during this period the Cunarder finally underwent her long-awaited trooping conversion. This was accomplished by packing several thousand hammocks and wooden bunks into her already austere passenger cabins, creating sick bays in several of her larger public rooms, and setting up a small but well-equipped surgical suite complete with an X-ray room. The liner's First Class dining room was converted into a mess hall for enlisted troops, while the Tourist Class dining room was set aside for embarked officers.

There were other additions as well. Sandbags were stacked around some of Queen Elizabeth's more vulnerable areas and hinged blast shutters were welded over her bridge windows. The ship was fitted with additional fresh water storage tanks and several of her cold-storage rooms were enlarged to accommodate the massive amount of food she would carry on each voyage. In recognition of the fact that soldiers will be soldiers even at sea, one of the Cunarder's larger storage rooms was converted into a stockade, complete with barred cells. And, finally, the ship was provided with scores of large life rafts and 2,000 flotation rings.

Workers laboring around-the-clock were able to complete Queen Elizabeth's trooping conversion in five weeks, and on 1 April the liner left Sydney for Hobart, Tasmania. Though the short voyage gave the liner's crew a chance to fine-tune some of the changes made to the ship during her conversion, its real purpose was to make space in Sydney Harbor for the incoming Queen Mary. The port simply could not accommodate both Cunard queens at once, because there was not enough space for the anchored ships to "swing" with the tides. Once the older liner took aboard her load of 5,000 troops, she departed for Jervis Bay, a coastal

Eight days after leaving Nuku Hiva in the Marquesas Islands, *Queen Elizabeth* is moved alongside her pier at Esquimalt, British Columbia. The ship arrived in Canada on 23 February 1942, but her great draft required her to wait two days for a high tide before moving into dry dock. *National Archives of Canada*

anchorage to the south, so that *Queen Elizabeth* could enter Sydney to embark her own load of troops. The two liners exchanged places on 9 April, meeting at sea for the first time as both passed Sydney Head.

Queen Elizabeth took aboard 5,600 Australian Army, Air Force, and Navy personnel in the two days following her return from Tasmania, and on 11 April sailed from Sydney on her first wartime trooping voyage. The occasion was doubly memorable because it also marked the first time *Queen Elizabeth* sailed in company with *Mauretania, Nieuw Amsterdam, Ile de France,* and *Queen Mary.* Meeting off Jervis Bay, the liners formed the largest troop convoy yet seen in the war as they departed for Suez escorted by the cruiser HMAS *Australia.*

The first leg of the passage was uneventful, and upon arrival in Freemantle the convoy split up. *Queen Elizabeth* and *Queen Mary* set out for Trincomalee, in northeast Ceylon, escorted by the cruiser HMAS *Canberra.* The other liners, still attended by *Australia,* set a course for Colombo on Ceylon's southwest coast. The Cunard queens

encountered no problems on the crossing and arrived safely in Trincomalee on 26 April. After pausing for barely six hours to refuel, *Queen Elizabeth* pressed on in company with *Canberra.* The two ships were rejoined by *Queen Mary* the next day, and all three vessels turned west and set out across the Arabian Sea.

Though the voyage to Africa was unhindered by enemy action, it was nonetheless almost literally hell for the troops embarked aboard *Queen Elizabeth* and *Queen Mary.* The liners had been designed for the frigid North Atlantic and therefore had no air-conditioning and too few ventilators. Daytime temperatures soared well past 110° Fahrenheit in the troop berthing areas, causing heat stroke and outbreaks of fighting among the Australians. Conditions were little better for the liners' crews, though they at least had the running of their ships to help keep their minds off the discomfort. And though the temperatures actually increased after the convoy entered the Gulf of Aden at the end of April, the knowledge that the voyage was nearing its end was enough to cheer crew and passengers alike.

Canberra left the convoy at Aden, leaving the Cunard queens to enter the Red Sea on their own. Once through the straits, *Queen Mary* increased speed to 27 knots in order to enter Egypt's Port Tewfik first. Just south of the Suez Canal's southern end, the harbor was too small to accommodate both ships at once and the risk of air attack made it imperative that each liner off-load and depart with haste. *Queen Elizabeth* was able to enter the port on 3 May, and stayed only long enough to put ashore her load of Australian troops and take on fuel and water. That done, she sailed on 6 May for Singapore, where she went into the yards for a thorough cleaning.

Queen Elizabeth was back in Australia by mid-June, and over the next five months undertook three round-trip voyages to Suez. On each outbound passage she carried an average of 5,500 Australian and New Zealand troops to Port Tewfik by way of Freemantle and Trincomalee; on each return trip she carried both Allied wounded and Axis POWs. The first two voyages were made in company with *Aquitania* and *Queen Mary*, while the third was in convoy with *Queen Mary* and the cruiser HMS *Cornwall*.

Japan's 7 December 1941 assault on the U.S. Pacific Fleet at Pearl Harbor brought *Queen Elizabeth*'s duty as a "Suez shuttle" to an abrupt conclusion. The liner was underway from Trincomalee to Australia when the Japanese struck, and when the ship reached Sydney on 15 December she had new orders. She was to proceed to Esquimalt, British Columbia, for a comprehensive overhaul, after which she would make her way south to San Francisco. There she would embark some of the first U.S. troops to be sent to the Pacific following the United States' entry into the war. It would be a historic voyage for the liner, because she would be the first of Cunard's queens to visit North America's West Coast.

Queen Elizabeth remained in Sydney for nearly two months while her senior officers finalized plans for the voyage with Royal Australian Navy and Cunard Line representatives. The liner's gun crews made good use of the time, practicing endlessly with the ship's 6- and 3-inch guns and getting used to the two 20 mm cannons and 10 .303-caliber machine guns that had been installed during the Cunarder's last visit to Port Tewfik. *Queen Elizabeth* was to receive two additional 3-inch guns in

Canada, and workers in Sydney built mounts for the weapons on the liner's foredeck.

The first leg of *Queen Elizabeth*'s voyage to North America began with her 6 February 1942 departure for New Zealand. She arrived in Auckland two days later, and left on 10 February after taking on fuel and fresh water. Her next landfall was at tiny Nuku Hiva in the Marquesas Islands, where she stayed only long enough to take on fuel from the tanker *Bishopdale*. That done, the Cunarder set off for Canada at full speed. Her speed averaged about 26.5 knots, and the liner's bridge watch sighted the coast of British Columbia on the morning of 23 February, just eight days after leaving Nuku Hiva.

Both the Royal Canadian Navy and the U.S. Navy had received reports of enemy submarines operating off the coast of the Pacific Northwest, so five RCN corvettes and several seaplanes met *Queen Elizabeth* at sea. They escorted the liner into the Strait of Juan de Fuca, leaving her only after she dropped anchor in Esquimalt's Royal Roads. The Cunarder's great draft forced her to wait for suitable tides before entering the dry dock, which she finally did on the morning of 25 February. By the time she emerged a week later, she had been thoroughly fumigated, her hull had been cleaned and given a new coat of gray, and she'd been fitted with two new lifeboats and an additional pair of 3-inch guns.

Queen Elizabeth spent four days in Vancouver after leaving dry dock, during which she took on fuel, water, and provisions for the trip south to San Francisco. That voyage was to be made with a U.S. Navy escort, which appeared on the afternoon of 10 March in the shape of the Seattle-based destroyer USS *Fox*. A World War I veteran recalled to active duty in September 1939, the four-stacker had been ordered to Vancouver just that morning. Her captain, Lieutenant Commander C. T. Caufield, had been told only that his charge was a "vessel of great importance," though he recognized *Queen Elizabeth* as soon as *Fox* entered Vancouver's Boundary Bay.

This first-ever military collaboration between the liner and the U.S. Navy did not begin well, however, at least from Caufield's point of view. He and several members of his staff crossed to *Queen Elizabeth* by small boat at about 4:15 P.M., and soon found themselves sharing tea with the Cunarder's captain in the liner's staff lounge. Several hours of polite and seemingly aimless conversation went by before Caufield, perturbed at what he considered

High and dry at last, *Queen Elizabeth* sits securely in the Esquimalt dry dock. During her weeklong overhaul, her hull was scraped, her troop accommodation spaces were cleaned and fumigated, her coat of gray camouflage was redone, and she was fitted with additional armament. *National Archives of Canada*

to be excessive chitchat, finally got the information he had come for and returned to his ship.

By 8:15 the U.S. destroyer and her British charge were ready to get underway. The move toward the open sea did not go well, however; during the passage through Boundary Pass and Haro Strait, overzealous Canadian searchlight crews on shore obscured the vision of *Fox*'s bridge crew and continually played their searchlights full upon both the destroyer and *Queen Elizabeth*.

The ships finally cleared Cape Flattery at 4 A.M. on 11 March and set a westerly course. Eight days earlier, Caufield and his crew had reported a possible submarine contact in the same area, so the cautious destroyer skipper directed *Queen Elizabeth*'s captain to begin zigzagging and ordered his own crew to General Quarters. No threat materialized, however, and by 9 A.M. *Fox* had reached the limit of her escort area. Caufield signaled *Queen Elizabeth*'s master that the destroyer was leaving and, after

adding a final "good luck and safe voyage," turned his elderly warship for home. The Cunarder, on her own in potentially hostile waters, increased speed and set a course for San Francisco.

As *Queen Elizabeth* hurried south, the U.S. Navy's Western Sea Frontier headquarters on San Francisco's Treasure Island was arranging an impressive reception. Early on 13 March two destroyers, the World War I-vintage USS *Sands* and the newer USS *Talbot*, had been dispatched to intercept the Cunarder. The escorts rendezvoused with the liner off the coast of northern California shortly after 4:30 A.M. and at first light Army and Navy patrol aircraft dispatched from San Francisco arrived over the convoy. Within an hour a Navy anti-aircraft defense ship arrived to join the growing flotilla, which arrived unhindered off San Francisco just before 7 A.M. After a brief wait for low tide to allow the liner to clear the bottom of the Golden Gate Bridge, the ship sailed into the bay.

Seen from the deck of the escorting destroyer USS *Fox*, *Queen Elizabeth* builds up speed for the voyage from British Columbia to San Francisco. This passage marked the first time the liner was attended by U.S. warships, as well as the first time she was escorted by U.S. patrol aircraft: U.S. Army B-25 light bombers and U.S. Navy Catalina flying boats met her upon her arrival off the coast of California. *National Archives of Canada*

Queen Elizabeth's arrival in San Francisco was impossible to hide. She was the largest commercial vessel to visit the city up to that time, and crowds jammed the Embarcadero to watch as she moved toward her berth at Pier 35. Still more onlookers packed adjoining piers as she was carefully moved alongside by tugboats, a painstaking and time-consuming process because of her size. Scores of armed troops cordoned off the pier once the ship was berthed, and the commander of the Army's San Francisco Port of Embarkation boarded the Cunarder to begin talks with her master and his staff.

In keeping with the U.S. government's desire to quickly dispatch troops to Australia, the U.S. port commander immediately suggested that *Queen Elizabeth*'s troop capacity be increased from approximately 5,500 to 8,000. This could be done, he said, through the installation of additional bunks and by placing mattresses in wind-protected deck areas. The liner's master agreed to the plan

with only minor changes, and work began the following morning.

The modifications made to *Queen Elizabeth* during her stay in San Francisco were carried out by about 100 workers from the Bethlehem Steel Corporation, which had undertaken similar work on *Mauretania, Ile de France,* and several Matson Line ships. Though the task consisted primarily of installing the additional bunks and renovating the troop berthing areas, the workers also upgraded the liner's galleys, renewed her anchor and mooring chains, and improved the splinter protection around her bridge and radio room.

The work went on around-the-clock, and by the evening of 17 March the port commander was able to begin loading the first of the U.S. troops. These were mainly engineer, quartermaster, and transportation soldiers, though some Army Air Force and Navy personnel were manifested as well. This first embarkation of U.S.

Queen Elizabeth passes Sydney Head upon her 6 April 1942 arrival in Australia bearing the U.S. troops she had taken aboard in San Francisco. The passage south had been an eventful one; the near collision with the destroyer USS *Alden* had been prevented only at the last possible moment. *Australian Department of Defence*

units went remarkably smoothly given the haste with which it was conducted and boarding was completed just before midnight the following day. *Queen Elizabeth* fueled and provisioned as the troops were loading and was ready to sail by mid-morning on the 19th.

Tugs began backing the liner from her pier shortly after noon and she passed under the Golden Gate about two hours later. Once outside the bay, *Queen Elizabeth* was joined by the converted liners *President Coolidge* and *Mariposa*, the escorting destroyers *King* and *Talbot*, and two Catalina patrol bombers. Once past the Farallon Islands the convoy was joined by the cruiser *Chester*. The destroyers and Catalinas returned to San Francisco at nightfall, and the remaining four ships set a course for the Marquesas.

The voyage south was uneventful, and on 27 March the troopships and their escort rendezvoused with the tanker *Torres* in Nuku Hiva island's Comptroller Bay, the same place *Queen*

Elizabeth had refueled on her voyage to Canada just six weeks earlier. The Cunarder and *Chester* had to wait outside the anchorage as *President Coolidge* and *Mariposa* filled their tanks, then moved in alongside the tanker once the smaller troopers put to sea. After completing their own refueling, the liner and her escort rushed to catch up, at times reaching speeds of almost 28 knots.

It was on this last leg of the voyage to Australia that *Queen Elizabeth* came close to disaster for the first time in her military career. Soon after leaving the Marquesas, the Cunarder was alerted by *Chester*'s commander that the convoy would be gaining another escort, a U.S. destroyer patrolling between New Caledonia and Fiji. Since *Queen Elizabeth* had forged well ahead of the other vessels, she would be the first to encounter the warship, with the rendezvous set for a point northeast of Norfolk Island.

The sailors aboard the World War I-vintage four-stack destroyer USS *Alden* had been told

Queen Elizabeth's first transatlantic shuttle trip carrying 15,000 embarked troops ended safely in the Firth of Clyde on 5 September 1942. She is seen here during off-loading the following day, with smaller lighters ranged alongside to take off the departing troops. Three days after her arrival in Scotland, she was underway for the return passage to New York. *U.S. Army Transportation Corps Museum*

only that they were to meet an unnamed "very important vessel" at a specific spot in the ocean. They were not enthusiastic about the new assignment; their aged vessel, not in the best shape before the outbreak of war in the Pacific, was nearly worn out after four months of continuous service in the Philippines, the Battle of the Java Sea, and on patrol duty out of Australian and Polynesian ports.

Alden was thus not at her best when she met *Queen Elizabeth* late on the evening of 3 April. When the two ships sighted each other the liner signaled *Alden* to take the lead on a zigzagging track. But when the tired warship quickly proved incapable of staying a safe distance ahead in the moderately heavy seas, *Queen Elizabeth*'s master ordered the destroyer to stop zigzagging and take up a straight course. Even this did not solve the separation problem, so the liner broadened her own zigzag pattern and reduced speed.

This last change seemed to be working when, just before midnight, *Alden* experienced what her log later referred to as a "steering casualty"—a foreign object rolled into the helm's ropes and jammed them. The warship started drifting uncontrollably to one side and *Queen Elizabeth*, rushing up from behind on a starboard-to-port zigzag leg, charged toward *Alden*'s fantail. The destroyer's bridge watch could only turn on their vessel's masthead lights and hold their breath as the liner bore down on them. Just as it seemed a collision was inevitable, the Cunarder veered sharply to one side and *Alden*'s sailors cheered as the huge liner passed safely by just 75 yards away.

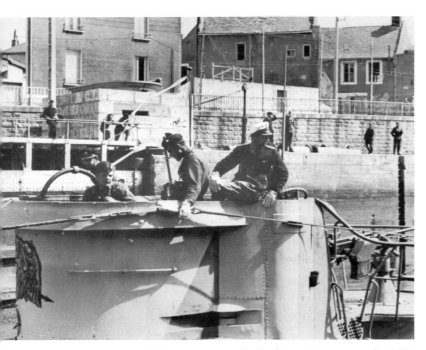

Kapitänleutnant Horst Kessler (in white cap) prepares to take *U-704* to sea from St. Nazaire during the fall of 1942. In November of that year Kessler and his crew, returning to their French base from a less than successful Atlantic patrol, sighted and attacked a vessel they identified as *Queen Elizabeth*. The questions arising from that action remain unanswered. *Author's Collection*

Queen Elizabeth arrived off Sydney Head on 6 April, just as *Queen Mary* was departing for New York after delivering her own load of Americans. It was the second time the liners had met at sea, and they duly saluted each other with siren blasts. The younger Cunarder entered the harbor, unloaded her troops, and awaited new orders.

When they came, those orders brought a significant change in *Queen Elizabeth*'s trooping career. In keeping with an agreement signed just weeks earlier by British Prime Minister Winston Churchill and U.S. President Franklin Roosevelt, the liner was to be shifted from the primarily Australia-Middle East service on which she had been engaged to a New York-UK-Suez route. This new route was intended to shift U.S. forces to Britain and British troops to the Middle East. The change would bolster the U.K.'s defenses, while at the same time providing troops to counter Axis advances in North Africa.

Queen Elizabeth embarked upon her new assignment on 19 April, sailing from Sydney for the last time just before noon. Her route took her to Freemantle and from there to South Africa. In

Cape Town the liner took aboard 2,000 German POWs bound for camps in Canada, then sailed for Rio de Janeiro. Pausing in the still-neutral Brazilian port only long enough to refuel, the Cunarder was at sea again within 10 hours of her arrival.

The liner arrived off New York on 24 May, nine days after leaving Rio. The only excitement on the voyage north had been a hasty call to Action Stations off Natal when an unidentified ship appeared briefly on the horizon, and by the time the Statue of Liberty appeared, *Queen Elizabeth*'s crew was ready for some shore leave. Their enthusiasm for New York was only slightly dampened by the sight of the French Line's *Normandie*, which had burned and capsized at her nearby pier four months earlier.

While *Queen Elizabeth*'s crew took time off, workers from Todd Shipyards added 2,000 bunks to the liner's already well-packed troop berthing areas. The increase in the ship's capacity was the result of a U.S. Army Transportation Corps plan to give each of the Cunard queens the ability to carry 10,000 troops on each eastbound Atlantic crossing. The work also included another upgrade of the ship's toilets and kitchens, as well as modifications to her degaussing girdle.

The liner's enhanced capabilities were soon put to the test; on 2 June the first of 9,850 soldiers began embarking for *Queen Elizabeth*'s first US-to-UK trooping voyage. Preparations were completed by the night of 3 June, and the liner cast off early the next morning. The passage to Scotland took five days, and while still a day out of Gourock the Cunarder was met by two Royal Navy escorts and a handful of patrol aircraft.

Though *Queen Elizabeth*'s return to Britain after a two-year absence was cause for celebration, the deteriorating situation in North Africa ensured that festivities were kept to a minimum. Field Marshal Erwin Rommel's forces were advancing in Libya, and the defending British Eighth Army desperately needed reinforcements. *Queen Elizabeth* was tapped to participate in a large-scale troop lift around the Cape of Good Hope to Suez, and on 15 June began embarking the first of 10,000 desert-bound British troops.

The liner sailed for Egypt on 17 June, escorted by eight destroyers and an anti-aircraft cruiser. Two days into the voyage a lone Luftwaffe patrol bomber chanced upon the convoy well off the northwest coast of Spain, only to be driven away by gunfire from *Queen Elizabeth*'s escorts. Soon afterward the ships encountered a dense fog bank, under cover of which the Cunarder signaled farewell to the warships and headed south at maximum speed. She called at Freetown on 25 June to refuel, and a week later anchored at Simonstown naval base near Cape Town. She departed for Suez on 5 July, and made the passage up the African coast and through the Red Sea in 13 days.

As she had on her previous visit to Port Suez, *Queen Elizabeth* took aboard German POWs once the British troops had been put ashore. On this particular occasion the loading process was interrupted by a German air raid, so the liner left for Cape Town with only about half of her usual complement of 2,800 prisoners. The Cunarder stopped briefly at Simonstown and Rio de Janeiro, and was safely at rest in New York's Hudson River by 19 August.

After turning the Germans over to Canadian troops for the final leg of the journey to POW camps, *Queen Elizabeth*'s crew set about preparing their ship for what they assumed would be another US-UK-Suez run. Allied war planners had other things in store for the ship, however; she had been tapped to join *Queen Mary* on the sort of two-ship, transatlantic shuttle service for which they'd been designed. Each liner would carry up to 15,000 troops on each eastbound crossing and would return to North America with smaller numbers of wounded soldiers, prisoners of war, and civilian evacuees. *Queen Mary* had inaugurated the GI shuttle service with her 2 August departure from New York, carrying 15,125 troops bound for Gourock.

Before *Queen Elizabeth* could join her sister on the new service, her troop capacity had to be increased from 10,000 to 15,000. This was done by removing all of the wooden bunks and hammocks installed in Australia and replacing them with standee bunks. Tiers of these folding metal units were installed throughout the existing berthing areas, as well as in other parts of the ship not previously used to house troops. Indeed, virtually the only parts of the ship not packed with bunks were the passageways.

The Todd Shipyard workers contracted to do the renovations also installed several single-barreled 20 mm anti-aircraft guns along *Queen Elizabeth*'s upper works. Grouped around the base of each funnel, these weapons significantly increased the liner's firepower. Additional 20 mm

With cameramen and members of the ship's company looking on, the U.S. crew of one of *Queen Elizabeth*'s 3-inch mounts prepares for gunnery practice during a shuttle crossing. Though the liner never fired her guns in anger, her weapons and their crews were kept ready for action at all times when the ship was at sea. *U.S. Army Transportation Corps Museum*

cannons would be added on the ship's subsequent visits to New York, as would dual- and single-barreled 40 mm guns. And, finally, a team of U.S. Navy specialists quietly installed an early surface-search radar set, which was to be operated by Royal Navy technicians permanently assigned to the ship.

The conversion work was completed by 29 August, and two days later *Queen Elizabeth* sailed for Scotland with just over 15,000 troops and 860 crew members. This first "full division" voyage was a learning experience for both the troops and the ship's complement because, like those on *Queen Mary* before them, they had to adapt to the special challenges of living on and operating a vessel so densely packed with human beings. For the troops this meant staying in their assigned areas and eating and sleeping in shifts. For the liner's crew, on the other hand, the most important adjustment was to her new and often disturbing handling characteristics. Always a "lively" ship, the liner became even more prone to rolling when loaded with troops and facing even moderate seas.

Fortunately for all aboard, the most serious challenges faced on this first GI shuttle voyage were missed meals, soldiers unable to find their bunks, and the occasional need to calm those prone to claustrophobia. *Queen Elizabeth* arrived in the Firth of Clyde on 5 September and off-loaded her troops over the next two days. She took aboard a mixed load of Axis prisoners and Allied troops

A helmsman on *Queen Elizabeth*'s bridge takes up a new course given him by the liner's captain. On her wartime voyages the ship was always commanded by the Cunard Line's most senior and experienced masters, while her military contingents often included Royal Naval Reserve members with equally impressive credentials. *The Cunard Line*

being sent to North America for training or reassignment. The liner sailed for New York on the 8th and arrived without incident six days later.

Over the next eight weeks *Queen Elizabeth* made two additional round-trip Atlantic crossings, one originating in New York and one in Halifax, Nova Scotia. Both voyages were unremarkable except for the harsh weather typical of the season, and each ended safely on the Clyde. However, it was on the return passage to New York at the end of the second voyage that *Queen Elizabeth* apparently had her closest call, though to this day there is controversy about just how near the liner came to disaster[3].

On 5 November 1942 the German Navy's Kapitänleutnant Horst Kessler took the submarine *U-704* to sea from St. Nazaire to join Wolfpack Panther in the waters south of Greenland. He rendezvoused with the other boats six days later, and on 16 October attacked and sank a 5,000-ton Allied cargo vessel. Three days later Kessler was

ordered to join a second wolfpack operating farther to the west, though *U-704*'s time with Group VEILCHEN was not productive. She made no attacks between 19 October and 7 November, and on 8 November was herself damaged after being caught on the surface by an Allied patrol plane. The air attack caused water leakage around the forward torpedo tubes where they passed through the boat's pressure hull, and there was some topside damage from gunfire. With his boat low on fuel and in need of repairs, Kessler decided to return to St. Nazaire.

U-704 began the return voyage to France on the evening of 8 November, and by noon the following day was about 650 miles west of Ireland. The going was tough for Kessler and his crew; the surfaced submarine was plowing through high seas and buffeted by fierce winds. Snow flurries and wind-driven sea spray cut visibility to less than two miles, and the lookouts belted to the U-boat's conning

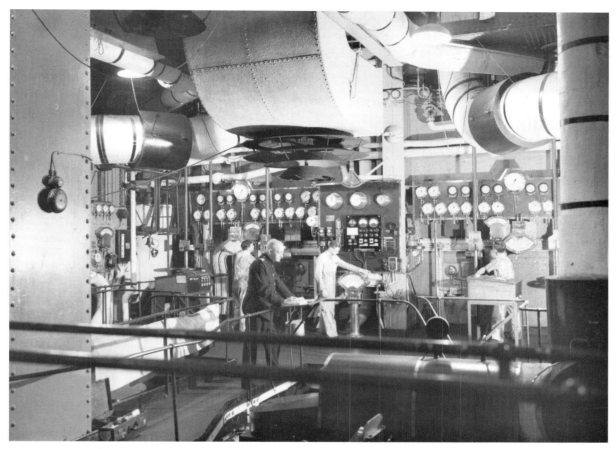

If *Queen Elizabeth*'s bridge was her brain during the trooping voyages, the engine room's main control station was most certainly her heart. Seen here during the course of a 1943 passage, the station includes the engine order telegraphs, gauges, and other instruments necessary to translate the captain's orders into movement. *The Cunard Line*

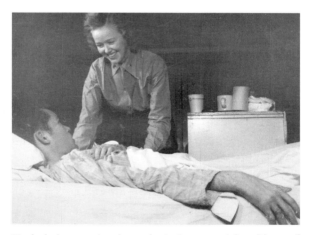

Tender loving care, American style. An Army nurse jokes with one of her patients aboard *Queen Elizabeth* during a 1944 voyage from Britain to New York. Both of Cunard's queens evacuated large numbers of wounded soldiers to the United States, carrying up to 1,800 bed-bound and several hundred ambulatory patients on each westbound crossing. *U.S. Army Transportation Corps Museum*

tower couldn't use their binoculars because of the constantly overcoming swells. It was thus something of a shock to the bridge watch when, shortly after 1 P.M., the weather suddenly cleared enough to reveal a giant ship crossing the submarine's path six or seven miles distant, racing westward.

By the time Kessler made it to the bridge, the unidentified ship was close enough to make out with the naked eye. The vessel was huge, with two large funnels, two masts, and a stepped-aft superstructure. A quick search through his ship-recognition book convinced Kessler the giant steamer could only be *Queen Elizabeth*, and he decided to make the most of his chance encounter with the liner. He had four torpedoes left in his forward tubes and one in the aft barrel, and he was determined to make them count.

Ordering the bridge cleared, Kessler sounded the action alarm and took *U-704* down to periscope depth. The heavy seas and blowing snow periodically obscured his view through the raised scope, but he was able to confirm the liner's identity and estimate her speed at roughly 28 knots. After setting his boat onto an intercept course, Kessler ordered all forward tubes ready, planning to fire a fan of torpedoes from a range of about 2,000 meters. Just nine minutes after the initial sighting, *U-704* was in position and, after a final look through the periscope, Kessler ordered the four torpedoes away and then took the boat down to 20 meters to await the impact.

He didn't have to wait long; just two minutes later *U-704*'s hull shuttered with the reverberation of one torpedo's detonation. Soon afterward the submarine's hydrophone operator reported that *Queen Elizabeth*'s screws had stopped, and Kessler ordered the boat to periscope depth to check the damage to the apparently disabled liner and set up a killing shot with his one remaining torpedo. Dense snow gusts had again cut surface visibility to less than 100 meters, however, so the submarine's captain ordered the engines full ahead and set a course toward the liner's assumed position.

But before *U-704* could close with *Queen Elizabeth*, the liner's screws sprang back to life and she moved off at high speed. Immensely disappointed that he had not bagged the huge steamer but firmly convinced he had hit her with at least one torpedo, Kessler radioed St. Nazaire his position and added that he had fired a "fan of four against *Queen Elizabeth*, one hit certain; snow gusts, course of enemy 270, speed 28 knots."

Hoping that another U-boat might finish off the liner, Kessler closely monitored both Allied and Axis radio signals for any news as *U-704* headed toward France. On 11 November he was stunned to hear Radio Berlin announce the sinking of the British battleship HMS *Queen Elizabeth* and he immediately sent off another message stating that the ship he had attacked was the superliner, not the warship. He heard no further news about the liner's fate, however. Upon *U-704*'s return to France on 23 November, Kessler was informed that intelligence reports indicated the Cunarder had not been damaged by his attack.

The controversy over Kessler's claim to have attacked *Queen Elizabeth* deepened even further when, during a House of Commons speech several weeks later, Winston Churchill labeled the German assertions "an outright lie." This despite the fact

Gambling was always in style among *Queen Elizabeth*'s embarked troops. Here, Army Air Force personnel shoot craps in one of the liner's crowded berthing areas during the first 1945 repatriation voyage. Homeward-bound personnel often had large amounts of cash on hand, and one win during a shipboard game could make or break fortunes. *U.S. Army Transportation Corps Museum*

that the liner had indeed been roughly in the position Kessler reported at the approximate time of the attack, and that several U.S. soldiers returning to New York aboard the ship later reported hearing a muffled bang just before the liner came to a brief stop. No accounts of the alleged attack appeared in the Allied press owing to wartime censorship rules,

A returning soldier's favorite greeting graces Cunard's New York pier in April 1945. During the course of her five U.S. troop-repatriation voyages, *Queen Elizabeth* carried 70,000 Americans home from Britain. On her eastbound passages, she carried home British children sent to the United States during the height of the Blitz. *U.S. Army Transportation Corps Museum*

With troops packing every inch of topside space, *Queen Elizabeth* arrives in New York at the end of her first troop-repatriation voyage. The welcome accorded the liner was tumultuous, with cheering throngs lining the piers to welcome the troops home. *U.S. Army Transportation Corps Museum*

however. *Queen Elizabeth* continued her transatlantic shuttle service without interruption and the incident was soon forgotten[4].

German submarines were not the only menace *Queen Elizabeth* faced during her Atlantic shuttle crossings. Indeed, the only damage done to the liner during the war years (other than by souvenir-hunting soldiers) was caused by Mother Nature. On several occasions heavy weather battered the ship unmercifully, breaking windows and portholes, carrying away lifeboats, and even bending hull plates.

By far the worst pounding occurred during a February 1944 westbound passage when a freak "monster" wave slammed into *Queen Elizabeth* from dead ahead. The roller hit with such force that the ship heeled sharply to one side as thousands of tons of water drove her down. The impact shattered most of the bridge windows and knocked the quartermaster away from the helm. The forward 3-inch gun mounts were destroyed, storage rooms above the forepeak flooded, and hatch covers, stanchions, and ready-ammunition lockers went over the side. Though the Cunarder was able to complete the crossing unaided, the

damage was extensive enough to warrant a nine-week yard stay in New Jersey.

Fortunately, most crossings were not nearly so dramatic. Indeed, the vast majority of *Queen Elizabeth*'s more than 30 wartime Atlantic crossings were routine, if understandably tense, events. After loading troops in New York or Halifax the liner would speed to the Clyde ports, unload, and take on a cargo of prisoners and patients bound for North America. She would then race westward, usually escorted only when close to her final destination. It was a routine as monotonous as it was vital to the war effort.

On the westbound passages *Queen Elizabeth*, like her elder sister, performed an extremely important if little-known task. This was the evacuation to North America of wounded and ill Allied military personnel, most of them Americans being sent home for further treatment or reassignment. During the early stages of the GI shuttle service, each of Cunard's queens was capable of transporting 1,800 bed patients and as many "walking wounded" as could be accommodated in the berthing areas. However, improvements made to each ship during the war

Refurbished after her wartime service, *Queen Elizabeth* finally entered the commercial service for which she had been built. The liner remained a favorite of the traveling public from 1947 until her 1968 retirement and, as seen here, even her arrival in Hong Kong following her sale by Cunard was cause for celebration. *Hong Kong Government Information Services*

continually increased the number of bed patients each could carry in the ambulance transport[5] role, though *Queen Elizabeth*'s westbound patient capacity was always 500 more than *Queen Mary*'s.

Fittingly, it was wounded soldiers going home to the United States who had the honor of joining *Queen Elizabeth* on her last wartime Atlantic crossing. About 3,000 patients boarded the liner in Gourock on 7 April 1945, and six days later disembarked at New York's Pier 90 to the sound of military bands and the cheers of welcoming civilians.

The accolades could just as well have been for *Queen Elizabeth* herself because the liner had con-

tributed immeasurably to the Allied victory during her almost five years "in uniform." She had carried nearly 750,000 people—troops, wounded, diplomats, and prisoners—and steamed nearly a half-million miles. She had eluded enemy warships and aircraft, battled her way through storms, endured tropical heat and frigid cold, and through it all had never lost a single passenger or crew member to enemy action. *Queen Elizabeth*'s early voyages to the Pacific and Middle East had helped shore up the Allies' defenses during times of dire need, and by shuttling massive numbers of Canadian and U.S. troops to Britain she had helped speed the liberation of Europe.

Her wartime career was, in short, one of which her crew, her owners, and her nation could be immensely proud.

But the end of the war in Europe did not bring *Queen Elizabeth*'s military service to an end because there was much left to be done. Like *Queen Mary* and *Aquitania,* she turned her efforts toward repatriating U.S. and Canadian troops, many of whom were earmarked for participation in the planned Allied invasion of Japan. Working together, the three Cunarders could move the largest number of men in the shortest possible time, the same ability that had made them so important to victory in the European Theater.

Queen Elizabeth remained in New York for nearly two months after VE-Day, during which time all of her 20 mm and 40 mm anti-aircraft guns were removed. She retained the 3-inch and 6-inch weapons that had been her first armament, though these were scheduled to be removed once the liner arrived in Scotland. She kept her degaussing girdle and mine-sweeping paravane equipment, however, because even with the end of the war in Europe the North Atlantic remained littered with both Axis- and Allied-sown mines.

Early on 14 June *Queen Elizabeth* departed for Gourock on the eastbound leg of her first troop-repatriation voyage. It was a vastly different crossing than her last one, because on this passage she had no need to zigzag. Nor was there any reason to maintain a blackout, so the Cunarder blazed with light as she raced toward the Clyde. She was oddly quiet, too, because she carried fewer than 1,000 passengers. Most were British subjects—children evacuated to North America at the beginning of the war or diplomats returning from duty in Washington and New York—though the liner also hosted several dozen high-ranking Allied officers and about 40 relief workers bound for duty in newly liberated Europe. The ship reached Gourock on the 19th, and six days later sailed for New York with 15,000 homeward-bound U.S. troops.

Queen Elizabeth's reception at the end of her first repatriation voyage was ecstatic. The liner was escorted upriver by fireboats shooting geysers hundreds of feet into the air, by dozens of gaily decorated pleasure craft, and even by a low-flying blimp. Vessels of all sizes saluted the liner with sirens, whistles, and the cheers of passengers and crew. Thousands of New Yorkers added their voices to the tumult and were answered by the soldiers lining *Queen Elizabeth*'s decks.

The scene was much the same in mid-July when *Queen Elizabeth* returned to New York bearing the entire U.S. 44th Infantry Division. As it turned out, this was the last westbound crossing to originate from Gourock; all subsequent loadings in the United Kingdom took place in Southampton. Newly dredged to accommodate the Cunard queens, it was a far more efficient terminus than the Clyde. *Queen Mary* began sailing from the southern England port in early August, and *Queen Elizabeth* followed her lead near the end of the month. The liner made three more voyages to New York by mid-October, each time carrying between 12,000 and 15,000 troops.

A new set of orders was waiting for *Queen Elizabeth* upon her return to Southampton at the end of that third crossing. In keeping with a June agreement between Britain's Ministry of War Transport and the U.S. Army Transportation Corps, the liner was to join Cunard's *Aquitania* in repatriating Canadian troops, with both ships operating between Southampton and Halifax. *Queen Elizabeth* took on 12,500 Canadians beginning on 20 October and embarked on her first Commonwealth repatriation voyage two days later.

The liner's 26 October reception in Halifax was no less tumultuous than those it had received in New York, though there was an undeniable undercurrent of tension. *Queen Elizabeth* had sailed to Nova Scotia against the advice of her recently appointed Master, Captain James Bisset, who felt that Halifax's lack of an enclosed dock and the harbor's vulnerability to heavy southeast swells put the liners at risk, especially in the harsh weather of a Canadian winter. Though the first two Commonwealth repatriation crossings ended in Halifax as planned, primarily in deference to Canadian and British public opinion, Bisset's well-reasoned arguments eventually won out; *Queen Elizabeth*'s 10 subsequent westbound voyages all ended in New York, with the Canadian troops traveling onward by rail.

Queen Elizabeth's last voyage as a troopship ended in Southampton on 6 March 1946. With the troop repatriation effort essentially complete, her wartime task was finally over, and she was now to undergo her long-delayed commercial fitting out. It would be a massive effort, carried out over several months by the

A sad end to a proud and fabled ship: *Queen Elizabeth*, renamed SS *Seawise University*, burns in Hong Kong on 9 January 1972. Gutted by fire, she capsized and sank at her moorings, and was eventually scrapped on-site. *Hong Kong Government Information Services*

most skilled shipyard workers in Europe. The task would begin on the Clyde at the hands of John Brown and Company, then *Queen Elizabeth* would return to Southampton for the finishing touches that would make her the world's ultimate passenger ship.

Before her transformation could begin, however, the liner had one more challenge to overcome. Early on the morning of 8 March, a worker taking a forbidden smoke break in one of *Queen Elizabeth*'s storage areas sparked a fire that soon engulfed much of her Promenade Deck. Though ultimately brought under control by firefighters called in from throughout the area, the conflagration damaged much of the liner's aft superstructure and warped the structural members supporting her

Boat Deck. Much cleanup work was done in anticipation of her movement to Scotland, though she still bore the scars upon her 31 March arrival at the Tail-of-the-Bank.

The first part of *Queen Elizabeth*'s conversion from troopship to luxury liner took 2,000 workers three months to complete. It was an extraordinarily complex task because it entailed the repair of the fire damage, the removal of all the military accouterments she had gathered over the course of six years' service, and the installation and testing of literally thousands of new items. All of the liner's staterooms, public rooms, and passageways were stripped bare, refurbished, and equipped with new fittings, floor coverings, lighting fixtures, and draperies. Her toilets, galleys, and service areas were rewired and equipped with new hardware; her decking was renewed; her electrical and plumbing systems were inspected and upgraded; and her lifeboats were overhauled.

Queen Elizabeth's Clydeside conversion also included the installation of thousands of pieces of furniture. Many of the objects had never been aboard the ship and had remained in British warehouses since 1939. Other items had been removed during the Cunarder's wartime wanderings and had to be collected from as far away as Australia and Singapore.

The first stage of *Queen Elizabeth*'s conversion was completed in early June 1946, and on the 16th of that month the repainted and revitalized liner sailed for Southampton for the second stage of her metamorphosis from battered trooper to ocean-going grande dame. On 6 August she entered the George V graving dock, and over the following two months underwent a comprehensive hull cleaning and restoration of her screws and rudders. This was completed by the end of September, and on 5 October the liner left for Scotland to undergo her long-postponed sea trials. These took place in the Firth of Clyde on 8 October with Queen Elizabeth and the princesses Elizabeth and Margaret on the bridge.

Queen Elizabeth was the first of Britain's major passenger liners to be refurbished after the war's end, and her commercial debut was almost as important to Britain's national pride as it was to Cunard's economic well-being. Her gala 16 October maiden departure for New York thus sparked widespread jubilation throughout a United Kingdom beset by postwar austerity, and the more than 2,200 passengers who sailed with her were treated to tumultuous receptions during the liner's call at Cherbourg and upon arrival in New York.

From this auspicious beginning, *Queen Elizabeth* went on to become one of the world's most popular express liners. Paired with *Queen Mary* after that vessel's return to civilian life in the summer of 1947, the Cunarder built a solid reputation as an elegant and capable ship. She retained a loyal worldwide following even after the advent of jet aircraft doomed the transatlantic passenger trade in the early 1960s, and her 1968 retirement from service was greeted with almost universal regret by those fortunate enough to have known her.

Sadly, *Queen Elizabeth*'s end did not live up to her long and proud life. The liner spent two years rusting in Florida while a consortium of local entrepreneurs vainly attempted to turn her into a tourist attraction. In 1970 she was sold to a Taiwanese shipping magnate who planned to convert her into an oceangoing center of international studies. Renamed *Seawise University*, the now-dilapidated liner made a long and trouble-plagued voyage to Hong Kong, where on 9 January 1972 she was gutted by a fire of mysterious origins. The famed and once-proud ship capsized and sank at her moorings, and was eventually scrapped on-site.

CHAPTER NINE

QUEEN ELIZABETH 2

Builder: John Brown and Company, Clydebank, Scotland.

Launched: 20 September 1967

Length overall: 963 feet

Width: 105 feet

Gross tonnage: 65,863 tons

Propulsion: Double-reduction steam turbines driving twin screws.

Top speed: 28.5 knots

Capacity:

  Commercial crew: 920

  Wartime crew: 650

  Passengers: 564 First Class, 1,441 Tourist Class

Troops: 3,150

Armament: Three .50-caliber Browning heavy machine guns, several 7.62 mm general-purpose machine guns, and multiple Blowpipe AA missile launchers.

Disposition: Remains in service (as of 1997).

Few events of modern maritime history have been as unexpected, as exciting, or as terrifying as the spectacle that unfolded at England's Southampton harbor on 12 May 1982. On that day thousands of cheering people lined the historic port's quays as the Cunard Line's *Queen Elizabeth 2* moved toward the open sea, her decks crowded with troops headed for the far-off Falkland Islands.

The ship's departure for the South Atlantic was unexpected because it had been nearly 40 years since a superliner had been called to serve her nation in wartime. Though the P&O Line's 44,807-ton cruise liner *Canberra* had been called up for trooping duty over a month before *QE2*'s departure, most observers had assumed that Cunard's opulent flagship was too large, too important, and too visible a national symbol to risk in what many saw as a comic-opera conflict with a second-rate banana republic.

And yet, *QE2*'s majestic progress down the Solent was undeniably exciting. Here was the world's sole remaining superliner being sent into harm's way with all the pomp and circumstance a grateful nation could muster. The cheering crowds and military bands, the salutes of other vessels, and the flotilla of small boats that shepherded *QE2* toward the sea all evoked farewells given her fabled predecessors a generation before. To many, the Cunarder's departure for the war zone was both an expression of national resolve and a demonstration of the long-ignored military value of the great passenger steamships.

In a scene strongly reminiscent of World War II, *Queen Elizabeth 2* races toward the Falkland Islands in 1982 (though the Sea King helicopter above her fantail firmly fixes the scene in more modern times). Britain's need to dispatch a large ground combat force to the war zone, coupled with the impossibility of building an "air bridge," virtually ensured that *QE2* would be called up for trooping service. *The Cunard Line*

But as stirring as it was, *QE2*'s departure for the South Atlantic was also terrifying for those who understood the risks she faced. Though the most advanced and most capable passenger vessel then afloat, the liner nonetheless was intended for commerce, not conflict. Tremendous technological advances had been made since the last time great liners sailed off to war, and the advent of satellites, supersonic aircraft, high-speed submarines, and over-the-horizon anti-ship missiles made the world's oceans vastly more dangerous for *QE2* than they had been for *Queen Mary* and *Queen Elizabeth*.

That the last great superliner would face such peril was something her designers could not have foreseen. When they began their work in the early 1960s, the primary threat with which they concerned themselves came from the jets that over the previous decade had come to dominate international travel. Like all of the world's great passenger steamship companies, the Cunard Line had been driven to near extinction by the airliner's increasing popularity. *Queen Mary* and *Queen Elizabeth* had been losing money for some time, and Cunard's directors knew the only hope for the survival of the firm's passenger business lay in the creation of a modern and innovative vessel combining the allure of the transatlantic express steamer with the economic viability of a cruise ship.

Queen Elizabeth 2's design incorporated structural and mechanical features well suited for both types of service. At 963 feet and 65,863 tons she would have the size and stability needed to confront the North Atlantic's worst conditions, yet would still be able to transit the Panama Canal and call at virtually any Caribbean harbor. Double-reduction turbines driving twin screws would give her a speed of 28.5 knots at an economical 520 tons of oil a day. Two pairs of stabilizers and twin bow thrusters would make her easy to handle both at sea and in port. The most extensive computer network yet installed in a commercial vessel would reduce the size of the liner's crew while improving the ship's overall performance, as would her state-of-the-art communication, navigation, and self-monitoring systems.

The Cunarder's passenger accommodations were to be equally impressive. She would have 687 Tourist Class and 245 First Class rooms, as well as 46 luxury suites and two split-level penthouses. On her transatlantic voyages *QE2* would embark 564 First Class and 1,441 Tourist Class passengers, though on cruises she would carry 1,350 guests in one-class splendor.

QE2 was to be a showcase of modern style. The dark woods, heavy brocades, and country-house trappings that had characterized Cunard's previous flagships were replaced by glass, steel, polished aluminum, and colorful fabrics. This bold and vigorous look was carried through in her public rooms, which included three restaurants, two nightclubs, two main lounges, a theater, and a boat-deck coffee shop.

Work on the liner began at John Brown and Company's Clydebank yards in June 1965 and Cunard's new flagship was launched on 20 September 1967 by Queen Elizabeth II[1]. Over the next 12 months, workers completed *QE2*'s powerplant and its supporting systems, finished her interiors, and installed her furnishings, carpets, and other appointments. Media interest in the liner remained high and was especially intense when she sailed from the Clyde on 26 November 1968 to begin her builder's trials.

Unfortunately, *QE2*'s first time at sea was a widely publicized embarrassment. Problems with her turbines plagued the voyage, and the liner limped back to Clydebank for repairs. Cunard refused to accept the vessel until the faults were corrected, though the delay forced the postponement of *Queen Elizabeth 2*'s much-advertised January 1969 maiden crossing. The delayed voyage eventually had to be canceled when further mechanical problems cropped up, and it wasn't until 18 April 1969 that Cunard accepted the vessel from her builders.

Queen Elizabeth 2's long-awaited commercial debut took place on 2 May, when she sailed from Southampton for New York. Though she made good time on this first westbound passage—just over 4 days, 16 hours—her subsequent performance was not up to her owner's expectations. Indeed, the liner's operating costs were considerably higher and her ability to draw sufficient passengers somewhat lower than expected; by the summer of 1971 *QE2* was deeply in the red. When the Cunard Line was bought that August by Trafalgar House Investments Ltd., there was widespread speculation that the liner would be withdrawn from service or sold for scrap.

Cunard's new owners decided on a less drastic course of action, however. Concluding that the best way to improve *QE2*'s drawing power was to improve her appearance and amenities, they ordered a comprehensive, £2 million facelift. The work was conducted between sailings throughout the last half of 1972 and included the upgrading of her kitchens, enlargement of her restaurants, installation of additional First Class accommodations, and revision of the decor in several of her public areas.

These measures made *QE2* one of the most "passenger-friendly" vessels afloat and helped improve her economic performance, but could do nothing to prevent the string of mechanical breakdowns and other unfortunate occurrences that seemed to plague the liner over the following decade. A complete breakdown of all three boilers set the Cunarder helplessly adrift in the Caribbean in April 1974; a collision with a Bahamian coral reef cut short a 1976 cruise; and an engine-room fire forced her to abort a westbound crossing in 1976.

Queen Elizabeth 2 soldiered on, however, making it into the 1980s without falling victim to the forced retirement many maritime experts predicted for her. Periodic refurbishments kept her stylish,

and she remained popular with those travelers to whom the "how" of reaching a destination was far more important than either the "when" or the "how much?" Though she remained an economic underachiever, Cunard seemed content to keep the liner on the alternating transatlantic/cruising service for which she had been designed.

The decision to keep *QE2* operational was to have important, if entirely unforeseen, military significance following Argentina's 2 April 1982 invasion of the Falklands. Though the assault did not come as a complete surprise to the British government[2], London was ill-prepared to move a significant number of troops 8,000 miles to the remote and inhospitable battle zone. Aircraft could transport men and materiel only as far as Ascension Island, about a third of the way, because there were no secure airfields or staging areas any closer. Moreover, successive defense cuts since the end of World War II had transformed the once-mighty Royal Navy into a force tailored specifically for anti-submarine warfare in European waters. Britain's senior service thus lacked the troop transports and support vessels necessary to mount the

Once her initial teething troubles were solved, *Queen Elizabeth 2* soon became a popular ship with the public. Though she continued to be plagued by a series of mishaps, regular refurbishments kept her stylish. She remained on an alternating transatlantic/cruising service throughout the 1970s and early 1980s. *Shaum Collection*

logistically daunting "out of area" operation necessary to retake the Falkland Islands.

Fortunately, the Royal Navy could get STUFT. The appropriately droll acronym stood for Ships Taken Up From Trade, a contingency plan under which the British government could requisition British-flagged merchant vessels to fill gaps in the Royal Navy's order of battle. Though the plan was primarily intended to supply oil tankers, repair and salvage vessels, ocean-going tugs, and bulk cargo carriers, it also provided for the requisitioning of ships suitable for trooping. This latter category included the 12,988-ton North Sea passenger ferry *Norland*, the 44,800-ton P&O Line cruise ship *Canberra*, and *QE2*.

Despite her presence on the STUFT list of merchant vessels, few knowledgeable observers initially believed Cunard's superliner would actually be called up for service. *Queen Elizabeth 2* was, they reasoned, too large and far too valuable to be put at risk. This point of view seemed to be borne out when she was not among the ships requisitioned in the weeks following Queen Elizabeth II's 4 April approval of the Order in Council that initiated the call-up of merchant shipping. That *Canberra* and *Norland* were requisitioned so early in the process—the former on 5 April and the latter 12 days later—was seen by many as further proof that *QE2* would not be drafted for South Atlantic duty. The Cunard Line's directors were not convinced their flagship had avoided call-up, however, and near the end of April took the precaution of securing additional insurance to cover the vessel should she be requisitioned.

This proved to be a wise move. As planning continued for Operation Corporate, the name given to the mission to free the Falklands, it became obvious that *QE2*'s participation would be essential. Though the initial British assault would be made by the 3,400 troops carried aboard *Canberra*, *Norland*, and the Royal Navy assault transports HMS *Intrepid* and HMS *Fearless*—the 2nd and 3rd Battalions, The Parachute Regiment, and the Royal Marines' 40, 42, and 45 Commandos—a 3,500-man follow-on force was to go ashore as soon as possible. Known as 5 Infantry Brigade, this force would consist primarily of the 2nd Battalion of the Scots Guards, the 1st Battalion of the Welsh Guards, and the 1st Battalion of the 7th Duke of Edinburgh's Own Gurkha Rifles. *Queen Elizabeth 2* was the only vessel capable of moving the brigade to the South Atlantic quickly and as a coherent unit, a fact that made the liner's participation in Operation Corporate a certainty.

As is often the case in wartime, those most directly affected by a particular decision are often the last to know of it. So it was for those aboard *QE2*. The liner had departed Philadelphia on 29 April bound for Southampton. Throughout the voyage there had been widespread speculation among her passengers and crew about what role, if any, *Queen Elizabeth 2* might play in Operation Corporate. Captain Alexander Hutchinson had received no word on his vessel's fate, however, and it was thus something of a shock when on 3 May the ship's communications room monitored a BBC bulletin announcing that *QE2* had been requisitioned for military service. Hutchinson wisely requested confirmation of the report from Cunard's directors and, after receiving it, announced over the liner's public address system that upon her arrival in England the ship would be transferred to Royal Navy control.

Queen Elizabeth 2's requisitioning took place soon after she came alongside her Southampton pier before dawn on 4 May. Shortly thereafter Hutchinson turned command over to Captain Peter Jackson, a veteran of World War II service in the Royal Navy and a long-time Cunard officer whose early service included stints as navigator aboard both *Queen Mary* and *Queen Elizabeth*. Though Jackson would be responsible for the day-to-day operation of the ship and the command of its crew, he would officially be under the orders of Captain Noel James, the liner's Senior Naval Officer.

QE2's passengers disembarked later on the morning of 4 May, and work crews spent the remainder of the day off-loading the normal detritus of a transatlantic voyage. Late that night tugs nudged the liner into the basin so that she could be turned in preparation for her next departure, and on the morning of 5 May the ship's transformation from luxury liner to troop transport began.

As with other great liners in earlier times, the first step was the removal of the ship's better furnishings and most fragile fittings. Workmen labored nonstop to take ashore furniture, artwork, silverware and glassware, plants, delicate electronic equipment, and all the other impedimenta that would have no place on the coming voyage. Many items that could not be removed because of size or complexity were protected in other ways. Decorative glass panels and murals were covered with tarpaulins, wooden railings were wrapped in sacking, and sheets of wood were laid over carpeting in the liner's public areas, main passageways, and many of her staterooms.

Military equipment came up *Queen Elizabeth 2*'s gangways even as her civilian trappings were taken ashore. Workers brought aboard more than 1,000 folding cots to augment the berths available in the liner's existing staterooms, boosting her troop capacity to 3,150. The ship's food storage areas, kitchens, and toilets were upgraded as needed, and her medical facilities were provided with additional equipment and supplies. Technicians even installed an updated (and internal) version of the proven degaussing girdle intended to reduce the liner's vulnerability to magnetic mines.

Up to this point the steps taken to prepare *QE2* for war had differed little from those undergone decades earlier by *Queen Mary* and *Queen Elizabeth*. But much had changed in the years since, and *Queen Elizabeth 2*'s trooping conversion included entirely modern aspects that those who sailed to war aboard her predecessors could not have foreseen.

Perhaps the most obvious of these was the installation aboard *QE2* of helicopter landing pads. The aircraft would undertake most of the ship-to-ship and ship-to-shore transport tasks once performed by lighters and tenders, and providing suitable deck space was a priority. Technicians from Vosper Thornycroft's Southampton works created an aft landing and maintenance area by removing the ship's upper deck lido all the way to the quarterdeck level and positioning a girder-and-plate pad over *QE2*'s aft swimming pools. A second, smaller landing area was built forward of the bridge by attaching a reinforced pad to the forward edge of the quarterdeck and extending it over the anchor capstans.

Because *Queen Elizabeth 2* could not carry enough fuel for a round-trip voyage to the Falklands, Royal Navy planners decided to equip her with something never before seen on a great liner, a naval-style refueling-at-sea system. This consisted of receptacles set just inside the midships baggage hatch on the vessel's starboard side, which fed into pipes running through passageways to the liner's main fuel tanks six decks below. Though not the safest system—a refueling acci-

dent or a hit by an enemy weapon could rupture the pipes and send blazing fuel oil throughout the ship—it was essential given the length of the voyage planned for *QE2*.

Also vital to the success of the liner's military mission was the ability to communicate immediately and securely with other ships of the British fleet, with aircraft of the Royal Navy and Royal Air Force, and with senior commanders in London. Though *Queen Elizabeth 2*'s extensive navigation and communications suite included a variety of commercial-band radios, radio-telephones, and an International Maritime Satellite (INMARSAT) link, it lacked the necessary military systems. This was corrected during the conversion in Southampton through the installation of UHF receivers in a radio room set up behind the bridge. More importantly, *QE2* was also equipped with a military-standard Satellite Communications/Onboard Tracker (SCOT) system, installed in vans bolted to the top deck aft of the penthouse suites.

Given the effort dedicated to providing *QE2* with the latest in high-tech communications gear, some of the 640 crew members[3] who had volunteered to stay aboard for the ship's trooping service were baffled by the absence of equally sophisticated weapon systems. Where, some asked, were the radar-guided anti-aircraft missiles, the large-caliber automatic guns, even the 20 mm and 40 mm cannons that had defended her predecessors? Indeed, the only indication that the ship would be armed at all was the installation of primitive gun mounts at several points on her upper works. That these would hold nothing more lethal than World War II-vintage .50-caliber machine guns did not inspire confidence in the militarily uninformed, nor did the news that the guns would be augmented by fewer than a score of shoulder-fired Blowpipe missiles brought aboard by Army air defense troops.

The relative lack of weapons was the result of several factors. First, Royal Navy planners intended to use satellite imagery and other intelligence assets to keep *Queen Elizabeth 2* far enough from enemy forces that she would not require defensive weapons. Second, equipping the liner with modern radar-based gun or missile systems would increase the chances that Argentine ships or aircraft might locate her through her electronic emissions. Third, only the most sophisticated systems would provide a viable defense against sea-skimming missiles or attack aircraft launching guided weapons from beyond visible range. Those weapons in the British arsenal capable of fulfilling these requirements were either already installed aboard warships more likely to encounter the enemy or were earmarked for such installation and, as the 4 May sinking of the destroyer HMS *Sheffield* by an Argentine Exocet missile had shown, even the installation of the most advanced weapons did not guarantee a ship's survival. To a large extent then, *QE2* would have to rely for protection on the same assets that had protected her kind in previous wars: reliable information, high speed, and stealth.

It was an indication of *Queen Elizabeth 2*'s military importance that her transformation into a troopship was accomplished in barely a week. Equipment, supplies, and provisions had begun coming aboard halfway through the conversion, and the first troops arrived on the afternoon of 11 May. These vanguards were joined early the following morning by the first 5 Infantry Brigade unit, the 1st Battalion, The Welsh Guards. Troop loading continued into the afternoon and by 4 P.M. *QE2* was ready to sail.

At exactly 4:03 P.M. the Cunarder moved slowly away from her pier to the cheers of several thousand well-wishers and the music of regimental bands. Aided by five tugs, *Queen Elizabeth 2* moved briefly upriver to turn about. That done, she moved majestically toward the open sea—cheering troops lining her rails—returning with her own siren the salutes offered by virtually every vessel in Southampton Water. It was in all respects a modern version of the farewells given other great liners in earlier wars; like them, it was a send-off truly fit for a queen.

As it happened, however, the much-publicized departure for the war zone wasn't what it seemed. Once clear of the Solent, and after taking aboard two HAS.2A Sea King helicopters of 825 Naval Air Squadron, *Queen Elizabeth 2* stopped off the Isle of Wight. Hidden from shore by an increasingly thick fog bank, she dropped anchor for the night.

QE2's unannounced overnight stop in the Channel was intended to give shipyard workers a chance to finish overhauling the liner's three huge boilers, a task that was to have been completed by the time of the ship's scheduled departure for the war zone. It wasn't, but government officials ordered her to sea anyway to reap the greatest pos-

Embarked troops manned 7.62 mm general purpose machine guns like this one aboard *QE2*, fixing them to the ship's bridge wings. The weapons were intended for use against small boats and low-flying aircraft, though their effectiveness against the latter was widely questioned by some of the liner's crew and embarked troops. *UK Ministry of Defence*

sible propaganda value from her on-time departure. *Queen Elizabeth 2* had thus come down the Solent on one boiler, and was to have the other two on line in time for an early morning departure for the South Atlantic.

Unfortunately, a massive leak in the liner's vital distilled-feed-water system made the job of bringing the two remaining boilers on-line more time-consuming than planned. This raised the specter of an extended and extremely embarrassing delay in *QE2*'s actual departure for the war zone; with only a single working boiler she would hardly be capable of movement, let alone the high speeds required for a safe passage south.

Such a debacle was avoided, however, through the skill and determination of *Queen Elizabeth 2*'s engineering crew and of the workers from Southampton. By working through the night they solved the feed-water problem and brought a second boiler on line, thereby ensuring the ship could make at least 20 knots. Just after 9 A.M. on 13 May Captain Jackson ordered SLOW AHEAD on all engines, and *QE2* gathered speed as she set out on the first leg of her voyage, the 2,956-mile passage to Freetown, Sierra Leone.

The trip to Africa would not be a pleasure cruise, of course, because there was much to do to make *Queen Elizabeth 2* and those aboard her ready for whatever the future brought. The first order of business, a boat drill for the troops, took place on the first morning at sea. Just after 10 A.M. the liner's lifeboats were swung out as more than 3,000 soldiers attempted to find their assigned mustering stations. Initial chaos soon gave way to a semblance of order as the troops, formed into single-boat loads of 25 men each, practiced moving from their berthing spaces to the boat deck. Similar drills became a regular feature of life aboard *QE2*, as did lectures on damage-control procedures, fire-fighting, and survival at sea.

Queen Elizabeth 2's first full day at sea was also marked by her introduction to "rassing," the difficult and potentially dangerous art of refueling at sea. Just before 6 P.M. the liner slowed from 21 knots to 12 to allow the tanker *Grey Rover* to overhaul her. Once in position 150 feet to starboard of *QE2*, the tanker fired over the first of three connected lines of increasingly larger diameter. The last of these was itself connected to an 8-inch-wide fuel transfer line, which was plugged into the receptacle in the midships baggage hatch. Once the attachment was made, *Grey Rover* pumped several tons of fuel oil across to ensure that the plumbing worked as advertised, then reeled in the hose and its guide lines. The exercise complete, the tanker dropped astern as *Queen Elizabeth 2,* her third boiler now on-line, surged ahead.

Over the next few days, life aboard *QE2* settled into a familiar routine. While the liner's crew operated, navigated, and maintained their ship, the troops prepared themselves for war. This entailed daily mass-runs around the deck to maintain physical fitness, nearly constant small-arms practice, and frequent intelligence briefings on the current status and disposition of Argentine forces in the

Falklands. Nor were the embarked Sea King helicopters idle; their crews practiced takeoffs, landings, and the range of specialized maneuvers they would be called upon to perform once the liner reached the war zone.

Though *Queen Elizabeth 2*'s departure for the South Atlantic was heavily covered by the news media, once clear of the Bay of Biscay the liner disappeared from public view. As directed by his Admiralty sailing orders, Jackson stayed well away from the regular shipping lanes and minimized *QE2*'s electronic emissions. Though these measures would not hide the vessel from high-flying reconnaissance satellites—both the United States and the Soviet Union were tracking the liner's progress—they eliminated the possibility of a news organization revealing *QE2*'s exact position to the world, and thus to the Argentines.

So effective were these efforts to mask *Queen Elizabeth 2*'s movements that her 18 May appearance off Freetown was as much a surprise to local journalists as it was to the port's officials. As the former vainly attempted to get word of the liner's arrival to the major European news services, the latter arranged for the Cunarder to take on fresh water and fuel. *QE2* had made the passage from Southampton at an average speed of 24 knots and, when added to the 4,000 tons remaining in her bunkers, the 1,867 tons of fuel oil she took on in Freetown would allow her to make the trip to the war zone without having to refuel. That the port was able to play as vital a role in *QE2*'s wartime operations as it had in those of liners-turned-troopers in earlier conflicts was one more indication that, at least in military matters, the advance of technology does not always invalidate the lessons of history.

Queen Elizabeth 2 stayed in Freetown barely 11 hours before resuming her voyage south. Her track took her toward Ascension Island, the British-owned but U.S.-operated mid-Atlantic base that was serving as a marshaling point for British forces headed toward the Falklands. The troops embarked aboard *QE2* made good use of the three-day passage, pausing in their training only for the traditional "crossing the line" ceremony when the Cunarder crossed the Equator on the night of 19/20 May.

The only other unusual incident of the Freetown-Ascension passage occurred the following morning, when the Soviet intelligence-gather-

The Blowpipe short-range anti-aircraft missiles brought aboard *Queen Elizabeth 2* by the troops of 43 Air Defence Battery offered somewhat better protection against Argentine attackers, though the missiles could only lock onto an aircraft once it had made its attack and was climbing away. *UK Ministry of Defence*

ing ship *Primorye* appeared on the horizon. The antenna-laden vessel accompanied *QE2* at a discrete distance for some time before departing, and Jackson and his senior officers could only assume the spy ship had transmitted *Queen Elizabeth 2*'s course and speed to Moscow. This was not seen as a direct threat to the troopship, however, because the Soviets were known to be unsympathetic to Argentina and were unlikely to pass *QE2*'s whereabouts to the anti-communist Buenos Aires regime.

For security reasons *Queen Elizabeth 2* was forbidden to call at Ascension, so personnel and equipment waiting on the island for transfer to the liner were to come aboard by helicopter. The first of these transfers took place soon after the departure of the Russian trawler, when *QE2* rendezvoused with HMS *Dumbarton Castle*. The 1,427-ton North Sea fisheries-protection vessel had been drafted into wartime service primarily because she was equipped with a helicopter landing pad, and made good use of it well into the afternoon. The

warship held position off *QE2*'s starboard side as the liner's Sea Kings transferred a score of passengers and several tons of equipment.

Among the most important "cargo" to come aboard *Queen Elizabeth 2* as she steamed past Ascension Island was Major General Jeremy Moore, Operation Corporate's Commander, Land Forces, Falkland Islands. Moore and his staff had flown out from Britain on 20 May, and boarded *QE2* by helicopter the following morning. As significant as the general's arrival was, for most of the embarked troops it was overshadowed by the fact that the stream of Sea Kings that brought him and his staff aboard also carried 10 tons of mail. For many of the soldiers it was the first word from home since leaving their camps in England and morale soared.

The effect was short-lived, however; late on the evening of 21 May those aboard *Queen Elizabeth 2* heard the sobering news that British forces had begun landing on the Falklands. Though the first units ashore at San Carlos on

Physical training, weapon drills, and intelligence briefings helped keep *QE2*'s embarked troops sharp on the long voyage south, as did nearly constant helicopter embarkation practice. Here a Sea King touches down aboard the liner as the deck landing crew stands ready. *UK Ministry of Defence*

East Falkland had encountered only scattered resistance, British commanders expected the Argentines to react with increasing force. And since it was assumed that the enemy knew many of the British troops participating in the invasion had arrived in the war zone aboard the converted liner *Canberra*, it was logical that the Argentines would attempt to find and sink the ship carrying the bulk of the British follow-on forces: *QE2*. The liner's departure early on 22 May from the waters around Ascension thus marked the beginning of the most dangerous part of her voyage, a fact of which everyone aboard was well aware.

Of primary concern to Jackson, Moore, and the other senior officers on *QE2* was the Argentine Navy's hodgepodge but no-less-capable fleet. Despite the 2 May loss of the cruiser *Belgrano* to the British submarine *Conqueror*[4], the Armada Republica Argentina could still field one aircraft carrier, eight destroyers, five frigates, and four submarines. That the majority of the ARA's vessels were elderly and unreliable did not diminish the threat they represented to the British task force or to *QE2*.

Almost as dangerous to the Cunarder were the Fuerza Aerea Argentina's three long-range maritime patrol aircraft. These modified Boeing 707s of the FAA's Grupo 1 de Transporte Aereo had begun conducting long-range, unescorted patrols from a forward airfield on 21 April. They had

located the main British task force on that first mission and had shadowed its ships on and off ever since. It was thus not unreasonable to assume that they would be searching for *QE2*. If they found the liner and reported her position, the probability of an attack by aircraft or submarine would increase dramatically.

To decrease the likelihood of both detection and attack, *Queen Elizabeth 2* assumed a full wartime footing in the days after passing Ascension Island. As with other liners that had sailed in wartime, the first order of business was to black out the ship's portholes and windows. This was accomplished using taped-on sheets of black plastic, which were found to be as effective as the more traditional black paint.

Another form of "camouflage" put into effect during this period was a total cessation of electronic emissions. In order to avoid betraying *Queen Elizabeth 2*'s position, Jackson ordered her radar turned off, relying on extra lookouts to warn him of danger. The ship's radios were set to "receive only," and they and the SCOT satellite receiver would be *QE2*'s one-way link with the outside world until the ship reached the war zone.

The final and most symbolic change made to *Queen Elizabeth 2* as she headed south from Ascension was the installation of her armament. Mounts on each bridge wing and aft near her former shopping arcade were fitted with .50-caliber machine guns intended to detonate floating mines or dissuade the close approach of small vessels. What anti-aircraft protection the liner was to have was provided by 7.62 mm machine guns and shoulder-launched Blowpipe missiles sited around her funnel and upper works. Manned by soldiers of 43 Air Defence Battery, the Blowpipes were effective only at relatively close range, making them useless against aircraft launching sea-skimming missiles from over the horizon. More significantly, the heat-seeking Blowpipes could lock onto a target only from the rear, meaning enemy aircraft could be engaged only when they turned away after dropping or launching their weapons.

The troops aboard *Queen Elizabeth 2* had little time in which to ponder the effectiveness of the liner's defenses because the tempo of their training increased each day. Helicopter embarkation practice continued, as did weapon drills, physical training, and lectures on enemy strength and disposition. Nor were off-duty hours any less full: the soldiers entertained themselves with sports competitions and the nonstop card games that are a staple of troopship life. Though all this activity helped to lessen the anxiety of approaching combat, it could not eliminate the sense of loneliness some felt as they gazed out on the seemingly empty sea.

Queen Elizabeth 2 was not as alone as she might have seemed, however, because on her voyage south from Ascension she was part of a widely separated convoy. A day ahead of the liner were the Townsend Line's *Baltic Ferry* and *Nordic Ferry*, twin 6,455-ton vessels carrying 5 Brigade's heavy equipment and additional troops. And just out of sight astern of *QE2* was *Atlantic Causeway*, a Cunard-owned 14,946-ton container ship loaded with personnel, equipment, and 10 Sea King HAS.2A anti-submarine warfare helicopters. Each vessel would have an important role to play in the retaking of the Falklands.

Just how costly that victory was proving to be was illustrated by news from the war zone monitored aboard *QE2* during the voyage south. Late on the evening of 23 May came word that the frigate HMS *Antelope* had been destroyed by Argentine bombs while protecting the British beachhead at San Carlos. On 25 May the news was even worse: two British ships had been lost. The destroyer HMS *Coventry* was bombed while patrolling near the entrance to Falkland Sound and sank with the loss of 20 men. Soon afterward FAA Super Etendard attack aircraft launched two Exocet missiles at ships of the British task force; decoyed away from the carrier HMS *Hermes*, one of the missiles devastated the requisitioned container ship *Atlantic Conveyor*, sister to *Atlantic Causeway*.

Though still out of range of missile-firing Argentine aircraft, *Queen Elizabeth 2* was now close enough to the war zone to encounter enemy submarines. To reduce the threat, on the afternoon of 26 May, Jackson ordered the helmsman to begin zigzagging. Though the liner initially maintained 25 knots on the straight legs of her course, by the evening of the 26th increasingly heavy seas forced Jackson to slow somewhat and deploy the ship's stabilizers to smooth the ride for the embarked troops.

Jackson was forced to slow *QE2* even more when, late on the 26th, falling temperatures brought on freezing rain and thick mist that reduced visibility to less than a mile. In an especially worrisome development, the liner also began

to encounter icebergs more than capable of ripping her hull open. These conditions made reliance on human lookouts foolish at best, and after much consideration the liner's Senior Naval Officer agreed that Jackson should briefly turn on the ship's radar every 30 minutes. The wisdom of this precaution was quickly validated; the radar's first sweep of the area illuminated nearly 100 bergs of varying sizes. Jackson quickly cut *QE2*'s speed to nine knots and ordered all her watertight doors closed, then spent the remainder of the night threading the huge liner through the shifting berg fields.

Much to everyone's relief, *Queen Elizabeth 2* cleared the ice area on the morning of 27 May. Jackson increased speed because he had a rendezvous to make northeast of South Georgia Island, the Falklands dependency recaptured from the Argentines a month earlier.

The liner reached the mid-ocean meeting point shortly before noon and was soon joined by the guided-missile destroyer HMS *Antrim*. Heavily weathered and still carrying the scars of combat, the warship came to a halt near the waiting liner so that Moore and 5 Brigade commander Brigadier M. J. A. Wilson and their staffs could cross from *QE2* by helicopter and launch. *Antrim* then left to carry the senior land force officers to a meeting with British Task Force commander Rear Admiral John Woodward aboard *Hermes*, after which the soldiers would board the assault transport/command ship *Fearless* for the journey to the beachhead at San Carlos.

Queen Elizabeth 2 would not be following her former passengers to the combat zone, however, because the British government had judged the liner to be too valuable to risk in the hotly contested waters around the Falklands. Instead, the liner had been ordered to make for South Georgia. There she would transfer her load of troops to other ships for onward movement to San Carlos, then await further instructions.

QE2 arrived off South Georgia's Cumberland Bay East just after 6 P.M. on 27 May. The anchorage was cloaked in dense fog and getting the huge liner safely to her assigned position took 90 anxious minutes. The task was made even more challenging by the presence of 20 other vessels, among them P&O's *Canberra*, the ferry-turned-trooper *Norland*, the Royal Navy research ship HMS *Endurance*, and a variety of tugs and tenders. And though hidden from view by the fog, not far away lay a grim reminder of the war's seriousness: the Argentine submarine *Santa Fé* lay abandoned and half-submerged at a nearby pier, the victim of repeated missile and gun attacks by British helicopters.

The Royal Navy commander of South Georgia, a Captain Barker, was determined that such a fate would not befall the British ships sheltering in Cumberland Bay East. He was particularly concerned that the presence of both *QE2* and *Canberra* would attract the attention of the Fuerza Area Argentina, and sought to minimize the risk of an attack by ordering Jackson to begin transferring the soldiers of 5 Brigade to *Canberra* and *Norland* as soon as *Queen Elizabeth 2* was safely moored. This she was by 9 P.M., and soon thereafter the tug RMAS *Typhoon* moved alongside the Cunarder to begin off-loading the troops.

Over the next 14 hours small craft worked nonstop to complete the cross-decking. The men of the two Guards battalions were transferred to *Canberra*, while the Gurkhas were shifted to *Norland*. The need to maintain a strict blackout caused a few minor mishaps and several delays, and dawn was welcomed by all concerned. Sunrise also brought helicopters into the effort as *Queen Elizabeth 2*'s Sea Kings joined *Endurance*'s two HAS.1 Wasps in transferring bulk stores from the Cunarder to *Canberra* and *Norland*.

Anchored in South Georgia's Cumberland Bay East, *Queen Elizabeth 2* off-loads her troops on 28 May. Note that a Sea King is just lifting off from the liner's aft helicopter pad, which was created by removing the ship's upper deck lido all the way to the quarterdeck level and positioning a girder-and-plate pad over the aft swimming pools. *UK Ministry of Defence*

The movement of personnel was not all one way on the 29th, for having dispatched her troops *QE2* shifted to her secondary role as an ambulance transport by taking aboard 640 survivors of *Antelope*, *Ardent*, and *Coventry*. Each of the warships had been lost to Argentine air attacks, and many of the men brought aboard the Cunarder bore severe blast and fire injuries. The most seriously wounded were sent to *Queen Elizabeth 2*'s small but well-equipped hospital, while the uninjured survivors were accommodated in regular cabins.

The weather around South Georgia worsened during the cross-decking effort, and by the time the troop transfer was completed early in the evening of the 29th, huge swells were making life difficult aboard every ship in Cumberland Bay East. *Queen Elizabeth 2* was not immune, and her increasingly active rolling ultimately convinced Jackson that she would be better off in the open sea. His belief that it was time to leave was reinforced by the news that the tanker *British Wye* had been attacked by Argentine aircraft barely 400 miles to the north. Though the tanker escaped damage, the incident underlined the threat to the ships at South Georgia. Jackson lost no time in getting the liner underway, and she cleared the harbor just after 5:30 P.M.

By 7:30 P.M. *Queen Elizabeth 2* was well out to sea, making 18 knots through calmer waters as she approached the same ice field that had caused her crew such anxiety just days earlier. Jackson slowed the liner to 10 knots and guided her between the bergs, one of which provided an awesome spectacle by rolling completely over as the ship passed. For the next three-and-a-half hours *QE2* weaved through the starkly beautiful seascape, her blacked-out form hardly discernible in the darkness.

The liner cleared the main part of the ice field just before midnight. Soon afterward Jackson increased *Queen Elizabeth 2*'s speed to 25 knots and, in keeping with the sailing orders he had received at South Georgia, set a course for Ascension Island. There the survivors of the sunken British warships would presumably be put ashore prior to *QE2*'s expected return to the war zone.

The trip north was not an easy one; beginning just after dawn on 30 May the liner was buffeted by increasingly heavy seas and high winds. Though the bad weather helped hide *Queen Elizabeth 2* from

A requisitioned fishing trawler pulls away with troops off-loaded from *QE2* at South Georgia. The men of the Scots Guards, Welsh Guards, 7th Duke of Edinburgh's Own Gurkha Rifles, and various support units were transferred to ships thought better able to survive the journey to the Falklands. *UK Ministry of Defence*

Argentine ships and aircraft, the severe rolling it caused also made life uncomfortable for the liner's crew and passengers. More importantly, the mountainous waves prevented *QE2* from undertaking a planned 31 May refueling from the tanker *Bayleaf.* By the time *Bayleaf* was able to assume position off the Cunarder's starboard side at 9 A.M. on 2 June, the liner had barely 1,000 tons of fuel left in her tanks. Over the next 10 hours the ships ploughed steadily northward, separated by 150 feet of churning water and connected by a hose that was often pulled tight as the vessels rolled in opposite directions. By the time the ships parted, *Queen Elizabeth 2* had taken aboard 3,800 tons of fuel, more than enough to see her safely to Ascension Island.

As it turned out, however, the liner was bound elsewhere. By 3 June the situation in the Falklands had improved so much that the Ministry of Defence saw no need for *QE2* to return to the war zone. The liner was therefore ordered to bypass Ascension and make directly for Southampton to disembark the survivors of *Antelope, Ardent,* and *Coventry.* The news was greeted with mixed emotions by the liner's crew and embarked military

staff; though obviously pleased by the prospect of an early homecoming, many also felt *QE2* had much more to contribute to the war effort. However, they turned their attention to ensuring that the warship survivors enjoyed the voyage home to the fullest.

On the morning of 4 June *Queen Elizabeth 2* rendezvoused with *Dumbarton Castle* 50 miles southwest of Ascension Island. The meeting had been arranged so the liner could off-load 60 tons of ammunition not put ashore at South Georgia, as well as to disembark several critically injured sailors who would make the trip from Ascension to Britain by air. The cross-decking was carried out by an RAF Sea King and was completed by early afternoon. When the helicopter lifted off the Cunarder for the final time, Jackson ordered full ahead and shaped a course for Britain.

Even as *Queen Elizabeth 2* raced northward, preparations were being made in Southampton to honor her, her crew, and the survivors she carried. A mounting surge of public acclaim for all those involved in Operation Corporate ensured that the Cunarder—the first ship to return from

The "Whale," the P&O Line's 44,800-ton *Canberra*, stands by to take on the 5 Infantry Brigade troops off-loaded from *QE2*. The cruise ship played a vital role in Britain's campaign to retake the Falklands, carrying many of the troops landed at San Carlos. After the war she transported enemy POWs back to Argentina before returning British troops to the United Kingdom. *UK Ministry of Defence*

the war zone—would be treated to a spectacular welcome. Indeed, a 6 June message informed Jackson that the homecoming festivities would begin in the Solent, where Queen Elizabeth (the Queen Mother) would greet the liner from the royal yacht *Britannia*.

By the afternoon of 10 June *Queen Elizabeth 2* was back in home waters, cruising slowly to the northeast off the Cornwall coast as Sea Kings brought aboard new uniforms for the warship survivors. The helicopters were back again early the next morning, this time bearing Britain's First Sea Lord, Admiral Sir John Fieldhouse, Lord Matthews, chairman of Cunard, and 40 reporters and photographers. Fieldhouse departed after a brief shipboard press conference, but the others remained aboard as *QE2* steamed slowly up the Solent.

The liner's progress toward Southampton was nothing short of triumphant. It began with the Queen Mother's greeting from *Britannia*, a message cheered by the survivors of *Antelope, Ardent,* and *Coventry*.

Her wartime duty over, *Queen Elizabeth 2* was initially repainted in a light pebble gray color scheme that was widely denounced as unsuitable for a ship of *QE2*'s stature. Ultimately repainted to her traditional Cunard Line colors, she has led a somewhat troubled life since her postwar return to commercial service. A string of mechanical difficulties and a widely publicized run-in with the U.S. Public Health Service have clouded the future of the world's sole remaining Great Liner. *The Cunard Line*

Moving past Cowes toward Southampton Water, *QE2* was engulfed by the cheers of tens of thousands of well-wishers on shore and the massed sirens of virtually every vessel in sight. Scores of small craft darted about the liner as tugs turned her slowly about, then moved her alongside berths 38 and 39. A Royal Marine band played as flags and banners of every size, shape, and color snapped in the breeze. By noon all lines were secured; *Queen Elizabeth 2* was home.

The liner's return marked the official end of her brief but important military career. In service for just 37 days, she had played a vital role in the ultimate British victory by quickly and efficiently transporting the single largest element of the invasion force to the war zone. In so doing she conclusively proved that large passenger steamships can still play an important military role in a world dominated by jet aircraft, especially in those cases when deploying troops by air is not possible.

Her military duty completed, *Queen Elizabeth 2* underwent a comprehensive, £7 million refit intended to both erase the scars of her wartime service and update her somewhat out-of-date public rooms. Carried out at Southampton from mid-July to early August 1982, the work began with the removal of all military-specific equipment and structures installed during *QE2*'s conversion into a trooper.

Once these items were removed, *QE2*'s restoration and updating began in earnest. The most obvious changes included the replacement of the Lido Deck structure removed to create the aft helicopter landing pad, the transformation of the quarter-deck's Q4 Room into the Club Lido, and the installation of a posh Golden Door health spa in the former Turkish bath. Other alterations included the redecoration of the Queen's Grill and the ship's casino, upgrading of heating and air-conditioning systems, and the replacement of virtually all carpeting in passageways and public rooms. Finally, in a move intended by Cunard to symbolize *QE2*'s "lighter and more contemporary flair," the color of the ship's hull was changed from its traditional black to a light pebble gray, but then back to its original color.

Queen Elizabeth 2 returned to commercial service on 15 August 1982 with a fully booked crossing to New York. She has remained popular ever since, though she has been plagued by a series of highly publicized difficulties that have hindered her economic performance. These included repeated failures of U.S. Public Health Service sanitation inspections, engine problems that on several occasions forced her to curtail voyages, and a trouble-plagued 1994 Atlantic crossing that ended in her being briefly laid up in New York. As of this writing her future, though clouded, seems secure, and we who love the world's great liners can only hope that she will be with us for many years to come.

NOTES

Introduction

[1] An acronym drawn from the company's name in German: Hamburg-Amerikanische Packetfahrt Aktien Gesellschaft.

Chapter 2   Kronprinz Wilhelm

[1] In honor of Friedrich Wilhelm Augustus, Freiherr Von Steuben (1730–1794), the Prussian officer who volunteered his services in training General George Washington's Continental Army.

[2] Developed by Royal Navy Lieutenant Commander Norman Wilkinson, the dazzle concept sought to confuse enemy gunners as to the true direction, speed, and shape of the camouflaged ship. This was done by painting the vessel with a unique pattern of shapes, stripes, and false profiles. More than 495 Allied ships received individual patterns during World War I.

[3] Scholars estimate that in four months (October to February) the influenza pandemic of 1918–1919 killed 27 million people worldwide, whereas the total number of combatants and civilians killed during the four years of World War I is normally set at 10 million.

Chapter 3   Carmania

[1] *Baltic*, launched in 1904, and *Adriatic*, launched in 1907. The quartet of White Star liners was known, inevitably, as the "Big Four."

[2] Wirth and 19 of the ship's 319 crew members were killed during, or died as a result of, the duel with *Carmania*. Twenty others either drowned or were killed by sharks. The *Eleonore Wörmann* eventually made it to the Brazilian mainland where she, her crew, and *Cap Trafalgar*'s 279 survivors were interned for the duration of the war.

[3] However, upon hearing *Cap Trafalgar*'s final radio message announcing her imminent sinking, and believing that the German colliers would rescue survivors, *Kronprinz Wilhelm*'s captain, Korvettenkapitän Paul Thierfelder, turned back toward the main South Atlantic shipping lanes.

When later criticized for not pursuing the escaping *Carmania*, Thierfelder explained that he believed British cruisers were lurking in the area and felt that to heave-to near Trinidad would put *Kronprinz Wilhelm* in unnecessary danger.

[4] Present-day Recife.

[5] One such patrol stands out from the rest, however. On May 1, 1914, *Carmania* and the cruisers HMS *Essex* and HMS *Bristol* were searching for German vessels off the coast of New York when they briefly rendezvoused with Cunard's *Lusitania*, which was outbound for Liverpool. Two suspicious passengers, thought to be German spies, were transferred from *Lusitania* to *Carmania* for incarceration in the latter's brig. Six days later *Lusitania* was sunk by a German submarine off the Irish coast.

Chapter 4   Lusitania

[1] Most notably Colin Simpson in his controversial book *The Lusitania* (Little, Brown, 1972).

[2] Again, Colin Simpson's research is the most exhaustive and his theories the most persuasive.

Chapter 5   Vaterland

[1] This incident was related by Gleaves in his *A History of the Cruiser and Transport Service* (George H. Doran Co., 1921) and in his later memoirs.

[2] The event was related to Sir Bertram Hayes, commodore of the White Star Line, by the New York pilot. Hayes recounted it in his 1925 memoir, *Hull Down: Reminiscences of Wind-jammers, Troops and Travellers* (Cassell & Co., 1925).

[3] This conservation effort was undertaken despite the fact that *Vaterland*'s distillation plant was capable of producing 24,000 gallons of fresh water each day.

[4] Inevitably, the ship was most often referred to by her crew and the troops who traveled aboard her as the "Levi-Nathan."

[5] Of the 130,000 troops carried to France by the ships of the Cruiser and Transport Force at the height of the pandemic in October 1918, over 15,000 were incapacitated by influenza or pneumonia and almost 2,500 died.

[6] As was her sister *Imperator*. The ship was laid up in Germany throughout the war and was commissioned as the U.S. troopship USS *Imperator* after the Armistice. Following the end of the repatriation effort, the liner was withdrawn from Navy service and ultimately awarded to Britain's Cunard Line as a war reparation. The vessel served Cunard long and well as *Berengaria*, and was scrapped in 1946.

Bismarck, the third HAPAG supership, was also laid up in Germany during the war. Seized by the Allies after the Armistice, she was passed to Britain's White Star Line, which she served until 1936 as *Majestic*. She was scrapped in Scotland in 1943.

Chapter 6   Aquitania

[1] Ambulance transports are used for the rapid evacuation of wounded and are not normally fitted with the extensive medical facilities found aboard hospital ships. In contrast, hospital ships are normally fitted with state-of-the-art facilities and often anchor in one area for long periods to support on-going operations ashore.

[2] In British practice of that era, military hospital ships were brought into use only as needed, whereas naval hospital ships formed a permanent part of Britain's fleet and used the prefix HMHS (His Majesty's Hospital Ship).

[3] *Mauretania* remained out of service until October 1916, when she made two trooping voyages to Halifax. She was then laid up again until after the United States' 1917 entry into the war.

[4] *Shaw* was given a new bow during extensive repairs at Southampton and returned to service in May 1919. She was decommissioned in June 1922.

Glassford was absolved of any responsibility for the collision, and he and each member of the skeleton crew that took *Shaw* into Portland were later decorated for heroism. Nor was Charles held accountable; as master of the overtaken vessel he was not at fault.

[5] Formerly the Hamburg-Amerika Line cargo vessel *Steiermark*, *Kormoran* was commissioned as a commerce raider in October 1940 under the command of Frigattenkapitän Theodor Detmers. Her military career prior to her fateful meeting with *Sydney* was successful: In the nearly 12 months she was in service, *Kormoran* sank or captured 11 ships totaling 68,274 tons.

[6] This is the second ship of the name, built by Cammell, Laird & Co. and launched for Cunard-White Star in 1939.

Chapter 7   Queen Mary

[1] Ironically, *Queen Mary* was always the faster of the two despite her age and less businesslike mien.

[2] And in Washington as well. Even before the United States entered World War II, President Franklin Roosevelt suggested to his secretary of state, Sumner Wells, that both *Queen Mary* and *Normandie* be seized by the U.S. government and operated under U.S. registry. He saw them as partial repayment for war debts incurred by Britain and France, but the plan was abandoned after encountering British and French opposition.

[3] *Queen Elizabeth* was herself requisitioned soon after, as were 16 other Cunard-White Star vessels totaling 430,000 tons.

[4] Illingsworth was one of several veteran masters to command *Queen Mary* during the course of her wartime career. These gentlemen rotated command throughout the conflict, and Illingsworth had taken over from James Bisset in mid-August 1942.

[5] The Admiralty slapped a complete news blackout on the collision with *Curacao*, and it was not until 1945 that a formal court of inquiry was convened to examine the circumstances of the accident. After four years of legal maneuvering, British courts ruled that *Queen Mary* was one-third responsible for the collision and *Curacao* two-thirds.

Chapter 8   Queen Elizabeth

[1] Who would later become Queen Elizabeth II.

[2] And, it must be admitted, allowed Great Britain time in which to bolster her defenses and prepare herself for the inevitable conflict.

[3] This account was assembled from information provided to the author by Horst Kessler, from Kriegsmarine war diaries now held by the U.S. Navy Submarine Museum in Groton, Connecticut, and from published histories (see the bibliography for a complete listing).

[4] By virtually everyone except Kessler, that is. Though he went on to command a new boat, the Type VIIc *U-985*, the young officer steadfastly maintained that *U-704* had fired on *Queen Elizabeth* and that the liner had gone dead in the water soon after the torpedo's detonation. The British government has continued to deny that the attack ever

took place, despite the fact that postwar Royal Navy investigations apparently found that Cunard's records contained a document supporting Kessler's claim.

In a 1980 letter to the author, Kessler stated that the document was first mentioned by a Royal Navy officer participating in the 1947 British War Court hearings in Hamburg. The officer reported finding the document after earlier testimony by Kessler's senior watch officer had piqued his curiosity about the alleged attack on *Queen Elizabeth*.

According to the document, several members of the Cunarder's bridge crew reported a "heavy detonation" near the ship very soon after the time Kessler said he fired his fan of torpedoes. The document further stated, according to the Royal Navy officer, that *Queen Elizabeth* then went dead in the water for 15 minutes as her crew attempted to determine if the detonation had been caused by some sort of structural failure (despite the fact that stopping at sea for any reason was in direct violation of standing Admiralty regulations).

Unfortunately, this potentially helpful document has apparently not been seen since, and various researchers have reported that other Cunard records pertaining to *Queen Elizabeth*'s 1942 military activities have since disappeared. Kessler's claim remains unproven.

[5] Though each of the queens carried large numbers of wounded troops and were equipped with extensive medical facilities, the converted liners were not hospital ships. Under the Geneva Convention articles governing the conduct of war at sea, hospital ships must carry red or green crosses and hull bands distinguishing them from all other vessels. Moreover, hospital ships may not carry healthy combatant troops or military equipment, nor can they carry weapons other than small arms issued to shipboard security personnel. *Queen Elizabeth* and her companions were thus technically "ambulance transports" when their human cargoes consisted primarily of wounded, sick, or injured troops.

Chapter 9   Queen Elizabeth 2

[1] Cunard went to great lengths to explain—primarily for the benefit of over-sensitive Scottish nationalists—that the new liner's name did not stand for the royal title "Queen Elizabeth the Second," but merely indicated the ship was the second vessel to be named "*Queen Elizabeth*."

[2] Buenos Aires-based agents of Britain's Secret Intelligence Service (known as MI6) predicted the exact date of the landings a week before they occurred.

[3] Among whom were 23 women, including stewardesses and nurses in the ship's hospital.

[4] The submarine sank the World War II-vintage, 10,650-ton cruiser with two Mark 8 torpedoes. Though the subsequent 4 May loss of *Sheffield* to an Argentine Exocet had evened the score somewhat, the British government was justifiably concerned that QE2 would be a virtually irresistible target for an Argentine military looking to sink a British ship at least as large and as much a national symbol as was *Belgrano*.

BIBLIOGRAPHY

Behrens, C. B. A. *Merchant Shipping and the Demands of War*. In the series *History of the Second World War: United Kingdom Civil Series*. London: Her Majesty's Stationery Office, 1978.

Bonsor, N. R. P. *North Atlantic Seaway* (five vols.). Prescot, Lancashire: T. Stephenson & Sons, 1955.

Braynard, Frank O., and William H. Miller. *Fifty Famous Liners*. Cambridge: Patrick Stephens, 1989.

Brown, David. *The Royal Navy and the Falklands War*. London: Leo Cooper, 1987.

Bykofsky, Joseph, and Harold Larson. *The Transportation Corps: Operations Overseas*. In the series *United States Army in World War II*. Washington, D.C.: Office of the Chief of Military History, 1957.

Crowell, Benedict, and Robert Forrest Wilson. *The Transportation of Troops and Military Supplies, 1917-1918*. In the series *How America Went to War: The Road to France*. New Haven, Connecticut: The Yale University Press, 1921.

Dugan, James. *The Great Iron Ship*. New York: Harper & Brothers, 1953.

Gibbs, Vernon, Commander C.R. *Passenger Liners of the Western Ocean*. London: Staples Press, 1957.

Gleaves, Admiral Albert. *A History of the Cruiser and Transport Service*. New York: George H. Doran Co., 1921.
———. *The Admiral: The Memoirs of Albert Gleaves, USN*. Pasadena, California: Hope Publishing House, 1985.

Harding, Steve. *Gray Ghost: The RMS Queen Mary at War*. Missoula, Montana: Pictorial Histories Publishing Company, 1982.

Hayes, Captain Sir Bertram F. *Hull Down: Reminiscences of Wind-jammers, Troops and Travellers*. London: Cassell & Co., 1925.

Hickey, Des, and Gus Smith. *Seven Days to Disaster: The Sinking of the Lusitania*. New York: G.P. Putnam's Sons, 1982.

Hurd, Archibald. *A Merchant Fleet at War*. London: Cassell & Co., 1920.

Kludas, Arnold. *Great Passenger Ships of the World* (six vols.). Cambridge: Patrick Stephens, 1972.

Konings, Chris. *Queen Elizabeth at War: Her Majesty's Transport, 1939-1946*. Wellingborough: Patrick Stephens, 1985.

Maxton-Graham, John. *The Only Way to Cross*. New York: Macmillan, 1972.

Middlebrook, Martin. *Operation Corporate*. London: Penguin Books, 1985.

Miller, William H. *The Great Luxury Liners, 1927-1954*. New York: Dover Publications, 1981.

Plumridge, Lieutenant Colonel John H. *Hospital Ships and Ambulance Trains*. London: Seeley, Service & Co., 1975.

Preston, Anthony. *Sea Combat Off the Falklands*. London: Willow Books, 1982.

Rogers, Colonel H. C. B. *Troopships and Their History*. London: Seeley, Service & Co., 1963.

Schmalenbach, Paul. *German Raiders*. Cambridge: Patrick Stephens, 1979.

Shaum, John. *Majesty at Sea: The Four Stackers*. New York: W. W. Norton, 1981.

Simpson, Colin. *The Lusitania*. Boston: Little, Brown, 1972.

Snyder, Louis L. *The Military History of the Lusitania*. New York: Franklin Watts, 1970.

Sunday Times of London Insight Team, The. *War in the Falklands: The Full Story*. New York: Harper & Row, 1982.

U.S. Navy Department. *Dictionary of American Naval Fighting Ships* (nine vols.). Washington, D.C.: U.S. Government Printing Office, 1959.
———. *History of the Naval Overseas Transportation Service in World War I*. Washington, D.C.: U.S. Government Printing Office, 1969.

Villar, Captain Roger. *Merchant Ships at War: The Falklands Experience*. Annapolis, Maryland: Naval Institute Press, 1984.

von Niezychowski, Count Alfred. *The Cruise of the Kronprinz Wilhelm*. Garden City, New York: The Sundial Press, 1938.

Wardlow, Chester. *The Transportation Corps: Movements, Training, and Supply*. In the series *United States Army in World War II*. Washington, D.C.: Office of the Chief of Military History, 1956.

INDEX